Praise for *Stardust*

"Jaime Smith has long heard from friends, family and colleagues that he should publish a memoir. The first half of *Stardust* is just that, while the second half is a collection of essays that run the gamut from musings on the Finnish language to trans-continental trips by BMW motorcycle, from opera to trust and truth in the media. Smith is a modest, down-to-earth, learned man, something that shines through in his writing."

— Lorraine Graves
Science reporter

"Never shy of learning new ideas, Jaime Smith has climbed many peaks, both literally and figuratively. *Stardust* is the story of an astronomer, an actor, a motorcyclist, a draft dodger, a psychiatrist and an AIDS and gay rights advocate.

Smith's essays, presented in clear and efficient prose that can be read in any order, provide a veritable feast of reviews, ideas, explanations and reflections. From hilarious to sinister, from dystopic to historic, Smith is, after all, a realist without illusions and a survivalist with a sense of humour."

— Bruno Huber
Author of *Folly Bistro* and *Mariposa Intersections*

"An interesting life . . . from the motorcycle-riding, classical-music-loving, traditionalist progressive who moved from astronomy to psychiatry because of LSD and who writes essays in retirement to stave off thoughts of returning to stardust."

— Sheldon Goldfarb, *Ormsby Review*
Author of *Sherlockian Musings*

Praise for *Foxtrot*

"An autobiography may seek to explain, to persuade, to justify – or simply to recollect. *Foxtrot* does the latter and it's richer for the choice. It's a short book about a long life, a pathway with few straight lines and some sinuous curves, described with honesty and economy."

— Peter Ward, *Ormsby Review*
History Professor Emeritus
University of British Columbia

STARDUST

STARDUST

memoir and essays by an astronomer who became a psychiatrist

Publisher's Cataloging-in-Publication data
Names: Smith, Jaime, author.
Title: Stardust : memoir and essays by an astronomer who became a psychiatrist / Jaime Smith.
Description: Includes index. | Vancouver, BC, Canada: Granville Island Publishing, 2021.
Identifiers: ISBN: 978-1-989467-30-5 (pbk.) | 978-1-989467-31-2 (ebook)
Subjects: LCSH Smith, Jaime. | Astronomers—Biography. | Psychiatrists—Canada—Biography. | Literature—Essays. | Science—Essays. | Belief and doubt. | Art. | BISAC BIOGRAPHY & AUTOBIOGRAPHY / Personal Memoirs | LITERARY COLLECTIONS / Essays
Classification: LCC RC438.6 .S65 2021 | DDC 616.89/0092--dc23

Book editor: Jessica Kaplan
Copy editor: Rebecca Coates
Book designer: Jamie Fischer
Book indexer: Emily LeGrand

Granville Island Publishing Ltd.
212 – 1656 Duranleau St.
Vancouver, BC, Canada V6H 3S4

604-688-0320/1-877-688-0320
info@granvilleislandpublishing.com
www.granvilleislandpublishing.com

Author's Website
https://karhunluola.wordpress.com

Printed in Canada on Recycled Paper

for Cathleen — without her, nothing

Contents

FOXTROT 1

Preface 3

1 Childhood and BA in Humanities 5
Minnesota *1933–1955*
2 Family and Research 13
Astronomy in Argentina *1955–1963*
3 Graduate Studies in Astronomy 25
The University of Minnesota *1963–1966*
4 University Teaching in the Kootenays 29
Nelson, BC *1966–1972*
5 Medical School and Psychiatric Residency, UBC 35
Vancouver, BC *1972–1980*
6 Psychiatry and the AIDS Crisis 42
Vancouver, BC *1981–1994*
7 The Yukon's Only Psychiatrist 52
Whitehorse *1995–2001*
8 From the Arctic to Canada's Riviera 58
Sidney, Vancouver Island *2001–2011*
9 Warrior Woman 66
10 Notes from the Bear Cave 68
Victoria, BC *2011–*

MOSAIC 79

Preface 81

Homo scribens 83
11 Homo scribens 85
12 Bilingualism 86
13 Nineteen Ways of Looking at Wang Wei 87
14 Tu Fu 88
15 Writing as Therapy 89
16 Speaking vs. Writing 90
17 The Abominable Pronoun 91
18 The Emoji Code 93

19 Evolving Usage 94
20 Barfing and Babel 95
21 Invented Languages and Zamenhof 96
22 The Voynich Manuscript 97
23 Bibliography 98
24 A Library Miscellany 99
25 A Book of Book Lists 101
26 The Libraries of Alberto Manguel 102
27 The Pigmalion Bookshop and Lyall's 103
28 Writing about Reading 104
29 Reading 105
30 Slow Time and Broad Horizons 107
31 The Man Who Liked Dickens 107
32 A Bedtime Story: First a Murder, Then to Sleep 109
33 Finnish Crime Novels 111
34 Aleksis Kivi and the Seven Brothers 112
35 Kalevala 113
36 Karamazovshchina 114
37 Russian Memories 116
38 An Act of Kindness 117
39 Berlin Airlifted 118
40 Borges and Eco 119
41 Fabulous Monsters 120
42 Oliver Sacks 121
43 Alan Turing: The Enigma 122
44 The Quest for Corvo and Hadrian VII 123
45 *Pampa Grass* 124
46 Guevara and *The Motorcycle Diaries* 125
47 Mao's Little Red Book 127
48 On Writing a Memoir 128
49 Jan Morris in Her Tenth Decade 129
50 On Literary Gratitude 130

Homo cognoscens 133
51 Homo cognoscens 135
52 From Presocratics to Quantum Mechanics 136
53 What Is Life? 138
54 Beyond Schrödinger 139
55 Biophysics 140
56 Viral Pathogenesis and Vitalism 141

57 Order 143
58 Abstract vs. Concrete 144
59 Art in Science 145
60 Feigl, Wittgenstein and the Vienna Circle 146
61 Marie Curie and Cecilia Payne-Gaposchkin 147
62 Copernicus and Vesalius 149
63 Cosmology, Ufology and the Fermi Paradox 150
64 What Is (the) Time? 151
65 Punctuality 152
66 Regret 153
67 Carpe Diem 154
68 Forgotten, Not Gone 155
69 The Way of All Flesh 156
70 Can Medicine Be Cured? 158
71 Pseudoscience 159
72 Irrationality 160
73 Freud, Psychoanalysis and Self-Indulgence 161
74 Astrology and Psychology 162
75 Lunacy 163
76 Insomniac Dreams 165
77 Nosology: Psychiatry and Sexual Orientation 166
78 Global Gay 167
79 Tongzhi Living 169
80 Psychiatry and Pathogens 170
81 (Recovering) Environmentalist 171
82 Book, Bird and Avoidance 174
83 Withering 175
84 The Wall 176
85 The Exterminating Angel 177
86 Cannibalism 178
87 Hawking, Hope and the Curse of Cassandra 179
88 Extinctions 180
89 Lucid Melancholy 182

Homo credens 185
90 Homo credens 187
91 Faust 188
92 A View from the Cave of an Urban Hermit 189
93 Confucius 190
94 On Being: The Gauguin Questions 191

95	Ultimate Questions	193
96	Atheism	194
97	Battling the Gods	195
98	Mortality and the Ancients	196
99	The Lure of the Arcane	197
100	The Order of Knights Templar	200
101	The Lodges of the Enlightenment	201
102	The Rosicrucians of the Post-Reformation	202
103	The Madness of Occultism	203
104	Hell	204
105	Abortion and Neonaticide	206
106	Impure Thoughts	207
107	Slavery, Progress and Human Rights	208
108	Canadian Museum of Human Rights	209
109	Greed	210
110	The Dismal Science and Its House Organ	212
111	Wealth Management	213
112	Property Is Theft	215
113	Marx, St. Paul and Human Nature	216
114	Polybius and Anacyclosis	217
115	Exceptionalism	218
116	The Dawn Watch	219
117	Patriotism	220
118	What Is to Be Done?	221
119	Swimming in Argentina	222
120	The Herod Solution	223
121	Trust and Truth in Journalism	225
122	Curses	226
123	Hope	227
124	Life and Loss	228
125	We Were Only Human	229
Homo ludens		231
126	Homo ludens	233
127	Music	234
128	Music Criticism	235
129	A Non-lexical Dictionary	237
130	Earworms	238
131	Music and Metaphysics	239
132	Nibelungenlied and Walhalla	241

133	Two Words from Kundry	243
134	Fascinating and Unexpected Books	244
135	Poetastery	245
136	Fictional Linguistics	246
137	Europanto and Wordplay	247
138	Fausto Squattrinato and C.D. Rose	248
139	The Cynic's Dictionary	249
140	The Portable Curmudgeon	251
141	Eunoia	252
142	Narrative Constraint	253
143	Gallows Humour	254
144	The Colourful Five Percent	255
145	Dreamers	257

Postscript 259
Die Weltanschauung

Acknowledgements 261

Index 262

FOXTROT

memoir

Preface

What is the narrative, the becoming of being in a life? A biographical essay may attempt to dispassionately examine the forces that propel the trajectory and achievements of another person, but an autobiography or memoir treads more dicey territory, for the author needs reflection and self-examination to avoid the perils of unwitting self-praise or disparagement.

Beyond these pitfalls, since a memoir is only written in one's senescence, two major hindrances impair reliable composition — memory becomes increasingly fallible, and word searching less efficient.

Yet the alternative to writing a memoir is to do nothing at all, and sink mutely into the silence of the tomb (or be consumed in the flames of the crematorium).

With some reservations, then, I set myself the task of writing a memoir, and the search for an appropriate narrative led me to reflect on the English philosopher Isaiah Berlin (1917–97), who in 1951 wrote "The Hedgehog and the Fox," a celebrated essay describing contrasted lifestyles, inspired by the ancient Greek poet Archilochus, who wrote, "The fox knows many things, but the hedgehog knows one big thing."

Some educational psychologists have claimed that the average person requires at least three hours daily over ten years to attain mastery of some particular ability, although a few might have an inborn aptitude for proficiency in chess, music, sport or another skill.

However their abilities were acquired, such a person would have been seen by Berlin as a hedgehog, knowing one big thing. Celebrity scientists, artists, authors and others known for attaining a high level of accomplishment in their chosen fields would often seem to merit this title.

Then there are the foxes, lacking expertise in one major activity, yet knowing many things. Who are these people who display a wide range of knowledge or skill but lack full expertise in any one area? We all probably know a few, though they are not likely to be famous. Though devoid of some special inborn or acquired skill, they may yet be competent amateurs, turning pages for the pianist, members of a chorus, acolytes to priests, lab assistants for scientists, Watsons to Sherlocks.

Alas, we cannot all be hedgehogs, but there is no disgrace in being a fox. And in any event, the two traits tend to be mixed, with more of one and less of the other in any given individual.

Berlin's fox–hedgehog dichotomy has intrigued many since he suggested the distinction in his essay, ostensibly writing about Tolstoy's theory of history in *War and Peace*. He characterized Tolstoy as "a fox who wanted to be a hedgehog."

This suggests other questions: Are there perhaps hedgehogs who wish they were foxes? Or, unlike Tolstoy, foxes quite content to be what they are?

Berlin's essay also provoked a number of humorous responses, like suggesting there are two types of thinkers: those who divide people into two types, and those who don't.

A brilliant and witty parody of Berlin's essay, using imagery from Edward Lear's nonsense poem "The Owl and the Pussycat," appeared in *Punch* in 1954, written by English historian John Bowle.

Aristotle cautioned about devoting excessive attention to a single skill, advising that one should be able to play the flute, *but not too well.*

Even Freud cautioned about uncontrolled cathexis (overinvestment) in thought and activity:

> Higglety pigglety psychoanalysis
> Rewards self-indulgence by charging a fee,
> Converting neurosis to common vexation,
> "Where Id was there Ego shall be!"

I tend to regard myself as more of a fox than a hedgehog, and am content to have been a competent amateur who tried to understand things under, above and even *within* the sun.

1

Childhood and BA in Humanities

1933-1955

Minnesota

In 1933, the year Nazi leader Adolf Hitler proclaimed the foundation of the Third Reich, I was born in Appleton, Wisconsin, a Midwestern town noted for its Institute of Paper Chemistry, as well as for being the home of the infamous fascist Senator Joe McCarthy. Following my birth, my parents relocated briefly to Chicago before moving to Minneapolis, Minnesota.

My maternal grandparents, Anna and Charles Tolonen, were both born in the late nineteenth century in what is now Finland, which at the time had been a possession of the tsar of Russia since 1815. Like many Europeans hoping to start their lives in a new land of opportunity, they had each emigrated separately to northern Michigan, where they met and married. Being fertile Finns, they soon had eight daughters, of which my mother Irene was the second eldest.

Born in Houghton, Michigan, on May 29, 1900, the last year of the nineteenth century, my mother grew up in Duluth, Minnesota, in a large middle-class family, remaining close lifelong to her six sisters and their families. Although intelligent, she never acquired post-secondary education beyond training in secretarial skills following graduation from high school.

She married my father, Alfred Smith from Waupaca in central Wisconsin, whose father worked at a flour mill until he retired in 1940. My parents met in Duluth and married around 1930. I was their only child.

It was said that my dad was never abusive or unkind towards my mother, but unfortunately he became alcohol dependent, even swiping the grocery money to buy liquor. Finding it intolerable to continue in the marriage, my mother divorced him when I was around three years old, a daring move for an unemployed single mother at the beginning of the Great Depression of the 1930s.

My mother found a job as a legal secretary and hired a girl to look after me while she was at work, although the girl was abruptly fired when she was found teaching me to recite the rosary, a Roman Catholic prayer. I have no memory of this incident but wonder now if it may have been an inoculation against religious belief that persists to this day. For a brief period of time I was sent to Sunday school at a local Protestant church, but Bible stories didn't help in understanding the universe, though I did internalize the moral teachings, learned to be kind to others, tried to be honest and didn't steal.

After the divorce, my mother's large family rallied around her and my grandmother left Duluth to come live with us. Two of my mother's younger unmarried sisters visited periodically before I started school and, finding I was eager to learn, taught me to read before I was five. One book I remember was *The Little Engine That Could*, which promoted the virtue of trying hard to achieve success, perhaps implanting a positive attitude towards the Protestant work ethic that manifested in my later involvement with learning at school and university.

I also recall once being asked by one of my aunts if I knew whether the sun went around the earth or vice versa. When I gave the wrong answer I was corrected, thus ironically beginning my career in astronomy with a false assumption about a common, observed celestial event.

Knowing I was an early reader, an aunt bought me a young person's encyclopedia titled *The Book of Knowledge* and encouraged me to keep learning independently. I devoured the set throughout childhood, educating myself about the natural world and probably learning as much or more than I did at school. Going to the public library was a special treat. Classes at school were easy and, skipping kindergarten, I went directly into grade one. But being younger than my classmates impaired social adjustment and I repeated grade five.

I interacted well enough with my peers eventually, but being somewhat of a loner and a bookworm I formed no close friendships. I liked adult company and hoped I would soon mature. Having no siblings, I yearned for an animal companion and loved to visit other families that kept a cat or a dog, but we lived in apartment buildings where dogs were forbidden, and cats were ruled out because my mother had ailurophobia, a morbid fear of felines. My early life was not really lonely, just unique in its own way. I now appreciate my mother, who tried to provide me with an adequate childhood with her limited resources, and am grateful for the support given us by her mother and sisters.

The Second World War had little effect on us in Minneapolis and though my dad was in the US Navy, he was stationed in Alaska and so saw no actual combat. By then he had affiliated himself with Alcoholics Anonymous and maintained sobriety for the rest of his life. When I was a teenager he would appear occasionally and take me out for a meal, but for paternal guidance I became closer to my dad's father, Al Smith Sr., staying with him periodically in rural Wisconsin in the summer, canoeing on the nearby lakes, playing the card game Schafkopf, and picking and eating raspberries. Meanwhile my dad had remarried and was living in Dallas, Texas.

I started middle school locally for grades eight and nine. One of my teachers encouraged classical music and played short, accessible symphonic pieces for his class. I became hooked and began to attend free concerts for schoolchildren put on by the local symphony orchestra. When I was ten, one of my aunts sprung the money for a used upright piano and I started weekly lessons, quickly learning to read musical notation. I also learned how to swim at the YMCA and joined the Boy Scouts, going on camping trips in both summer and winter.

In September 1948, I enrolled in Central High School in Minneapolis for grade ten. Aptitude tests were given that year to encourage students to think about careers after leaving school, and venturing that I would like to become a professional musician, I was sent off to the music department at the University of Minnesota for an assessment of my hearing acuity. They confirmed that I had a tin ear and told me to think of something else. Though mildly disappointed, I assumed I would attend university after graduation and left it at that. Meanwhile, I expanded my interest in classical music, learning to play the piano and listening at home to radio broadcasts from the New York Philharmonic every Sunday afternoon.

Around this time, I developed a congenial friendship circle with a group of peers belonging to the youth organization of the local Unitarian

Society. I attended services, finding the major tenet to be that of individual freedom of belief. There was no mention of a supreme being called God, but rather a strong dedication to reason and human rights that stayed with me lifelong. Affiliating with the society led to an active social life; I no longer felt like a loner among others of my age as I had in the past.

Some of the older members of the Unitarian Society were also amateur musicians, meeting weekly to play string quartets. They invited me to come and listen, and I soon became captivated by the practice of playing classical music with a small group. They encouraged me to learn to play the viola, which would afford me the best opportunity to participate, for while violinists were a dime a dozen, violists weren't, and one could always find a spot to play with them. I discontinued piano lessons, bought myself a cheap viola, and found a teacher who was a violist with the local symphony orchestra. I practised scales as well as fingering and bowing techniques and had no problem reading musical notation, having learned from my experience with piano.

When I graduated from high school in June 1951, I had a summer job, a good friendship network, was seventeen years old and healthy, and was eagerly looking forward to my first year as an undergraduate at the University of Minnesota. Although without any specific occupational plans, I was aware that a career in business was surely not something I found attractive.

Upon admission in September, each incoming student was given a packet of welcome goodies, including small samples of branded personal grooming items and a mini package of cigarettes to promote early nicotine addiction. (I believe they were Luckies.) I registered for the mandatory course, English 101; for the required science course, Astronomy 101 (a fateful choice); and finally, to defer conscription, Military "Science" 101.

English 101 got off to a good start, with the first assignment being to write an essay about what one had done over the past summer. As it happened, I had somewhere found an old copy of George Eliot's 1861 novel *Silas Marner*, and out of curiosity had recently read it. Throughout the year I devoured a wide range of fiction, a genre previously unknown to this seventeen-year-old ingénue, and finished with top marks.

I had always found astronomy fascinating and Astronomy 101 was no exception. The professor was Willem Luyten, a lucid and soft-spoken Dutchman. When the student society held a contest for popularity of lecturers, I approached him one day at his office to ask for his consent to enter his name. He greeted me effusively and described his research on the proper motions of faint blue stars. Not only was his work interesting to hear about, but I was flabbergasted when he immediately offered me a job as a research assistant.

Being a poor student and working for minimal pay at part-time jobs around the campus, I leapt at the opportunity and was soon trained to measure stellar motions using a microscope and to examine and record images on glass plates of stars photographed by a telescope in South Africa. I quit the other part-time jobs and settled into my new role in the Astronomy Department, forgetting all about the student popularity contest. I later learned that Professor Luyten had been expecting a referral for a research assistant from the student employment agency when I knocked at his door, and he mistakenly thought that I was the one referred. I got an A grade in the astronomy course as well.

The so-called military science lectures were dull, and the labs were nothing but close-order drills. After a few weeks of this, one afternoon when we were commanded to "about face!" and "forward march!" I thought to myself, "This is stupid and ridiculous," and so just kept on marching out of the gate and never returned. It was the only course I ever failed.

In the second year of university, to fulfill the language requirement, I opted for courses in German, taught by the amiable Professor Pfeiffer. Quickly learning basic vocabulary and sentence structure, I could soon understand and haltingly speak the language — not fluently (which would require total immersion), but adequately enough to read a newspaper or a simple mystery story. I also took courses in political science, history, philosophy and sociology.

Becoming more aware of history, the origins of warfare, the persistence of poverty and the inequitable distribution of wealth in capitalist economies led me to develop my own political viewpoint, espousing democratic (not Marxist) socialism.

While exposed to a wide range of learning in many different disciplines, I continued to measure stellar motions for the Astronomy Department. Friends taught me how to drive a car and I bought a used 1937 four-door black Chrysler sedan for $90. I drove it for over a year, including a trip to visit my grandfather Smith in Wisconsin. I eventually sold it for $95, feeling smug about having made a profit.

Expanding my social life, I dated a couple of girls from the Unitarian club, which I had joined along with some pals from high school, once going for a hayride with Marjorie Benson. Marjorie's older sister, Cathleen, was a major in art history and was, at the time, studying sculpture at a famous Russian artist's studio in Paris. Mostly though, I socialized with my male peers, engaging in harmless activities such as target shooting with a rifle at a friend's farm, but also listening to recorded Bruckner symphonies and spending late nights drinking beer or wine while discussing the "meaning of life" and career plans.

Our Unitarian club had a tradition of public service, including collecting clothing for Palestinian refugees displaced by the Israeli theft of their land, as well as monthly visits to socialize with chronic patients at the nearby state-run "lunatic asylum," an early exposure for me to mental illness as it was treated in public institutions in those years. Another tradition was the "faculty visit," in which we would invite ourselves to the private homes of different scholars for an evening of talk and getting to know them personally, not only as academic lecturers. We visited a well-known poet, a professor of symbolic logic (who baked an excellent lemon meringue pie for the occasion), a scientist, a historian and other specialists we knew from the lecture halls.

At the end of second year, after having developed a wide range of intellectual interests from my initial total ignorance, I still had no concrete career plans. My mother was concerned that I wanted to continue in philosophy and not something more economically promising like sales or another area of commerce. Later, when I continued to work in astronomy, she was pleased that I had chosen, in her words, something more "down to earth." (Like *astronomy?*) Still later, when I trained in psychiatry, she hoped I wouldn't be working in an "insane asylum," but was reassured when I told her it was just a mental hospital. She was a kind person and a well-meaning parent, but like others in her large family, devoid of any sense of irony.

In the third and final year of undergraduate studies I formally identified my major as the newly offered nonspecific field of humanities and registered for a number of courses in philosophy, history and world literature, as well as a year-long seminar with the academic program chairman. This was a rich intellectual feast. I read authors from Santayana and Marx to Tolstoy and Dostoevsky, eagerly devouring the classics of Western culture, though I was still deficient in many areas, especially science and mathematics.

It had been an extraordinarily rich three years for this initially naive but intelligent and questioning youth. Now transitioning from adolescence to adulthood, I felt ready for more independent living. Clearing out a closet in the roof of the physics building, next to a dome with a small refracting telescope used for demonstrating the wonders of the visible universe to members of the unsuspecting public, I installed a camp bed, a desk and a bookshelf. Although this was probably not officially permitted, it was rent free, and the department head winked and said nothing. I brought with me a sleeping bag, clothes, a few books and my viola, which I continued to play in string quartets with other students and even with the student symphony in larger works. Violas, as promised, were always in demand.

On June 12, 1954, I was awarded the degree of bachelor of arts cum laude and tentatively registered as a graduate student in philosophy, actually beginning a seminar in epistemology after graduation, although ultimately dropping out because it was boring. Working as a teaching assistant in astronomy, I developed romantic feelings towards a female student who needed assistance in drawing ellipses to represent planetary orbits. Cathleen was the older sister of Marjorie, who I had dated previously, now returned from her year in Paris. I agreed to help her with the exercise after class and for payment asked if she could make me a meatloaf, my favourite dish. Cathleen was agreeable to this request. She passed the course, the meatloaf was delicious, and the rest was history for the remainder of the century and beyond.

Now that I was no longer a student, the army pressured me to accept conscription, even during the brief period of peace between the Korean and Vietnam wars. Alternative service was allowed for members of certain religious sects, but I was an atheist and didn't qualify, so instead of going to jail I decided to emigrate. Knowing some German, I considered the Free University of Berlin but was dissuaded by Professor Luyten because of European instability at the time. As an alternative, I thought next of Latin America and I began Spanish lessons with a classmate from the Unitarian group who was studying linguistics. Spanish was easier than German anyway.

Professor Luyten offered me a job photographing faint blue stars at the Argentine National Observatory, near the city of Córdoba (now the Astronomical Observatory of Córdoba), contingent upon obtaining a research grant for that purpose. Cathleen and I were now living together and she fully supported my plans to emigrate to Argentina. The research grant proposal was finally accepted on February 7, 1955, and after giving away most of my possessions and attending a farewell party hosted by the Unitarian group from the university, I left Minneapolis by train on February 21, accompanied partway by Cathleen, who then returned home to her family after we parted with mutual promises to maintain the relationship by long distance from Argentina.

I stayed a few weeks with an aunt in New Mexico, then went to the University of Arizona in Tucson for a period of training in astronomical photography with Professor Luyten at the Steward Observatory. At approximately 10:00 a.m. on March 22, 1955, I walked across the bridge over the Rio Grande from El Paso, Texas, to Ciudad Juárez in Mexico, feeling relief to be out of the US and beyond the reach of the detested American military authorities.

Thus began my exile from the land of my birth. I shed no tears, and felt a gratifying sense of irony that my departure was made possible by a federal grant from the US Department of Naval Research.

2

Family and Research

1955-1963

Astronomy in Argentina

Travelling by rail when possible, I took a direct train from Ciudad Juárez south to Mexico City, and after a few days exploring this historic city, continued on by air, touching down at a series of Central American capitals en route to Panama, where after chatting at the airport bar with a young German, I boarded a direct flight to Lima, Peru. I visited the national museum, rode a rattling old tram to the port city of Callao, and quenched my thirst on Inca Cola, the Peruvian soft drink alternative to the excellent Pilsen Callao beer.

After two full days in Lima, I travelled overland all the way south, first by rail to Huancayo, in the heart of the Andes, on what was at the time the highest railway in the world (before China built a line to Tibet in the following century). Because of the high elevation of the pass (4,800 metres), oxygen was available for those passengers affected by the altitude, although I didn't require this amenity. From Huancayo, the following days were spent on a combination of three scary bus rides through the mountains to Cuzco. The drivers chewed coca leaves to remain alert as we tore along narrow unpaved roads up and down precipitous mountain passes. I stayed at the ancient Inca capital for several days and took a side excursion to the extraordinary ruins at Machu Picchu.

A final day by rail brought me to Puno, on the shores of Lake Titicaca, Peru, and an overnight steamer across the high Andean lake to Guaqui, Bolivia. From there it was another short hop by train to La Paz, where I boarded the ninth and final train of my journey. This was a 72-hour narrow-gauge international service, with comfortable sleeping compartments and a dining car where I could practise my Spanish with amiable and educated Bolivian passengers as we slowly trundled through arid landscapes to lower elevations. On the second day, we crossed the Argentine border at La Quiaca, continuing further south through the provinces of Jujuy, Salta, and Tucumán to my final destination — the city of Córdoba.

I arrived at the Alta Córdoba station on the evening of April 14, 1955. There were no available taxis, due to a political demonstration demanding the return to Argentina, from the UK, of the Islas Malvinas (Falkland Islands). Instead I went by horse-drawn sulky down to the city centre and took a room at the inexpensive but slightly shabby Hotel San Martín on the main plaza. I spent the next few days walking around the town, with its Spanish colonial-style cathedral and municipal buildings, including the oldest university in the country.

Unlike the nineteenth-century capital, the metropolis of Buenos Aires, Córdoba was founded by Jesuits in 1573 and nicknamed *la docta* (the learned). I rode trams to familiarize myself with the area and made friends with a medical student my age who also was living at the hotel. I travelled to the National Observatory complex, located in a large park not far from the centre of town, and met the director and members of the scientific staff.

The Bosque Alegre Astrophysical Station was forty kilometres from the city. The telescope dome and support buildings were perched on a mountaintop west of Córdoba, near the town of Alta Gracia. The town itself was the former home of the Spanish composer Manuel de Falla and the recent home, unbeknownst to me at the time, of a medical student named Ernesto Guevara, nicknamed "Che" when he became a revolutionary in Cuba. I worked there intermittently for the following six months, photographing faint blue stars on moonless nights with the giant 1.54-metre reflecting telescope.

Taking photographic plates of faint blue stars all night, I would sleep in the mornings and develop the exposed plates the following afternoon. My night assistant, David MacLeish, was a fifty-year-old Kiwi with hemorrhoids and an agreeably vulgar sense of humour. On cloudy nights we played a card game called *chinchon* with Spanish cards and drank yerba mate with the caretaker of the site, Don Pancho, whose wife Angelica and her mother, Doña Adelina, were respectively cleaning lady and cook.

On a free day I would borrow a horse and ride an hour or so down to the *estancia* (ranch) also called Bosque Alegre (Happy Forest), below the mountain, where I befriended the manager, the cheerful Scotsman Johnny Nairn, and his wife. We drank tea, ate oatcakes and talked about rural life in the Argentine. When not working at Bosque Alegre Station, I stayed in Córdoba at a nearby flat with friendly university students, from whom I quickly learned idiomatic Argentinian Spanish (including all the taboo words). It was the last year of the Perón dictatorship and they were all pro-democracy, anti-government radicals.

After a period of intermittent protests, the revolution to overthrow Perón boiled over in mid-September. I was offered a gun to carry by one of the students but declined, preferring to use my wits if I got into trouble, which I did. One day returning to Bosque Alegre on foot from the city, I was stopped by an armed rebel soldier, who searched me, then apologized and gave me a ride partway to nearby Alta Gracia, which was held by government forces at the time. In Alta Gracia I was stopped and searched again at subsequent checkpoints, but I finally made it up to the observatory and the telescope dome. I still retained my American passport, which I found useful when stopped by either side.

When my six-month contract ended at the end of September, it was not immediately renewed due to the unstable political situation. I temporarily moved to Uruguay, unsuccessfully seeking employment. At the end of the year I returned to Buenos Aires, where I eventually found a job as a reporter with the United Press news agency, renting a room in an apartment in the centre of the city. I was given assignments to interview celebrities, such as racing driver Sterling Moss, and to research and write dry articles on commerce, on topics such as trade relations between Portugal and Argentina (exporting *quebracho* oil for tanning leather to Portugal and importing corks for wine bottles to Argentina).

In Buenos Aires, I haunted the Pigmalion Bookshop and bought some books in English, no doubt rubbing shoulders with the Argentine author Jorge Luis Borges, who I later learned was a regular patron. I enjoyed exploring the city and environs when not at work, finding restaurants I particularly liked, as well as a Danish bar called Wivex, across from the renowned opera house Teatro Colón.

Bored with the work at the news agency, I thought about pulling a Joseph Conrad and working as a seaman but also of enrolling in university for more education, perhaps in literature or philosophy. But the local political situation stabilized and I was offered another contract to photograph faint blue stars at Bosque Alegre. I quit the agency, returned to Córdoba, and resumed work at the observatory.

Without a companion, I felt lonely and wrote to my girlfriend Cathleen back in Minnesota suggesting that she join me in Argentina. She enthusiastically agreed, and plans were made for her to travel to Buenos Aires by sea on a Norwegian freighter that August. Prior to her arrival, I rented a modest house in nearby Alta Gracia and bought furniture, utensils and crockery. The small whitewashed house by a small stream at the edge of town was owned by the estate of a recently deceased professor of botany and boasted a profusion of flowers, grape vines and fruit trees planted in the extensive garden.

A pleasant older woman, Señora Dominguez, had worked for the deceased professor and asked if she could continue to help us, and I readily agreed. There was only a kerosene stove and no refrigerator, but the property was adjacent to the local ice factory. An insulated icebox was adequate for storing food short term, and we were only a five-minute walk from the main street with shops. Winters (June through August) could be chilly, but there was a tiled stove providing heat on cold days. By the entrance was a patio sheltered beneath a huge wisteria vine with fragrant hanging purple blossoms.

In August I travelled to Montevideo, Uruguay, where Cathleen and I were married, first legally in a civil ceremony at the registration office, and then in a Quaker ceremony at the home of a pacifist American couple, the director of the local zoo and his wife, who had both been supportive of my leaving the US. They were active in an anti-war group that I was referred to by Cathleen's parents back in Minnesota. At that time, Uruguay was more stable and less militaristic than Argentina. There, before others, Cathleen and I affirmed that we would take care of one another as long as we each lived. Following the ceremony there was a reception at the French cultural centre with our hosts, witnesses, a few students I knew and the captain and officers of the Norwegian freighter that brought her from New York.

I joined Cathleen on board the ship for the overnight crossing to Buenos Aires. We stayed at a hotel for a few days before taking the train to Córdoba and Alta Gracia, where we settled in and befriended some other people in the town. My student friends from Córdoba came to visit us, as did Fraülein Dobermont, the librarian at the National Observatory. She was a friendly middle-aged German woman who loved classical music, and

I played my new recording of Bruckner's Fourth Symphony for her. At the dramatic conclusion she commented, "Vell, zat iss ze ent av ze vhite race!" I thought it an odd remark at first, later realizing she must have been an ex-Nazi. I didn't ask her about lampshades in the Third Reich.

But Cathleen and I were happy and in love in our cozy little home in Alta Gracia, with our big white dog León, given to us by Don Pancho, and our little gray pussycat, Grisette, a gift from our wedding hosts. After a few months of glorious springtime in Alta Gracia, of warm and sunny days amid the wisteria blossoms and with long walks in the mountains and countryside, the southern summer began in January 1957 with a written order from the US military for me to "report for examination and induction to the army base in Panama."

Taking immediate action to avoid compliance, I travelled to the American consulate in Buenos Aires, where "as provided by section 349 of the Immigration and Nationality Act" I swore that "I hereby absolutely and entirely renounce my nationality in the United States and all rights and privileges thereunto pertaining and abjure all allegiance and fidelity to the United States of America." I sent copies of my declaration to the military authorities in the US and surrendered my American passport, thus becoming stateless. Travel outside Argentina was no longer possible, at least until I acquired Argentinian nationality after five years as a permanent resident. Despite the change in my legal status, I felt no different than before, perhaps a bit more at ease by having cut all legal ties to the US.

I returned to Córdoba and we resumed our idyllic life in Alta Gracia and periodically up the mountain at the observatory at Bosque Alegre. We shared meals and played bridge with friends and went to concerts in Córdoba, only a half-hour trip by bus. One good friend, with whom we shared an interest in music and literature, ran the United States Information Service. He didn't care about my conflicts with the US military or my new statelessness, and at that time I had no negative feelings about American values or culture.

I took some courses in science and mathematics from the University of Córdoba, and after a local American hired me to be a science tutor for his teenaged daughter, I began to see myself as a potential teacher. Wanting to see more of the country, one week I took a bus to the western province of Mendoza and up to the border with Chile, beside Aconcagua, the highest peak in the Andes. I began to think of mountains as challenges, inviting ascents.

Cathleen and I talked about discontinuing contraception and starting a family, and we did so after that first summer. We were both fertile and by the end of the year the nosy neighbour ladies on our street were assuring her that she was carrying a boy. My closest friend at the observatory, astronomer José Luis Sersic, was also expecting a child with his spouse, Hebe. We were all young and excited at the prospect of becoming parents.

Meanwhile I continued my monthly ten-day sojourns up on the Bosque Alegre mountaintop, photographing faint blue stars on clear moonless nights. I learned to play chess on cloudy nights with my assistant, David, who always won. I enjoyed playing Bach's unaccompanied suites for cello in transcription for viola, sometimes while suspended on a platform in the great dome of the telescope, watching the Milky Way slowly rise over the perfectly flat horizon of the dark Argentine pampas.

Our first daughter, Anna, was born on February 25, 1958, at the Alta Gracia clinic. I was there for the easy birth and noted that our daughter was a redhead when she popped out. I had no qualms about leaving mother and child to fend for themselves while I absented myself periodically to continue stellar photography at the astrophysical station, but I thought it prudent to acquire some transportation should I need to hurry down off the mountain if there were a problem. Not being able to afford a car, I settled for something better than a horse and bought a used NSU Max 250cc German motorcycle, the first of what turned out to be fifteen different motorbikes acquired over the next half century — once bitten, I was smitten by the exhilaration of motorcycling, the wind in my face and the bugs in my teeth.

As well as the nocturnal observational work at Bosque Alegre, I had to take the developed photographic plates down to Buenos Aires periodically for shipment to the Astronomy Department at the University of Minnesota to be analyzed. I usually travelled overnight both ways by train and while there would stay at a club for foreigners in the centre of town, affiliated with the Córdoba English Club, with rooms for transients and a common lounge that often held bridge games for low stakes.

A second pregnancy went well and our daughter Kjerstin was born in Alta Gracia on March 18, 1959. On the day of her birth, I had promised an American astronomer from Denver that I would take him on my motorcycle from Bosque Alegre down to the estancia for tea with the Scottish manager. An hour after the birth, both mother and baby were content and doing well, and Cathleen said to go ahead and keep the appointment: "All is well here." So I did.

A periodic researcher at the observatory was the American astronomer Ira Epstein from Columbia University, known to his friends as Izzy. We became close friends, staying together at Bosque Alegre, especially on cloudy nights when stellar photography was impossible. We talked about music, Wagnerian opera in particular, and he relished describing details of *Parsifal* and the *Ring* cycle with inimitable gusto.

The observatory work was intermittent, and now with two small children, I considered more regular employment. An English-speaking primary and secondary school was set up in suburban Argüello near Córdoba, drawing students from both communities. As I had already been tutoring in science in Alta Gracia, it seemed reasonable to offer my services as a teacher at the new school. At the end of the year we relocated with our two little daughters to suburban Argüello, thus ending the first phase of our sojourn in Argentina. I was then twenty-five, a quarter of a century old, no longer a youth but not yet mature, as I prepared to take on a new identity.

Our nearby neighbours in this somewhat more elegant community of detached villas were Josef and Patricia Krasinski, a Polish engineer, his English spouse, and their four daughters. Josef and Patricia had met when he was in the Polish air force during the Second World War and assigned to live with her family when she was but an early adolescent. They fell in love, the English schoolgirl and her dashing Polish officer. After the war, they married when she was of age and emigrated to Argentina, where he found work at the wind tunnel of an air base near Córdoba.

Josef owned a Czech-made Jawa motorcycle, which made him my pal. We threw shot put together and went polar bear swimming in a creek on the southern winter solstice in June. For exercise, I began working out at a gym downtown and when free on weekends would sometimes head off on long hikes, once even rising at 4:00 a.m. and walking forty kilometres out to the estancia of Bosque Alegre for tea. I also took an interest in the history and technical aspects of mountaineering, scrambling up some peaks in the nearby sierras.

With the beginning of the school year in March, I began teaching science in grades eight to twelve at the Academia Argüello, a short fifteen-minute walk from home. The classes were small, from three to eight students, primarily of American families, though some were from European national backgrounds. I enjoyed the teaching, felt I was effective as an instructor, and at home was content with our little family and friendship network. But there remained a nagging sense of needing something more in life beyond what I was doing in terms of a career.

In January 1961, one of the Americans working for the Kaiser Company invited me to accompany him on his drive south from Córdoba to Patagonia. With no objection from Cathleen, who by now was engaged in preschool work with local children and had reliable home support from Paca, a local young woman with experience as a helper with household management and child care, I agreed to go. We initially headed west across the pampas to Mendoza, visiting local vineyards before turning south along the foothills of the Andes. After two days of somewhat arid and bland countryside we arrived at the province of Rio Negro.

At this point the road left the foothills and entered the mountains of the southern Andes, and the landscape was transformed into a temperate rainforest with broadleaf vegetation unique to the region. We arrived at the town of Bariloche on the south shore of Lake Nahuel Huapi, famous as a winter sports destination from June through August and a mecca for mountaineering in the summers, December through February. Here we parted company and I rented a room with a friendly Polish family for two weeks.

Exploring the town, I found the Club Andino and bought their guidebook to climbing and camping in the surrounding Nahuel Huapi National Park. I chatted with staff about options for an enthusiastic novice mountaineer in terms of accessible climbs and hiring a guide, and after studying possible climbs in the guidebook, I chose two significant but easy ascents. The first was to Mt. Bonete, on the north side of Lake Mascardi, south of town.

At the club, I met and hired an experienced guide from Slovakia, Peter Strukelj, and we set off for a two-day excursion to the peak. The weather was splendid and we were both in good physical shape, hiking uphill the first afternoon and sleeping under the stars after a supper of oatmeal. The next morning we continued up to the summit, having to abseil down a short cliff along the way. I signed the guest book for climbers, kept in a cairn on the summit, and feasted on the wonderful expanse of the mountain range, forests and lakes before descending and returning to the town of Bariloche. This was my first real climb as a beginner, not difficult except for the abseiling bit and enormously rewarding.

Three days later I headed west along the lake towards the Chilean border and up Mt. López. Halfway to the summit, the Club Andino maintained an overnight hut for climbers that was managed by a German guide who was available upon request to accompany one up to the top. After a healthy meal and a good sleep in the cool mountain air, we headed up the trail. After a lot of scrambling and no technically difficult patches (although we were roped together in case of an unexpected fall), by noon we were on the summit.

The sight from the top was again spectacular, with two glaciated volcanic peaks visible: to the north was Lanín Volcano, seismically active, and to the southwest, on the Chilean border, the massive El Tronador (the thunderer), not active but so named because of the roaring caused by glaciers breaking off and falling with a thunderous boom. El Tronador was readily accessible with a certain amount of planning, and I vowed to return and ascend it in the future.

Returning to the picturesque faux-Bavarian town of Bariloche, I bade farewell to the friendly Poles and returned to Córdoba — and to my little family — by train over four days via Buenos Aires. At the beginning of the school year I resumed teaching science at the Academia Argüello, but in December Cathleen and I stored our furniture and left by train with our two little girls to spend the following summer in Bariloche and its surroundings.

In early January, I took the train back to Córdoba and spent a week at Bosque Alegre photographing faint blue stars on another contract from Minnesota before returning to my family in the Patagonian Andes. While I was absent, Cathleen took the two girls for daily walks up the hill behind town, each day going one kilometre further than on the previous day. When I returned they were doing ten kilometres daily. Not bad for ages three and four!

During that summer I made two technically challenging ascents for an aspiring mountaineer.

The first was to the snowy peak of El Tronador with Josef, who had done some climbing back in Poland and wanted to do more in the Patagonian Andes. A two-day procedure, this was a proper ascent, with ice axes and crampons on boots. The first day was on horseback across the Chilean frontier to a refuge hut maintained by the Club Andino, and the second an ascent to the summit, to where the Andes' chain of mighty peaks was revealed to us as to a condor in flight.

I was roped together with Josef, who insisted that chewing garlic improved breathing in higher elevations. I was, however, unconvinced and not always successful at staying upwind. At the top we were both rewarded with the unfolding of the grandiose and seemingly endless prospect of lower peaks amid green forests and sparkling blue lakes, a memory to treasure for the rest of one's life.

The second climb was at Cathedral Mountain, closer to Bariloche, a technical scaling of a rock face to the summit of a pillar, where I signed the visitor's book before abseiling down the cliff like a spider from a net. It was both scary and exhilarating. In retrospect, I now shudder at what at the time seemed more like solving a technical climbing problem than being daring. It was not foolhardy, though, as I used proper gear.

Before returning to Córdoba, Cathleen and I spent a week with Mrs. Newbery, a ninety-three-year-old pioneer woman, and her sixty-five-year-old daughter at their remote home across Lake Nahuel Huapi. Cathleen had met Mrs. Newbery in Bariloche while I was off climbing, and she had invited us to come and stay for a few days. She and her husband had lived here since emigrating from Ohio in the late nineteenth century. There was no electricity, but they managed quite comfortably. In the sunny days, we explored the area and picked pails of raspberries.

In the evenings we were regaled with tales of early days, and how her husband pressured the government to create the surrounding national park. I was asked to look at some documents left by her late son, Diego Newbery, an author and frontier bush pilot whose book *Pampa Grass* I had read and admired. Among his papers I discovered an article written by hand in the 1930s, by the eminent Spanish philosopher Miguel de Unamuno, and with her consent I sent it to the director of the National Library in Buenos Aires, Jorge Luis Borges.

After the summer I resumed my teaching at Academia Argüello, but I was becoming bored with the unchallenging routine and considered further study towards a postgraduate degree in astronomy. Although this could be done in Argentina, I knew it would be more easily accomplished back in Minnesota, and as I was still periodically doing observational work for Professor Luyten at Bosque Alegre, I contacted him about the possibility. He was encouraging and I began to make plans.

First, I would need to obtain Argentinian citizenship, which I easily did after having lived blamelessly in the country for over five years. I then obtained an Argentinian passport to enable overseas travel, now no longer as *James* Smith but as *Jaime* Smith. (Argentine law required all first names of citizens to be in the Spanish language.) At the end of 1962 I flew to the US to visit family and to organize graduate studies back at the University of Minnesota, having changed both my name and nationality.

Returning via New York, I boarded the Norwegian freighter MV *Buenos Aires* for the three-week voyage down to Buenos Aires by way of Savannah, Georgia; Rio de Janeiro and Santos, Brazil; and Montevideo, Uruguay, where Cathleen and I had been married six years prior. I enjoyed a commodious private cabin, three plain Scandinavian meals a day in the company of the captain and ship's officers, and the flying fish and my bag of books for company. It was a wonderful journey.

I was back in Córdoba in good time for the birth of our third daughter, Emilie, on April 3, 1963. I spent the first night with mother and baby at the downtown clinic in Córdoba, because there was another insurrection underway. Outside on the street we could hear rifle fire, a fitting start to life for our youngest daughter, who later in life became radicalized as an Anglican priest supporting Latin American groups opposing US colonial commercial exploitation.

I resumed teaching for my final year at the Academia Argüello. We packed a trunk with our treasures, to be taken to Michigan by an American friend who was returning to the US, sold or gave away unwanted possessions and had a farewell party with our friends on August 21, before departing on Aerolíneas Ini, a fly-by-night budget Argentine airline. We flew to Minnesota via Lima, Panama and Miami. I registered at the University to complete the prerequisite courses in physics and mathematics, before being admitted to the graduate program in astronomy as a native-born foreign student.

Looking back at our time in Argentina, I now confess to feeling nostalgic for an agreeable lifestyle unlike anything I had previously experienced. I was plunged into a different culture with a new language, and I made new friends, gained expertise in scientific research and started a family with a loving partner (all with minimal but adequate income). Yet I was still hungry to learn more.

I fondly remember the Italian-based cuisine popular in local Argentine restaurants; the delicious scent of grilled chorizo sausages wafting from the carts of street vendors; sentimental tangos and wistful folkloric tunes in the air; and the earthy, spontaneous and friendly people who were helpful to strangers and always ready to laugh and poke fun at the pompous Catholic priests and military officers (curas y militares) who took religion and politics too seriously and interfered with the fun of just being happy and alive.

It was our good fortune to live there long enough to become familiar with the Spanish slang unique to the New World, where Castilian Spanish was the subject of mockery, as in the joke of a recent immigrant from Spain asking a policeman, "¿Donde puedo coger un taxi?" (Where can I grab a taxi?), to which the cop replies, "No se, señor, tal vez por el caño de escape" (I don't know, sir, maybe in the exhaust pipe). In Spain, the verb coger commonly means "to grab," but in Argentina it means "to fuck."

Returning to Argentina a couple of times over the years for visits, I would quickly feel at home in familiar surroundings, even beginning to dream in Spanish again. Despite all the political and economic vicissitudes suffered there over the years, I continue to cherish the days of my youth in the vast pampas of the gauchos and the craggy Patagonian mountains of the Southern Andes that became my second home after leaving the land of my birth.

3

Graduate Studies in Astronomy

1963-1966

The University of Minnesota

After arriving back in Minnesota in September 1963, Cathleen and I borrowed a car and retrieved the items that had been sent by our American friend in Córdoba to his home in Michigan. We found an apartment near the University of Minnesota, in the Prospect Park neighbourhood, close to Cathleen's sister Marjorie and her mathematician husband, Leon Green.

I felt no qualms about my national identity, though I was now in the unusual situation of being a foreign student in my hometown, with a passport from Argentina and a student visa for the US. These formal legal identities were vital, necessary masks for survival in a potentially hostile environment. Perhaps I was an imposter of sorts. But I wasn't troubled, for I had lost any sense of patriotism years before, and though now formally a citizen of Argentina, I felt emotionally detached from that or any other nation state. This more mature understanding of myself was a second awakening, the first having been my post-secondary studies in humanities.

I began classes in physics and mathematics at the University and again worked part time in the Astronomy Department, calculating stellar motions, while Cathleen found ill-paid employment teaching elementary-level classes at a suburban Roman Catholic school, the low salary doubtless compensated by reduced post-mortem time in purgatory. On November 22, 1963, the day US president Kennedy was assassinated, Cathleen's car was struck by a school bus, causing dental injuries. She sued and in the settlement was awarded sufficient funds to return to college for a year and acquire a full teaching certificate. She was then able to find a better-paid position in the public-school system, working in the Head Start program among young minority children mostly from Black, impoverished families in St. Paul.

Sadly, Cathleen's sister Marjorie developed myocarditis in early 1964 and died in the hospital, leaving their two small children, Sarah, four, and Eric, but one year old, without a mother. We considered options with Cathleen's brother-in-law, Leon, and he bought a duplex house in St. Paul, wherein we combined our families. Leon lived in the upper level with his children and their Norwegian elkhound, Haakon, while Cathleen and I lived on the lower level with our three daughters. The house was quite close to the Como Park Zoo, and at night we could hear seals bark and lions roar.

With some mathematician colleagues of Leon's, I began playing string quartets once more. I also convened a small group of fans of Anton Bruckner, the nineteenth-century Viennese composer, whose lengthy symphonies, recorded by different conductors, would feast our ears. One faithful member of our Bruckner Society was Herbert Feigl, a member of the Vienna Circle of empiricist philosophers in the years before the Nazi *Anschluss* of Austria, who was now teaching philosophy of science at the University. He had been my professor when I was an undergraduate, and we now reconnected.

I completed the required prerequisite courses in June 1964. In particular, I appreciated the abstract art implicit in pure mathematics, writing an essay about a method of transforming differential equations into algebraic ones to facilitate solutions, as described by Polish mathematician Jan Mikusinski. I was able to find errata in his (translated) book, guaranteeing me an A in the course. Becoming able to appreciate the abstract beauty of pure mathematics, I was tempted to learn more, but didn't pursue further studies in this field.

I started graduate school in the fall, studying astrophysics and stellar statistics in preparation for writing a thesis for the master of science degree in astronomy. The material for my dissertation was collected from my observational work in Argentina. Quasi-stellar objects (quasars) had recently been discovered, and my thesis, "A Search for Quasars Among Faint Blue Stars," was timely in terms of methodology for identifying these then-mysterious objects from other photographic images in a field of stars.

Though I wasn't specializing in astrophysics, it helped to quench my thirst for understanding the origins and processes within stars, accumulating the beginning of a working knowledge of the *how* but not the *why* of what and of who we are. Articulating these questions laid a physical (though not yet a biological) foundation for later constructing a consistent world view, or *Weltanschauung*.

Meanwhile, in 1965 the American government continued to expand their imperialist war in Vietnam, massacring civilians and bombing cities, all in the name of "preventing communism" in Southeast Asia. Many students and other young people were rising in protest against this American foreign policy, and Cathleen and I began to feel increasingly uncomfortable about paying taxes and continuing to live in the US.

At a dinner party with an old schoolmate of Cathleen's, I had a total meltdown, abusively confronting her husband, who insisted on the need to prevent the so-called domino effect of "losing" Vietnam to the communists, as though (like the US government) he considered the country to be an American possession. We had to leave the premises. This was the first of only two such episodes in my life. Normally I was reserved and kept my cool, but being human, I wasn't perfect.

I reacted strongly to the American atrocities, refusing to enable them and withholding income tax, which resulted in being declared delinquent by the federal government for the second time. Evidently it would not be possible to remain in the US once I completed my studies, and in late 1965 we began to consider alternatives: Should we return to Argentina? Relocate to Europe?

By early spring I had completed my dissertation, and I received the master of science degree in June. Another signpost of achievement, but for what end? Survival, yes, but survival for what? Anyone can climb a mountain with stamina and the right equipment, but upon reaching the summit what can one do other than admire the view? That was an unanswered question.

Meanwhile, in planning a second departure from the US and reviewing possible destinations, I thought that moving north to Canada would be a good choice. I wrote to different universities, enquiring about teaching positions in science, and was offered a position teaching physics, mathematics and astronomy at a small Catholic university in the mountains of British Columbia. The pay wasn't attractive, but it would be a location from which I could no doubt move on to something better, and best of all, it was in the mountains, an attractive location after my days of hiking and climbing in Patagonia. I accepted the offer and prepared to leave the US for a second time.

At the time of our departure, the Vietnam War was heating up, and the local conscription authorities wrote to me at my last known address in Argentina, at the National Observatory in Córdoba, attempting to compel me yet again to join their bloody army. I replied by sending them another copy of my 1957 oath of renunciation of American nationality, essentially telling them to fuck off. I cunningly enclosed the reply within an envelope and mailed it to the Córdoba Observatory, instructing them to send it back from there to the draft board in Minnesota. I departed for my new job in Canada at the end of the summer of 1966. Cathleen and our three daughters were to follow at the end of the year.

Instead of a Canadian visa on my Argentine passport, only available from the Canadian consulate in Buenos Aires, I was admitted at the Canadian border by an order-in-council from Ottawa as a permanent resident, having an offer of employment to teach science, thus becoming an exile from the country of my birth for the second time.

4

Teaching at Notre Dame University and Selkirk College

1966-1972

Nelson, BC

Arriving in Nelson in early September 1966, I was surprised to be met upon my arrival at the bus station by a bagpipe band. It transpired, though, that they were not meeting me, simply returning from a Labour Day parade. I was met, however, by Señor Espinoza, a Spanish teacher from Notre Dame University of Nelson (NDU), my new employer. Señor Espinoza greeted me in Spanish as Jaime, now my legal name.

From that day onward I was forever known as Jaime instead of the former Jim or James. It took a while to become accustomed to the usage, but the legal name stuck. By the time Cathleen and our daughters arrived in December, everyone knew me as Jaime. Whenever I was introduced to new people, they often assumed my name was Hymie and that I was Jewish. That didn't bother me, but I would reply *muchas gracias* and explain I was a recent immigrant from Argentina and so had a Spanish name.

In those first few months in Nelson I made many friends among the staff at NDU. I also visited Argenta, a nearby anti-war Quaker community that Cathleen's mother had recommended I contact, where I made many new and lasting friendships among those living this remote and secluded lifestyle, all of whom were supportive of US draft resisters who found their way there.

The small town of Nelson, on the shore of the west arm of Kootenay Lake, was congenial and welcoming. I lived in a downtown rooming house with another faculty member, historian Arthur Bartsch, an expert on Immanuel Kant and the Enlightenment, with whom I still remain in touch, both of us now in our late ninth decade. One weekend Arthur and I drove 600 kilometres to Vancouver, my first visit to the city that would one day become my home. On another weekend I took the NDU rodeo team to an intercollegiate rodeo in Edmonton, Alberta. I soon knew my way around the roads of southeastern BC.

My family joined me just before Christmas, having taken the train from Minnesota to Spokane while the VW Beetle was driven separately. They arrived on a snowy December day, and the roof of the little car was loaded with bundles of our possessions. With a government loan, we bought a small house on the mountainside above the town, with a panoramic view to the west, down Kootenay River valley, framed by successive ranges of misty mountains. A railway track behind the property, with only two freight trains weekly, led directly to the University, and I would run to work each day along the line, sometimes surprising a bear engaged in searching for food.

After classes I would often go with colleagues for beer at a downtown hotel pub, at the time still divided into separate sections for "men" and "ladies & escorts." The tasty cold Kokanee lager would be served to us by waiters in white shirts on terrycloth-covered little tables. One day, Arthur gestured to one of his young students at a nearby table and invited him to join us. Joel Christy, like many other young American men, had recently entered Canada as a tourist to avoid US military service. Joel and I had even more in common, for he was not only born, like me, in central Wisconsin, but also had the same birthdate of November 18. I was thirty-three and he twenty. We became good friends and indeed still are, celebrating our common birthday together each year, either in the UK, where he now lives with his wife and granddaughter, or in Victoria with me and my family. For a while Joel lived with us in the house on the mountainside, and with the help of one of the anti-war Quaker residents of Argenta, he was later admitted to Canada as a permanent resident.

Cathleen also found part-time work teaching art history at NDU. Among her students were members of the local Nelson Maple Leafs hockey team, who would come to morning class at times with eyes nearly swollen shut after a particularly brutal night on the ice. We built a large deck at the front of the house and relaxed many fine evenings, watching the sun set behind the panorama of mountains, happy to be safe at home in our peaceful community in southeastern BC and away from the warmongering Americans. But there were rumblings of discontent among the faculty at the university, suggesting a problematic future for teachers in local academia.

I managed to escape some of the religious and political conflict by embarking on a tour of secondary schools all over the interior of BC, giving students illustrated lectures about astronomy, hoping to entice them to attend NDU. Around this time, Cathleen's father died in St. Paul, Minnesota, shortly after retiring as a lifelong steel worker. Her widowed mother, Marjorie, left St. Paul and came to live with us in Nelson with her two yappy Scottie dogs, Tammy and Opal. We built her a small house next to ours, designed by our Quaker friend from Argenta, who had earlier sponsored Joel's immigration by offering him work as a carpenter.

Cathleen pursued her passion for creativity at the nearby Kootenay School of Art, where she studied ceramics with potter Walter Dexter, and I played my viola with two local violinists and a cello player. Together we formed the Kokanee String Quartet, playing primarily for our own pleasure at home every Saturday afternoon and later presenting free public concerts at NDU and elsewhere. We were only semi-competent amateurs, playing mostly relatively easy works by Haydn and Mozart, but it was great fun. I also played viola with a small amateur community orchestra in a nearby production of Gilbert and Sullivan's *Pirates of Penzance.*

I was asked once to be a substitute grade-eight science teacher at the local middle school and accepted thinking that it might be fun. At the beginning of the first day, all the pupils rose to sing in unison "God save the Queen." When afterward they remained standing, I asked why they didn't sit down, and was told that first they had to recite the Lord's Prayer. I told them it was only optional and to be seated and went on with the class. I wasn't asked back.

After teaching art history at NDU, Cathleen began her involvement in early childhood education with the founding of the Nelson & District Family Daycare Association, the first of its kind in British Columbia. I continued to teach at NDU, but after three years, and becoming frustrated with the constant turmoil between faculty and administration, I began thinking of moving on. The public post-secondary institution Selkirk College had recently opened in Castlegar, a community a half hour's drive down the Kootenay River valley to its confluence with the larger Columbia River. At the end of the year I applied for a position teaching astronomy and mathematics and was offered the job, to begin in September 1969. Although double the salary of the position at NDU, it was, alas, without a guarantee of any time off purgatory.

One of the other instructors at Selkirk was from Saskatchewan, and formerly played first violin with the Saskatoon Symphony Orchestra. As our first violinist in the Kokanee String Quartet no longer was with us, the addition of a new semi-professional player was a boost for our image, and we continued to present concerts in Nelson and Castlegar.

When I began teaching astronomy and mathematics at Selkirk, I considered investing in another vehicle so that Cathleen could have exclusive use of our little red VW Beetle. After my previous experience on two wheels in Argentina, buying another motorcycle the following spring seemed attractive, and I began looking at motorbike magazines while listening to Bruckner symphonies on cold and snowy winter nights in the mountains. In the spring I bought a new Triumph 500cc motorcycle, and once the snow had melted, began using it to commute between Nelson and Castlegar. I explored roads in and around the mountain ranges of southeastern BC, and in the summer I rode to a rodeo in Montana, meeting a former NDU colleague for a wild weekend of cowboy culture in a small western US town.

It being the mid-1960s, and consistent with the then-exploratory interest in marijuana, we planted some cannabis seeds a few metres beyond our property, by a culvert beside the railway tracks, and over the summer they grew into mature plants. We experimented with inhaling their fumes, as did most of our peers during those years, achieving mild highs and laughing, just as was described by the Greek historian Herodotus in 420 BCE, in his account of cannabis use in Central Asian nomadic cultures.

Later in the year, a ceramics student at the art school gave us tabs of LSD to try. My first experience with that powerful psychedelic agent turned out to be transformative, as it was for many others in those days. I recall lying stoned on the forest floor behind our home, examining in detail the structures of mosses and other microflora. This was when I realized that my scientific background was limited to looking up at the stars, and that my knowledge of the phenomena of living organisms was fundamentally deficient.

I registered for a course in biology at Selkirk in the fall, feeling a whole new area of interest becoming unveiled to me, while at the same time the prospect of teaching the same dry courses every year, calculus for science students and mortgage calculation for business students, was beginning to pall. Finding myself bored with teaching college, as I had been before when teaching high school in Argentina, I tried out for the part of Sir John Falstaff in a forthcoming college production of Shakespeare's *Henry IV Part One.* This was great fun, and I enjoyed learning and acting the part of the fat knight. We presented the play several nights at the college, also taking it on the road to Nelson at the NDU campus.

The science of biology in general led me to develop an interest specifically in human biology. The study of medicine seemed an appropriate next step. I consulted the University of British Columbia (UBC) calendar about requirements for medical school, and after taking organic chemistry and other courses at the college, applied for admission. I would take the medical college aptitude test (MCAT) and appear for an interview at the University the following year.

Cathleen was supportive, but I remember her saying she "didn't care to be just a doctor's wife," which I took to mean that she wanted to be known as a professional in her own right, not simply as an appendage to her spouse. She had developed a particular interest in early childhood education and planned to return to her studies to receive her graduate degree. I was totally in agreement with this, and we resolved, as before, to alternate working to support one another and our children while we each trained to expand our respective knowledge and skills.

Having taken part in the Shakespeare play the previous year, the following winter I tried a different angle and directed a production of the ancient Greek anti-war comedy *Lysistrata* by Aristophanes, first staged in 411 BCE. The lead role was played by English teacher and poet Rona Murray, and students were co-opted for supporting roles. A rock music finale was provided by a young Nelson musician who also was employed by the City of Nelson Sanitation Department as our garbage collector.

On June 26, 1972, at the Nelson courthouse, I became a Canadian citizen, my third nationality: American by birth, Argentinian by naturalization and Canadian by re-naturalization (though I retained the Argentine passport just in case). The judge asked each candidate a question to assess their knowledge of Canada, and one elderly Asian lady with almost no understanding of the language struggled to name a river in Canada until she was shown an atlas by a Mountie to help.

I also anticipated something simplistic, but when it was my turn, I was asked to compare the historical struggle for responsible government in nineteenth-century Upper Canada with the political situation in Argentina at the time. I was able to wing it by reflecting on Domingo Faustino Sarmiento, president of Argentina 1868–1874, who promoted compulsory education and founded the National Observatory. Both countries at that time were experiencing the need for codification of their political structures after loosening ties to the European lands initially involved in their colonial settlement. I passed and was presented a copy of the Holy Bible by the Canadian Bible Society, as was then customary.

I took the MCAT in the spring of 1972 in Vancouver, and my interview at the UBC medical school took place soon after. Among other questions, I was asked by the interviewer about my reasons for wanting to study medicine. I mentioned altruism, and the interviewer asked, "Then why not nursing or social work?" I replied that compared to medicine, neither of those disciplines were, for me, sufficiently based in science. A high score on the MCAT, together with top grades in the prerequisites, did the trick, and I was notified of my acceptance by mail the next week, with classes to begin in mid-September.

At the end of summer, I prepared to go to Vancouver, sold the bike, and bought textbooks and a microscope. Our plan was for me to live in residence on campus for the first year, while Cathleen and our daughters continued to work and attend school in Nelson, to join me in Vancouver the following year. So began another new intellectual mountain to climb.

5

UBC Medical School and Psychiatric Residency

1972-1980

Vancouver, BC

Enrolling in UBC's medical school at age thirty-eight, I was the oldest in a class of eighty first-year medical students (the second oldest was a veterinarian and the third a chiropractor). Most of the others were high-achieving science students but without backgrounds in another profession. We bonded well as classmates and I made many lasting friends among them. I lived in one of four suites on the top floor of a seventeen-storey student residence complex, together with five other mature students from different programs. We each had a small private room with bookshelf, desk and single bed, like a monastic cell but with a splendid view over the campus and city. We shared washroom and cooking facilities, and all being congenial, had no conflicts among ourselves.

Classes were primarily the basic sciences of anatomy, physiology and biochemistry, along with some initial supervision of patient interviews at the offices of participating family doctors. With my background in teaching and former employment in journalism, this came easy, but at times it was embarrassing, due to my initial lack of medical knowledge and its vocabulary. The physiology and biochemistry labs were particularly fascinating to one with a scientific bent, as they delved deeper into practical and observable details about the functioning of living body systems. I found these courses complemented the structural knowledge I gained from the anatomy course.

After the first year's final exams, I left the residence and returned to my family in Nelson, where I found a summer job as an assistant with the local health inspector, spending months flushing toilets at lakeside homes, tramping up and down Kootenay Lake testing for leakages from septic tanks. We found a few, including that of the local chief of police. Being reunited with my family, even for a few months, was a welcome decompression from the intensity of study. Cathleen and our three daughters all appeared to be doing well on their own and were looking forward to moving to Vancouver in a few short months.

At the beginning of my second year of medical school, I moved with my roommates from the previous year — Eugene from Ontario, Marvin from Montreal and Heinrich from Zurich — to a house near the university. The first semester was strongly academic again, with courses on the different specialties of medicine, as well as an introduction to the physical examination of patients' living bodies. Unlike in first year, where we only dealt with cadavers, this was now the "laying on of hands," not just interviewing about symptoms.

Having worked the previous summer with the Nelson health inspector, I developed a particular interest in public health and considered it a possible specialty after graduation. This was reflected by my top grades in microbiology.

Psychiatry lectures were fun, though given by a pompous professor who distinguished between mere eccentricity and mental illness by addressing a variety of psychological syndromes and then concluding each with the observation that thoughts or behaviours could be odd "but when prolonged are pathological." He smoked a pipe that always went out after a couple of puffs, so he was incessantly relighting it. We thought this was not only odd but, since prolonged, pathological. He had an abrasive manner and when a student asked him what "epistemological" meant he snapped, "Look it up!" He eventually came to a bad end, accused of sexually molesting patients, and left the department in disgrace.

At the end of the first semester and after five final exams on consecutive days, I returned to Nelson for the holidays. We loaded our worldly possessions into a U-Haul truck, and with Cathleen driving the VW Beetle with our daughters, we left Nelson after seven years in the mountains. We rented a house in Vancouver near where I had been living with the students, and Cathleen readily found a job at a community college teaching early childhood education, while our daughters enrolled in local public school.

Aware of the need for some diversion and creative activity away from the preoccupations of medicine and physical illness, and no longer playing the viola in quartets, I somehow found time to participate in the UBC theatre department's production of Ibsen's play *The Wild Duck*, and in later years performed in other productions.

The third year of medical school was essentially a combination of basic sciences, pathology and treatments, both pharmacological and surgical, of illness and injury, in preparation for the final year of working under supervision in a variety of clinical specialties, treating real patients. The third year was one of synthesis, adding up information obtained from the patient's history and examination, and formulating a diagnosis and treatment plan that could alleviate the presenting complaint(s).

A secondary interest also commanded my energy when the Medical Undergraduate Society (MUS) appointed me editor of their newsletter. Seizing the opportunity to indulge my literary whims, I founded and edited a magazine, *MUSings Quarterly*, publishing four issues throughout the year, for a total of 236 pages. I wrote editorials and book reviews, and selected reprint articles, also organizing an essay contest featuring rewards of bursaries of $500, $350, and $150 for the three best contributions from medical students.

There were controversial letters to the editor, and thoughtful replies, and the wide range of contributions included not only pieces about medical education but also articles on the provincial medical care plans in Canada, medico-legal issues, fitness, hypnosis, substance abuse, religion, euthanasia, and for lighter entertainment, medical humour, such as a reprint of a serious article from 1894 on masturbation by Dr. J.H. Kellogg, the inventor of Corn Flakes, called "Sexual Sins and their Consequences." The final issue, in the summer of 1975, was devoted to medicine and the arts, with contributions by staff of the Vancouver Art Gallery, on art and collectors; by my friend Joel, who was now working for a film distribution service, Pacific Cinémathèque, on movies and medicine; by UBC professor of music French Tickner, on opera; and by me, on music in general.

Since buying and reading the first Kinsey Report when I was sixteen years old in 1948, I knew that I was not really much different from many other men in having some same-sex erotic desires. But I was outraged that homosexuality was perceived as a sin by clerics, legally prosecuted as a crime by the police, and erroneously labelled as a mental illness by the psychiatric profession. I assured Cathleen that I cared only for her and had no intention of dumping her and running off with a male partner, as some married men did after coming out, but influenced by the nascent gay liberation movement, I became more open about my own same-sex feelings, which I had rarely expressed previously, giving public lectures on the subject in the community in Vancouver.

At that time in BC there was no specialized care providing service to the gay community. Yet in Vancouver, sexually transmitted infectious diseases like syphilis and gonorrhea were rampant. I found time to establish a small weekly STD-screening clinic for gay men at a community agency near St. Paul's Hospital in Vancouver's West End, where many lived. Every Monday night I saw drop-in patients with a registered nurse for counselling and testing, bringing the collected specimens of blood and anal swabs home, where they remained in our refrigerator overnight until in the morning Cathleen took them to the provincial STD clinic at Vancouver General Hospital. We counselled the use of condoms to prevent transmission a decade before the emergence of the epidemic of HIV disease.

Though a full-time third-year medical student, a writer and editor of a quarterly publication, and a community volunteer health worker (but not quite yet a licensed physician), I maintained my home life as a partner and father, socializing when possible with my family and friends as before, though I passed on the editorship of *MUSings Quarterly* to a new third-year student who had contributed to the magazine the previous year.

The fourth and final year of medical school was devoted to the clinical clerkship, which consisted of rotations through different specialties that exposed each student to a wide variety of genuine clinical encounters under supervision from an experienced senior physician. I both started and concluded my clerkship doing general medicine, learning how to appropriately interact with real patients both in examination and treatment in the emergency rooms of local hospitals, assessing patients who either walked in seeking help or were transported by ambulance.

To see a new ill person, take a history, perform a physical examination, and order appropriate investigation to confirm a potential diagnosis and then order appropriate treatment, seemed to me as close to being a "real" doctor as possible. One rotation in the clerkship was designated an elective, and I chose to spend time in neuroanatomy, sectioning and examining preserved brains to study detailed structures of the organ in health and illness.

I quickly adapted to the psychiatry rotation, assessing patients and when appropriate, their family members. Interviewing and writing consultation reports came readily to me after my background in journalism, and I applied for admission to the postgraduate psychiatric training program at UBC. Although surgery was fun, apart from the hours of work, and though I particularly enjoyed the challenge of microbiology and further studies in public health seemed appealing, I chose to continue with training in psychiatry, not just because of prior experience in interviewing but because the discipline covered a wilder field of interest in humanity than only becoming an expert in, say, diseases of the liver or malformations of the spine.

At the end of the year, I was asked to do one additional month in general medicine, after which I received my MD. Having already been accepted into the residency program in psychiatry, on July 1, 1976, I commenced the four-year postgraduate training at Vancouver General Hospital and completed eight six-month rotations through different hospitals. Since this involved assessing and treating patients under supervision, Provincial Health Services paid a small stipend for the work. Dazzled by the prospect of a small income, I invested in a little 600cc BMW motorbike to allow me to move between hospitals and mental health clinics. It was the first of many over the years to come.

Along with clinical work with severely disturbed patients at the four major hospitals in Vancouver, there was also training in psychotherapy. Unlike at an older, more traditional program such as at McGill University in Montreal, there was no special attention given to Freudian psychoanalysis, regarded at UBC at the time as historically interesting but of little clinical relevance. Some of the consulting rooms at older hospitals were furnished with couches, and at times a patient would enter and plop down, erroneously expecting "therapy," as always portrayed in shrink cartoons. They would be disabused of this expectation and invited to sit in a chair. At best, the couches were suitable for postprandial naps, particularly after an ample lunch if the patient failed to appear.

Psychiatry residents also participated in the teaching program for medical students. One method of instruction was to conduct an interview with a patient, with medical students and their instructor seated behind a one-way window to observe the interview technique and any indication of psychopathology displayed by the patient. One six-month rotation was devoted to child psychiatry, to practise developing rapport with recalcitrant teenagers and troubled families, sometimes requiring making home visits, usually within Vancouver but at times more distant.

An interesting training experience was at a dynamic group psychotherapy program called Day House, near the University hospital on campus. Small groups of non-psychotic patients, troubled by problems in their interpersonal relationships, were trained to act out their conflicts, as in a play, before supportive others, to gain insight into their own emotions and behaviours.

During this period, I became a member of the American Psychiatric Association (APA) in order to participate with other psychiatrists in lobbying against the inclusion of homosexuality in the official diagnostic nomenclature. Affiliating with the Gay and Lesbian Caucus, I argued for its elimination in sessions at annual meetings of the APA around North America and was the sole Canadian member in the group. In my final year of training I wrote a paper challenging the proposed new diagnosis of so-called "ego-dystonic homosexuality," and it was published in the peer-reviewed journal *Comprehensive Psychiatry* in early 1980. That diagnosis was subsequently eliminated from the official *Diagnostic and Statistical Manual of Mental Disorders*, and I felt gratified at having marginally contributed to a decision that was followed by significant social change.

Travelling with Cathleen to Mexico City in late 1979, I spoke at the World Congress of Sexuality, describing the changing psychiatric classification of homosexuality. A Spanish translation of my talk was later published in Bogotá, Columbia. An appropriate orgiastic conclusion to the conference was a dramatic display of fireworks at the final farewell party in a park outside the city. And in May I rode my motorcycle to San Francisco to attend the annual meeting of the APA along with other members of the Gay and Lesbian Caucus.

In late June 1980 I travelled by train to Toronto, where, with candidates from other Canadian programs in psychiatry, I passed my final oral examination. On my return I registered as a medical specialist, found a small office, bought furniture, and began seeing referred private patients, though I continued working periodically at St Paul's Hospital, covering different services as a locum, as needed.

For occupational variety, I also began providing psychiatric consultation services for family physicians from the town of Quesnel in the interior of British Columbia. I could travel directly by BC Rail from North Vancouver in the winter, but in the summer I preferred to make the trip by motorcycle, continuing this service for many years. I also began seeing patients at Simon Fraser University's student health services, covering for their regular psychiatrist when he went on holiday in late 1980. Unfortunately, he died in a car crash in Europe, so I perforce continued at SFU for another six months until they hired a permanent replacement.

The following year was one of settling into private practice, with periodic trips to Quesnel, running therapy groups for gay men at St. Paul's Hospital with a social worker, and attending professional conferences in Canada and the US. I had established what I thought would be my regular routine for years to come.

6

Psychiatry and the AIDS Crisis

1981-1994

St. Paul's Hospital, Vancouver

In early 1982 I continued my regular office practice and hospital coverage, along with bimonthly outreach visits to Quesnel. Among other professional duties, I was asked in early 1982 to give lectures at the BC Police Academy about sexual minorities and law enforcement. On May 6, Cathleen and I drove to Seattle for a festive dinner with the Seattle Psychoanalytic Society to mark Sigmund Freud's 126th birthday. The food and accompanied wines were unremarkable, but we purchased a memorable cookbook featuring recipes with bizarre names derived from psychoanalytic jargon, such as Transference Tortillas and Oedipal Omelets.

The following month, a biker friend and I rode our motorcycles to California to attend the celebratory San Francisco gay rights parade, but on the horizon were rumours of a rare skin cancer affecting gay men, a harbinger of acquired immune deficiency syndrome, first called the "gay plague" and subsequently AIDS or HIV disease.

The travelling continued and in October Cathleen and I made a brief visit to New York City, attending operas and visiting Izzy Epstein, our astronomer friend from the observatory at Bosque Alegre. In early December, we attended a conference of the American Academy of Psychoanalysis in San Diego, staying at the historic Coronado Hotel. While there, we went on an excursion to the renowned San Diego Zoo, where we were taken aback to see a gorilla munching on its own feces. Might this be a combined anal-oral fixation? We later learned it was a common way among primates to maintain gut flora, and that fecal transplantation in humans from a donor could actually assist in recovery from a loss of much-needed intestinal bacteria following their wipe-out occasioned by antibacterial treatment.

In early 1983 I relocated my practice closer to St. Paul's Hospital, sharing space with a family doctor while continuing part-time work there. And on May 5 at the APA annual meeting in New York, I gave a presentation entitled "Ego-Dystonic Nosology," cunningly satirizing the official nomenclature "ego-dystonic homosexuality," proposed by traditional psychoanalysts to describe patients who complained of unwanted homoerotic desire. The discussant of my paper was Robert Spitzer, editor of *The Diagnostic and Statistical Manual of Mental Disorders*, who on that occasion argued against my opinion. He eventually recanted, apologizing to gays on his deathbed at age ninety, many years later.

During my presentation, I convulsed the audience while responding to a comment suggesting that to remove the diagnosis would be a "step backward." I solemnly replied that "a step backward would be a step in the right direction, if one were initially facing the wrong way" (applause and cheers). Witty and amusing, yes. But on May 12, back in Vancouver, I interviewed my first patient with AIDS. Over the next decade I saw over 800 more. They all died of opportunistic infections and cancers. Sadly, many were colleagues and personal friends, including my biker companion from the trip to San Francisco who, unlike me, incautiously engaged in unsafe sexual practices.

On June 30, 1983, Cathleen and I flew to London, my very first trip across the pond. We trotted around London with our daughter Anna and her boyfriend, then crossed over to the continent and, taking the train to Zurich, visited my former university roommate Heinrich, before heading over to Vienna for the annual conference of the World Congress of Psychiatry. At Freud's university, I gave a presentation entitled "New Directions in the Psychotherapy of Homosexuality." The proposed discussant was a traditional analyst who averred the psychopathology of sexual variations but failed to appear. I guess I won the debate by default.

The gay and lesbian US medical association, still coyly calling themselves The American Association of Physicians for Human Rights, came to Vancouver in August for their annual meeting. Cathleen and I arranged their hotel accommodations, meeting rooms and social events, which included a boat cruise around the harbour and a final banquet at a restaurant in Chinatown. Meanwhile, the AIDS epidemic continued to expand dramatically and St. Paul's Hospital became the focal point of diagnosis and palliative treatment in Vancouver.

An AIDS care group was formed among the handful of specialists and private practitioners working with the gay population in Vancouver, and I became the psychiatric consultant, even making a presentation in September at medical grand rounds at Vancouver General Hospital, on the psychiatric aspects of acquired immunodeficiency disease, in the same lecture hall where I earlier attended these grand rounds as a medical student.

I had maintained contact with St. Paul's Hospital after my final six-month rotation in psychiatric residency, first maintaining a private office in a medical building close to the centre of town, then moving to an office across the street from the hospital. During this period, I continued to provide periodic service as a locum, but my principal work was with referred private patients as a consultant to family physicians, primarily in Vancouver but also to the community of Quesnel in central British Columbia. This pattern of practice changed when I became the appointed director of the eight-bed acute-stay inpatient psychiatry ward at St. Paul's.

I moved my office into the hospital, adjacent to the unit, and the first half of every day was devoted to supervision of a team of eight to ten psychiatric nurses providing 24-hour coverage. On arrival every morning I would review what had transpired overnight and inspect the chart of each patient. The average length of stay was usually less than one week, often sufficient to resolve the reason for admission and develop a plan to follow up after discharge, or if a longer sojourn in hospital was seen to be required, the patient would be transferred to the other inpatient unit for a longer period of treatment. If there had been a new admission overnight, I would meet individually with the patient and an assigned nurse to plan immediate treatment and consider eventual follow-up in the community.

In mid-morning I ran a group for all eight patients and nursing staff, with each patient being asked to summarize their state of mind and hopes for the future. We tried to encourage patients to regard their hospital stay as an opportunity for positive growth, and discharge planning always tried to provide follow-up to this end. Following the group meeting, we would have a staff conference and review each patient before lunch. This would conclude my formal daily attention to the unit, but my office being adjacent, I could be reached at any time there or at home by a pager that I always carried with me when in town. Coverage was obtained from a colleague when I was away.

I continued to see private patients, although fewer than previously, in the afternoons, many of whom were medically ill, most often with HIV-related illness. I would try to supply psychological support for out-patients and as necessary in hospital, even sometimes at their homes. I didn't go to funerals, though; there were too many.

In July 1986, the year of Expo 86 in Vancouver, we had an admission to the acute-care service of a gentleman from Melbourne, Australia, who, with his wife, was visiting the event as part of a world tour. The fellow was clearly in the midst of an acute manic episode requiring emergency hospitalization and mood stabilization. This was accomplished in a few days, and his wife decided to continue on the world tour alone, but he would have to return to Australia for continued care. It being required that a physician accompany him back to the hospital in Melbourne, at great personal sacrifice (as it were) I found myself on a trip to Australia with the now settled and compliant gentleman, my trip paid for by his insurance coverage. While there I was able to spend a week with Cathleen's cousin and her family in Queensland, where they kindly drove me around to all the local attractions.

Back in Vancouver, I resumed my work with the acute care service and the AIDS clinical care team, later travelling to Washington, DC, to attend an international AIDS conference, where I was able to meet and interact with colleagues from around the world. I continued to conduct bimonthly outreach visits to Quesnel throughout 1988 and weekly AIDS care meetings at St. Paul's with other specialists and family doctors caring for patients with HIV disease. Appointed as a clinical supervisor in the UBC Department of Psychiatry, I also began to provide instruction and supervision of medical students and residents in the postgraduate training program.

As a subspecialist psychiatrist working with HIV patients, I managed to combine my previous interest in public health and infectious disease with hospital-based acute care psychiatry. This entailed many trips away from Vancouver to connect with the many other colleagues working in this area in different parts of North America and elsewhere in the world.

Attending a conference in Phoenix, Arizona, on HIV disease and substance abuse, I learned of problems unique to this increasingly important cohort of patients with AIDS. Although, sponsored by Alcoholics

Anonymous, the meeting lacked a certain conviviality characteristic of these events. The major meeting of the year was the annual international AIDS conference in Stockholm, Sweden, in mid-June. Cathleen and I flew over to the UK and from there took an overnight ferry to Gothenburg, travelling by rail all the way to the north of the country, where we rented a car in Luleå.

We drove to the town of Haparanda at the Finnish border, where my maternal grandmother was born. We then ventured across the border into Tornio, the hometown of my Grandfather Tolonen, where we dined on reindeer stew at a restaurant called Ravintola. (I later learned that *ravintola* is just the Finnish word for restaurant.) These two northern towns lie at the top of the Gulf of Bothnia, the northernmost arm of the Baltic Sea, where the topography and climate resemble the area around Lake Superior in the US and Canada, where many emigrants in the late ninetieth century settled, including my maternal grandparents.

We headed south again by rail to Uppsala for a night, where Linnaeus developed the nomenclature for biological classification into genus and species, and visited his garden. From Uppsala, we continued an hour south to Stockholm to attend the international AIDS conference, where I presented two papers and one poster of my work at St. Paul's. We were given the use of a suburban apartment throughout the week, kindly provided by a Swedish colleague, and commuted daily by metro to the conference centre. From one of the presentations, I learned which psychological tests were the most useful in the diagnosis of HIV dementia, and later used them to confirm this unhappy complication of the still untreatable illness at St. Paul's.

Although I continued to head the acute care unit at St Paul's in 1989, increasingly my time was spent in the neuropsychiatric complications of HIV disease, doing patient assessments of dementia, writing academic articles, and attending conferences at the local, provincial, national, and international levels. In April, I spent three days at a World Health Organization meeting in Ottawa, and in May it was over to Winnipeg, where I gave a lecture on neuropsychiatry of HIV. At the end of the month I travelled to Montreal for the annual international AIDS conference, and at the end of the November I went to Victoria as a co-examiner for the final oral exam of a PhD candidate at the university who had written her thesis on the neuropsychiatry of HIV. She passed.

Meanwhile, consultation service to Quesnel and hockey games in Vancouver provided relief from the intense clinical activity at St. Paul's, along with brief trips to Seattle with Cathleen for opera performances. In May 1990, after five years, I resigned as director of the acute care psychiatry ward at St. Paul's in order to work primarily with the AIDS care service, though I was able to keep my office at the hospital. With my close involvement with the AIDS care group, I was now designated the team leader.

The international AIDS conference was in San Francisco that year, conveniently coinciding with a local presentation of the Wagner *Ring* tetralogy. Cathleen attended the first three operas with me, but before the final one (*Götterdämmerung*) she flew to Australia for a two-week visit with her cousin Florence and her family, returning to Vancouver in mid-July. I was accompanied to the final opera instead by the Swedish colleague who had provided us with accommodation at the 1988 meeting in Stockholm.

October found me in London again, attending an AIDS symposium at the Royal Society of Medicine and staying in rooms at the Domus Medica, a residence for visiting physicians at the Society, located at One Wimpole Street in the Marylebone district. This facility was conveniently located around the corner from Wigmore Hall, a prime London venue for chamber music concerts, and I attended a performance of the six Bartók string quartets, presented over two evenings.

I was also fortunate to hear a moving performance of Mahler's Third Symphony at the Royal Festival Hall by the visiting Vienna Philharmonic Orchestra. I remember walking back to the doctor's residence on the pedestrian bridge across the Thames with tears in my eyes.

These cultural experiences, along with my continuing outreach trips to Quesnel and locally cheering our NHL hockey team (the hapless Vancouver Canucks), helped to mitigate the stress induced by clinical work with so many tragic patients back in Vancouver.

But the epidemic was inescapable. When in London I visited the tomb and the home of Sigmund Freud, preserved with the famous couch and with his desk displaying his beloved arrangement of antiquities. I was accompanied by a psychiatrist colleague of mine from Vancouver, who died a few years later from HIV disease, one of several psychiatrists I knew personally who died of HIV, all closeted or undisclosed gay men. Such was the power of internalized and self-directed homophobia, notwithstanding the opinion of Freud himself, written in a letter to his British devotee and biographer Ernest Jones, that homosexuality was no reason to deny one's training in psychoanalysis. The letter may be seen in the Special Collections section of the library at Columbia University in New York, and I had read it there years earlier. Even a classmate of mine from medical school died, not from AIDS but from suicide, apparently from internalized homophobia. I only learned of this when his surviving boyfriend asked me for counselling.

More AIDS meetings with local physicians took place that November in Vancouver, and presentations were made to different specialists and community agencies. My primary work, though, was with individual patients with AIDS. I remember one fellow who continued to see me as an outpatient until he was too ill to come in, when I made home visits, as he had no one else to talk to. He was particularly fond of Jake, the dog who used to lie under a table in my office. On the day before he died, I brought Jake with me to his apartment; he was delighted to see Jake, who licked his face when cuddled and stroked.

Another guy was particularly fond of a cartoon by Leonardo da Vinci and asked me if I could get him a print from the National Gallery when I went to London, which I was able to do. He hung it on the wall of his hospital room, where he could admire it when awake, inducing a sense of calm in his last days. One very sad hospitalized patient with both AIDS and liver disease, in great pain, asked his family doctor for assisted death and was referred for my opinion, an uncomfortable duty requiring a thoughtful response.

Travel and meetings continued and I was able to combine international travel conferences with the opportunity to visit different parts of the world with their own problems associated with AIDS. In June 1991 Cathleen and I flew to Frankfurt. We continued by rail to Zurich, where we visited our Swiss friends for several days before heading over the alps to Padua in Italy, where I presented a paper on the neuropsychiatry of HIV at a conference on AIDS and psychiatry.

Back over the alps to Vienna, and Cathleen returned to Vancouver via Frankfurt, while I continued on to Moscow for a week of exploring the Russian capital by its renowned metro with palatial stations. One day, I hired a car and driver to take me south to Tula and the nearby estate of Leo Tolstoy, where on his little writing desk lay Dostoevsky's *Brothers Karamazov*, opened to the page of Ivan's dream of a Second Coming in which Jesus is rejected by the Church.

Returning, I stopped briefly to sample a glass of kvass, and back in Moscow, I attended a performance of the Tchaikovsky opera *Queen of Spades* at the Bolshoi Theatre, on a cheap ticket bought from a scalper by a friend of my nephew Eric, who was then working in Moscow for the diplomatic service of the US State Department and kindly facilitated my visit. This included a visit to the office of a psychoanalyst of the Freudian persuasion, who spoke of how delighted he felt that, now the repressive USSR was no more, he could practise therapy as he had been trained, in "scientific" psychoanalysis. He was obviously pleased and happy to exercise his training in the techniques of Freud, and courtesy compelled me to offer congratulations on his newly found freedom to treat patients and not to engage him in a discussion of the merits of this older approach to mental illness. I also visited a seedy-looking hospital for AIDS patients and shared my experiences with HIV patients in Canada with a physician.

On June 16 I left Moscow on the Trans-Siberian Railway and travelled all the way across Eurasia to the Russian city of Khabarovsk on the Amur River, close to the frontier of China, whose mountains were visible to the south. At one ugly town somewhere in Siberia, a crumbling statue of Lenin displayed the words *Lenin lived — Lenin lives — Lenin shall Live!* and I thought of Shelley's poem "Ozymandias," reflecting on the temporal fate of all-powerful kings.

I broke the seven-day journey halfway to Khabarovsk, spending a few days near Irkutsk as the sole guest in a rundown hotel at Lake Baikal. I had learned only a few words and phrases in Russian, but on the train was able to communicate with other travellers in French and German, if not in English. On July 4 I left Khabarovsk on an Alaska Airlines excursion flight across the Bering Strait, arriving in Anchorage on July 4, having dropped a day by crossing the international date line. I returned to Vancouver by way of Seattle and Bellingham, Washington, where Cathleen picked me up.

In midwinter 1982, a February trip to Quesnel was immediately followed by a midsummer trip to Argentina. I met old friends in Córdoba, where we used to live when I worked in astronomy, and visited a shabby hospital dedicated to infectious disease, making a presentation (in Spanish) about the neuropsychiatry of HIV. Touring the facility, I cynically noted that the pitiful AIDS patients were sweltering in over thirty-degree heat, while the physician director worked from an air-conditioned office.

Travelling by rail south to Patagonia, I found that unlike the efficient and punctual Swiss railways, the inefficient Argentinian rail system I knew in the 1950s had further deteriorated in both infrastructure and passenger comfort. Having read Paul Theroux's classic travel book *The Old Patagonian Express*, I resolved to experience a ride over this antique rail line in southern Argentina, not far from where I had climbed mountains in my youth decades earlier. I spent several uncomfortable days as an intrepid passenger, lurching along the decaying track bed, and later composed a droll account of my adventures in Patagonian railroading called "The Older Patagonian Express."

Later that year, while in the Netherlands, Cathleen and I stayed in the venerable old Hotel Amadeus on the town square of Haarlem, outside of Amsterdam. I commuted daily to meetings of the HIV neuropsychiatry group, followed by the eighth international AIDS conference. We visited museums and purchased a print of Rembrandt's portrait of Jan Six, which still hung on the wall of his private residence.

Back in Vancouver, a specialist in the AIDS care service described his outreach consultation work in Whitehorse, Yukon Territory, noting that there had been no psychiatrist serving the community of 20,000 for several years. Fortuitously, Cathleen was retiring from running the early childhood education program at Douglas College in New Westminster, at the same time that psychiatric input into acute AIDS care of patients infected with HIV was becoming less of an issue, with the illness becoming chronic and controllable with effective medication. This seemed like an opportunity for an anticipated change of venue.

In October I travelled north to Whitehorse and, envisaging the possibility of a future permanent move north, made enquiries of the local physicians, who welcomed the suggestion that I initiate a psychiatric outreach service. I duly registered as a physician with the Yukon Medical Council and a trial visit to interview patients was arranged for October. I assessed thirty referred patients that week and continued this service, as it transpired, for the following fifteen years. I was only in my sixtieth year, after all, and not ready to retire.

A midwinter trip to the North (where many are cold but few are frozen) in the first week of January 1993 was a bracing introduction to winter in Whitehorse, and I saw another thirty-eight referred patients. Back in Vancouver, I maintained some coverage at St. Paul's Hospital, consulted with the AIDS care committee and, when not working, attended language lessons, concerts and hockey games.

Meanwhile, in the summer of 1993 I was asked by the Canadian Border Services Agency to write an opinion about gay erotic material imported by Little Sister's bookshop in Vancouver. Shipments to the store had been seized at the border as possibly being harmful to the mental health of the Canadian public, so they sought an expert in the subject and were directed to me for assessment of the "filthy material." I told them I would be happy to assist and would bill them the standard hourly rate for my time, and they readily agreed, presenting me with a large carton of books and magazines.

I spent several weeks looking at each individual item when I had free time, keeping track of the hours, and advised them in a soberly written report that I considered it all harmless sexual fantasy material, irrelevant to the mental health of anyone who looked at it. They promptly paid my invoice for the time spent, but appear to have not used it in court, I assume because it was not consistent with their homophobic agenda.

My final year in Vancouver was 1994, when I worked at St. Paul's Hospital off and on between lengthy periods in Yukon. In Whitehorse that winter I averaged about forty patients weekly at the Mental Health Centre, staying in an apartment adjacent to the hospital complex. In mid-January, I went "down south" to Prince George in BC to speak about HIV issues at both the regional hospital and the mental health centre. I continued my social life in Whitehorse with an active and congenial group of fellow physicians, as well as periodically shared meals with my friend, journalist Ken Spotswood. Back in Vancouver in March, I took our three daughters to a performance of the appropriately named Chekhov play *Three Sisters.*

During the first week of August, I co-chaired an International Neuroscience of HIV conference at UBC that I had organized with colleagues. It was attended by about forty specialists in this field and featured the usual academic sessions and social events. Back in Whitehorse immediately after the conference, I worked for two weeks at the Mental Health Centre, and on a weekend went with Ken to Haines, Alaska, visiting the annual Southeastern Alaska State Fair. My teenaged grandson Abel flew up to join me, and after visiting the local hot springs, we spent four days driving back to Vancouver through northern BC.

I saw a few more patients at St. Paul's before Cathleen and I headed south at the beginning of September for another Wagnerian *Ring* cycle of operas in Seattle and a subsequent visit to Ashland, Oregon, to attend the annual Shakespeare festival and visit friends there. I made a final outreach visit to Quesnel after we returned to BC, and I arranged for a colleague from St. Paul's to take over my longstanding consultation service to that community. On October 31, 1994, I saw my last patients at St. Paul's.

That November I drove a rented U-Haul truck with many of our prized possessions from Vancouver north up the Alaska Highway to Whitehorse. No longer involved with the now receding epidemic of human immunodeficiency virus, I thought of a comment by Albert Camus in his novel *The Plague*: "*On apprend au milieu des fléaux, qu'il y a dans les hommes plus de choses à admirer que de choses à mépriser.*" (We learn in the midst of plagues, that in men there are more things to admire than things to despise.)

7

The Territory's Only Psychiatrist

1995-2001

Yukon

A fundamental characteristic of the Arctic is extreme seasonality, a consequence of the inclination of the axis of the earth's rotation to the plane of its revolution about the sun, which leads to long winter nights and long daylight hours in the summer. Distant from most of Canada's provinces and accessible by only a single paved highway or a two-hour flight from major population centres, Yukon is akin to a large island, with an area similar to that of France. It is one of the more sparsely settled regions of Canada, with different psychological consequences than those arising from living in crowded urban areas.

These two conditions help illuminate the background of life in the North and contribute to the quality of individual adjustments needed for comfort — indeed, for survival itself — in an inherently hostile environment. There may have been a tendency for patients with bipolar disorder to experience a seasonal variation of intensity of manic and depressive episodes, but if so, the difference wasn't obvious to me.

The remote location, however, was also manifested in what I termed "end-of-the-road syndrome," in which an urban discontent wanting to "get away from it all" would relocate north, only to find that the decision was ineffective and only based on wishful thinking, for an individual is always accompanied by their own personal temperament.

Accepting the challenge of working as a psychiatrist in this setting was unlike my previous experience with both chronic and acute patients in a major downtown hospital in an urban locale, though perhaps not so different from my outreach assessments in rural communities like Quesnel in the interior of BC.

On the morning of January 1, 1995, I flew from Vancouver to Whitehorse accompanied by our cat, Scrofula. Cathleen followed on the afternoon flight with our beloved mutt, Jake. We initially stayed in the slightly seedy Mountainside Apartments, part of the hospital complex across the Yukon River from the city centre. Settling in, we explored the town, watched the start of the annual Yukon Quest 1000-km dogsled race, and looked for temporary rental accommodation until the Vancouver house was sold.

In March we rented half of a duplex on the bluff overlooking the town and river, in the Valleyview district, moving in when our furniture arrived from Vancouver. It was originally built to house Canadian army officers, one of many created in an identical pattern and repeated in military bases across the country.

I began to work full time at the Klondyke Medical Clinic, assessing thirty to forty referred patients weekly, while Cathleen made friends in the community and considered what activity she might pursue in her newly retired status. After previously making a documentary on "special needs children" in the preschool setting, Cathleen thought to perhaps pursue a documentary on life in the North. I walked to the clinic most days but took the bus in severely cold weather, when the valley was shrouded in ice fog.

After the winter, spring and summer here were welcome. We travelled and entertained many friends and family who were intrigued by our move. In May we visited the neighbouring Northern communities of Atlin, BC, and Haines, Alaska. Two of my cousins and an aunt visited us in the long daylight hours, and we enjoyed showing them the sights in and around Whitehorse, such as the nearby Takhini Hot Springs north of town and the barren desert sands just a half hour's drive south.

In July our granddaughter Fiona visited from Victoria, and in August my medical school classmate Fred Solven flew across the country from New Brunswick to fish (unsuccessfully) in northern waters. Also in August, my colleague from the St. Paul's AIDS care group in Vancouver, dermatologist Alistair McLeod, and I made a scintillating joint in-service presentation at Whitehorse Hospital on dermatology and psychiatry, slyly announced as "The Ego and The Itch."

It was a good year for us, and we tolerated the bracing subarctic weather well, both having been raised in a northern climate in Minnesota. We survived a bitterly cold winter with prolonged periods of −40° (Celsius or Fahrenheit — they're the same at that point), but according to the locals, at least it was a "dry cold." The long winter nights didn't seem so dark and gloomy, for the snowy white ground cover gleamed in reflected moon- and starlight, and many a time the night skies blazed with a display of the aurora borealis.

Following local custom, in December we tramped through the snow out into the bush to cut ourselves a Christmas tree, and invited friends and colleagues over for tea on Boxing Day, as we had done for many years in Vancouver. After many years of living in the rainy and often gloomy coastal climate of southwestern BC, it felt good once more to feel snow crunching underfoot, and our dog Jake loved to frolic and roll around in it. Scrofula the cat, however, was not amused.

The Vancouver property was sold in February and we bought a large house in Whitehorse, over the bridge from downtown, across the Yukon river, with triple-glazed windows and plenty of room for visitors. Avoiding traffic congestion on the bridge during the so-called "rush minute," we moved into our new home in April.

There was no classical music performed locally that year in the northern cultural desert, but a local society brought in visiting groups for the occasional concert, such as a string quartet from Russia who came to town and played Shostakovich's Twelfth. I joined the local Rotary Club to expand my social contacts beyond the medical profession, attending lunches with a speaker every Friday, though I made no close friends among the businessmen.

I also affiliated with the local Canadian Legion post for more down-to-earth socializing among the local denizens, participating most Friday nights in their traditional meat draw. When asked why an American draft dodger would join a veterans' club, I may have thought to myself "cheap beer," but usually honestly said that I respected the Canadian Armed Forces, who participated in peacekeeping missions rather than trying to impose ideology on foreign countries as did the Americans.

I also did volunteer work, reading police-procedural detective stories in German to Hans, a retired miner with multiple sclerosis who was isolated in a chronic care facility. I also assisted in forensic services for the Territorial Ministry of Justice, assessing unhappy prisoners in the Correctional Centre (i.e., jail), where 80 percent of the inmates were Indigenous men. When one group of inmates completed an Alcoholics Anonymous course, I was invited to their graduation party, sharing "traditional First Nations cuisine" that included both moose stew and a bucket of Kentucky Fried Chicken.

Wanting to write something beyond psychiatric histories and academic papers on sexual variation and neuropsychiatric disease, I composed an item for the annual humour issue of the *Canadian Medical Association Journal*, an imagined 1901 psychiatric assessment of the miner portrayed in the Robert Service doggerel poem "The Cremation of Sam McGee," leading to the proposed diagnoses of cold intolerance and a morbid lack of heat sensitivity.

Many visitors appeared during summers, including grandchildren, cousins, and family friends. In early June Cathleen planted a garden in raised boxes in our backyard, and with nineteen hours of sunshine daily, the flowers and vegetables flourished: like eight-foot stalks of rhubarb. But once the snow started to fall again in mid-October, it was only our dog Jake who continued gardening, planting "Yukon tulips" over the winter, these being harvested in the spring as the snow melted in April and May.

In August, I attended the twentieth reunion of my medical class at UBC, and in September, Cathleen and I flew to the northernmost settlement in Yukon, Old Crow, above the Arctic Circle. I continued to see a few patients, and Cathleen met the elderly Indigenous journalist Edith Josie, later to become the subject of her documentary film. Now aged over eighty, Miss Josie had written a column for years in the *Edmonton Journal* and *Whitehorse Star* newspapers, titled, in her inimitable style, "Here Are the News," which chronicled life in the remote, mostly Indigenous, community of Old Crow, north of the Arctic Circle.

In 1997 life in Whitehorse continued in a stable pattern with occasional variations: daily work and hospital consultations with a wide variety of patients at the Klondyke Medical Clinic, reading German detective novels to Hans, and Friday Rotary Club luncheons and later meat draws at the Legion. Cathleen began her creative project, making a documentary film about Edith Josie with the help of grants from the National Film Board of Canada.

I spent several days in Ottawa in late winter, not at an AIDS conference as before but as a fan of the Dawson City Nuggets hockey team. They travelled there exactly as had their predecessors, by dogsled, ferry boat and rail, across the country to reenact a 1905 Stanley Cup game. A good time was had by all, the Nuggets (players) and the Nuggies (fans). One of the players was even the popular Dawson City family doctor.

I purchased another motorcycle to free up our Jeep SUV for Cathleen to use in my absence. There being no BMW dealer in the Territory, I settled for a Harley-Davidson Sportster, considered a good piece of farm machinery. Unlike in coastal BC, riding was unfeasible in the northern climate from mid-October to mid-April. But back on the road in the spring, I rode south down the Alaska Highway and across the Rocky Mountains to Edmonton in northern Alberta. Leaving the bike for servicing at the Harley-Davidson shop, I travelled by train across the prairie provinces and northern Ontario to Toronto, where I attended an annual meeting of the American Psychiatric Association. Meeting colleagues with whom I had corresponded about psychopharmacology, I also reconnected with members of the gay/lesbian group with whom I had worked for the elimination of homosexuality as a diagnosis from the psychiatric nomenclature.

I returned to Edmonton by air, retrieved the motorcycle, and over three days rode the 1,500 kilometres north up the Alaska Highway, over the mountain ranges to Whitehorse. Passing through a torrential rainstorm south of Fort Nelson, BC, I emerged into brilliant sunshine and, transfixed by the sight of a magnificent rainbow, parked the bike and photographed the display. It seemed to me a visual metaphor for the recovery from depression. The photograph was framed and has hung ever since in my office to share with patients. I also collected a speeding ticket, an unwelcome souvenir of the trip. But the cop was friendly, wanting to chat about the bike, and after giving me the ticket recommended a good place for a meal up the road.

I was happy that Cathleen had found a project that allowed her to express not only her artistic talent but also her devotion to promoting unique Indigenous talent in Canada's North. We flew up to Old Crow in the high Arctic, where she spent hours interviewing retired Indigenous journalist Edith Josie for her now-titled documentary film, *Here Are the News*, named after Miss Josie's column in the *Whitehorse Star*.

I continued working as the sole psychiatrist in the Yukon. By now having become somewhat of a local character, I was honoured to be included by writer and artist Jim Robb in a new edition of his popular book *The Colourful Five Percent*. For a complete change, in early spring I spent two weeks back in Argentina for a last nostalgic visit to where I had begun my adult life as an immigrant in a new country, after leaving the land of my birth and starting a family with Cathleen, now unable to travel overseas due to progressive chronic obstructive pulmonary disease.

In early May I bought a new Harley-Davidson 1,200cc motorcycle and during the summer rode up the Alaska highway to Fairbanks and later to remote locations all around the Yukon Territory, assessing patients in smaller communities. At the village of Mayo, located 300 kilometers north of Whitehorse, I stayed one night at the Bedrock Motel and the following day interviewed referrals at the local nursing station, enabling me to add to my resumé the distinction of having worked as a specialist at the Mayo Clinic.

On an unaccompanied visit to Old Crow in December to further interview Edith Josie, Cathleen suffered an acute asthma attack and needed to be evacuated by air ambulance to the nearest hospital at Inuvik, Northwest Territories. Because it was during a blizzard, she was encased in a body bag to keep warm. Because of her subsequent dependence on home oxygen therapy and limited ambulation, we made plans to relocate back to BC the following year.

Cathleen and I both liked living in the North and made many good friends in both the medical and First Nations communities. Our children, now on their own, had matured and produced seven grandchildren. At the beginning of our life in Whitehorse, Cathleen in particular had wondered aloud, "What am I going to do now in this place?" I reminded her that she had successfully adapted to all of the location changes throughout our lives together and I was confident she would do so again. And she did.

In April 2001 I viewed properties for sale around Victoria, on the south coast of Vancouver Island, returning in June to finalize the purchase of a small house close to downtown Sidney, a town just north of the capital and not far from the airport and mainland ferry terminals. The prospect of living in a milder climate, closer to medical care for Cathleen's chronic obstructive pulmonary disease, promised to make life easier, and being closer to our children and their families was a bonus. We sold our house in Whitehorse, held a gigantic garage sale, and in early August our youngest daughter, Emilie, came for a few days to assist in downsizing and preparing for the move south.

8

From the Arctic to Canada's Riviera

2001-2011

Sidney, Vancouver Island

Cathleen departed with Scrofula the cat on August 26, 2001, while I remained to do the final cleanup of the house in Whitehorse. Joel, by now an old family friend, arrived from the UK on the 28th to help with the move, and we loaded a small U-Haul trailer to tow behind the RAV4 truck. The movers came for the larger items on August 30, and Joel and I left the following day with Jake the dog. Although we experienced a brief delay in northern BC when the trailer suffered a flat tire, the U-Haul company arranged for a replacement within a few hours and we arrived in Sidney on September 4. The following days consisted of unloading the trailer and unpacking, after which Joel flew home to Yorkshire.

Our furniture arrived a few days later and the motorcycle was shipped separately, arriving safely at the local HD dealership in Victoria. We hired a landscaper, who created the beginning of a beautiful small garden and built a large shed in the backyard, both of which were sources of delight during our almost ten years living in Sidney. We also found a reliable local older fellow to help as a handyman.

I soon began to see referred patients at my shared office, only a four-minute walk from home, and the practice grew rapidly. I also flew north for working visits to Whitehorse, for as they had no other psychiatrist, I agreed to continue visits periodically on an outreach basis and possibly by a remote telepsychiatry setup later on. The relocation went smoothly and we were glad to be closer to our children and grandchildren. Cathleen and I felt we had made a good decision.

I had always enjoyed maintaining physical fitness, first going to a gym for weight training in Argentina while teaching, in Vancouver while working at St. Paul's Hospital, and later in Whitehorse. Before moving to Sidney, I had contacted the nearby recreation centre about continuing workouts, and I soon began attending for exercise beyond walking Jake twice a day. I preferred resistance training with free weights and alternated cardio on different machines, always followed by stretching in a sauna or steam room.

Cathleen's love of gardening had limited expression in the Arctic, but over a few months our backyard in Sidney displayed the beginnings of a green haven, while the new shed became a space uniquely my own: a place for tools, my motorcycle and bunk beds for visitors. I soon installed a wood-burning stove with a Jim Robb-style askew chimney to resemble a Yukon cabin, and also set in cement a flagpole to fly the Yukon flag. I then began interviewing referred patients from the Yukon directly from Sidney via a telepsychiatry connection.

For my first outreach visit to Whitehorse since our move, in July I rode the new motorcycle over to Bellingham, Washington, and from there sailed on an Alaska State Ferry for three days and four nights to Skagway in southeastern Alaska. Then it was only ninety minutes by bike over the coastal mountains to Whitehorse. It was fun to lash down the bike in the ship and settle into a stateroom that would be home as we steadily moseyed up the Pacific coast, first calling at Prince Rupert, BC, and then stopping at several Northern communities just long enough for a walk.

After a week of work at the Klondyke Medical Clinic, the hospital and the jail, I returned again by sea, but this time on the Alaska ferry only as far as Prince Rupert. I then sailed on BC Ferries aboard the ill-fated *Queen of the North* to Port Hardy, on the northern tip of Vancouver Island. One more day's riding brought me back to Sidney.

When my eldest daughter, Annie, informed me of a motorcycle club for gay men in Vancouver, I contacted them and they put me in touch with a similar Victoria-based group called Ferryriders. We met every Sunday morning at a coffee shop near downtown and (weather permitting) rode out in a small group of around six to many rural destinations around southern Vancouver Island. Our backyard shed was designated the official clubhouse, and the group occasionally met there over the following years for barbecues in the summer, flying the rainbow flag on the flagpole.

In 2003 I booked trips to Yukon every second month, beginning in January, until a local replacement was found, though I continued the telepsychiatry sessions from a corner in the shed. In the winter, the Ferryriders travelled together on a chartered bus to an annual motorcycle show near Vancouver. We sat on the new models and were bemused to find, among the many displays, the fierce-looking Hell's Angels and a cohort from the benign Christian Motorcycling Society, both similarly attired in leather and exhibiting their wares in adjacent booths.

As well as permitting year-round motorcycling, Victoria had an opera company, and Cathleen and I were impressed to see our grandson Hugh, then twelve, appear in a brief speaking role in a local production of Alban Berg's opera *Wozzeck*. In the following month we spent a weekend with family members at a resort west of Victoria, on the coast, visiting tidal pools at Botanical Beach near Port Renfrew.

In April Cathleen flew to Whitehorse for a few days to work on the production of her documentary, while I continued my routine office practice in Sidney throughout the rest of 2004. Whitehorse finally found another resident psychiatrist, so I initiated a new outreach consultation service with semi-monthly trips to nearby Pender Island, a welcome change from my office routine in town. After a thirty-five-minute early morning ferry, I rode to the local medical clinic, assessing referred patients throughout the morning and afternoon. Providing outreach consultations had always been an activity I relished, first when based in Vancouver and later in Whitehorse.

In late May I embarked on a lengthy motorcycle trip once again, this time with a longtime friend and colleague from Vancouver, psychiatrist Peter Constance. Over nineteen days, we visited many national parks in the western American states, before and after attending the annual psychopharmacology conference of the National Institute of Mental Health at Phoenix, Arizona (another "business trip," of course, heh, heh).

Having thought of getting certification as a fitness instructor at the local community recreation centre, in the winter of 2005 I took the St. John Ambulance first aid refresher course. As was the case in Yukon, friends and relations visited us in Sidney. Cathleen's brother-in-law Leon and his partner Jill, having briefly visited us in Victoria the previous year from their home in Minnesota, returned for a month, staying at a posh waterfront hotel and eating oyster burgers at the Boondocks pub in Sidney.

In 2006, becoming increasingly fatigued, I found that I had somehow become septic from an infection in my heart valves, requiring life-saving valve-replacement surgery. My general practitioner said that my subsequent rapid recovery was facilitated by having retained a high level of physical fitness, although after the surgery I decided to refrain from pursuing training as an instructor.

The new year brought continued work at my Sidney office, where, fully recovered from the surgery, I saw a total of thirty-seven referred patients in January alone. I also continued outreach trips to the Klondyke Medical Clinic in Whitehorse (who had asked me to return) and to the Pender Island Health Centre.

Over the winter our beloved dog Jake became increasingly frail, having to be lifted into the car. We sadly said farewell to him in May after fourteen years of him being our faithful companion, first in Vancouver, then in Whitehorse, and finally Sidney. We tried replacing Jake with a one-eyed black Lab who ran in circles, but we gave her up before long to the SPCA when she developed epilepsy.

Scrofula also completed her ninth and final life, gracefully purring herself to a final, long sleep one day in Cathleen's lap. Before long, two more kittens joined our household menagerie: Biscuit, a fluffy, long-haired multicoloured fussbudget who arrived in a biscuit box, and Ixie (named after a UK biker group), a short-haired black and white bossy number.

As the evenings became darker, I began reading aloud short stories by Nabokov, Maugham, Simenon and other favourite authors. Cathleen received a federal grant to complete her documentary film, and as always, on October 23 we ignored the anniversary of (biblical) creation in 4004 BC. In December I permanently closed my office in Sidney, after seeing a final fourteen referred patients. Although no longer assessing local referrals, I continued to make outreach visits north, flying to Yukon in the winter and spring.

Cathleen was occupied all year with the final editing of her documentary film about Edith Josie. We watched movies together at home, listened to lectures, visited the Thursday evening market in Sidney in the summer, went for drives in the vicinity and dined at various restaurants. Our three daughters and seven grandchildren visited, as did my cousin Ann from Seattle. I continued my routine fitness at the local recreation centre, even using hotel equipment when in Whitehorse.

In the spring we visited friends on Salt Spring Island, and my son-in-law Al Mackie and I attended a "beer dinner" in Victoria, where each course was created using a recipe with beer. My daughter Kjerstin and I attended a tea of the Monarchist League of Canada, held at The Blethering Place tearoom in Oak Bay. It was very proper and twee.

In June I travelled by land and sea (four days each way) to Whitehorse for continued work at the medical centre. In late summer I repeated the journey once again, but this time with Peter, who had accompanied me earlier to Phoenix. We rode up the Island, north to Port Hardy, and took a BC Ferry to Prince Rupert, then rode overland to Yukon through northern BC. Our return trip was even more interesting, for we rode all the way down the Alaska Highway to Dawson Creek, BC, and crossed into Alberta, where from Grand Prairie we headed south through Jasper and through the Rocky Mountains to Lake Louise via the Icefields Parkway.

On a warm summer evening in late August, the Ferryriders held a barbecue at one fellow's place on Pender Island. We contentedly watched the full moon rise over the pines, drinking beers and sharing tales of past adventures on two wheels by the crackling bonfire.

I fully retired from psychiatry on November 12, 2009, after seeing my final patient in the Yukon. Reflecting on my career as a psychiatric physician over the previous thirty years, I recognize that though at times I could have done better, I tried to do no harm. When I unexpectedly met three former patients on different occasions socially, they expressed gratitude, though I wasn't fishing for compliments. Especially important to me as a consultant were family physicians appreciating my thorough consultation reports with history, mental status examination, preferred diagnosis, and treatment recommendations, if any.

I felt this was important, particularly because I always functioned as a member of a team working together on behalf of our patients. It was psychologically important for my own mental health to know that I had supportive colleagues. I would not have felt comfortable being completely on my own, as were some psychiatrists who tended to distance themselves from general practitioners and other specialists.

The summit of my academic career was participation alongside a number of colleagues in the American Psychiatric Association in the shared effort that successfully led to the deletion of homosexuality from the psychiatric nomenclature, and clinical highlights arose from working with psychiatric issues in patients with HIV disease. I assessed on referral an average of two men with AIDS weekly at St. Paul's Hospital in Vancouver during the eight early years of the epidemic in the 1980s. Unlike now, at that time there was no effective medical treatment for the fatal infectious disease.

Besides the opportunity and honour of hearing the life stories of so many patients, it was also my fortune to have had the chance to attend many professional conferences and seminars, both in North America and overseas, making presentations and meeting colleagues from other countries and other cultures from Mexico to Moscow.

Always a source of satisfaction were the different outreach visits to assess referred patients, initially to Quesnel in the interior of BC, later to remote and isolated small Northern communities of the Yukon Territory, and finally to Pender Island in the Salish Sea, between Victoria and Vancouver. In addition to meeting a wide variety of people, I took pleasure in the travel involved, by air, railway, and coastal ferries, but especially by motorcycle in the summers.

After my retirement, I continued riding with the Ferryriders on Sundays to our favourite local destinations, such as Sooke, Duncan, Lake Cowichan, and other locales along the Saanich Peninsula. During the summer, Cathleen and I hosted beer-and-burger evenings at the shed in our backyard, adorned with the banner displaying the group's clubhouse and flying a rainbow flag on the flagpole.

Cathleen was fully supportive of both my professional work and my social interactions, ever since my first STD clinic for gay men when I was a medical student. She notably helped in disease prevention during the early years of the AIDS epidemic, handing out condoms or bringing samples from the free STD clinic to the lab. We became ever closer, sharing mutual interests in music, art, literature, and of course our family.

A major event of 2009 was the completion of her documentary film, which was shown at the Vancouver international documentary film festival, DOXA, on May 27. Many hundreds of copies were distributed to schools, libraries and other institutions across the country.

I chose to fully retire at the end of 2009 to provide care and companionship to Cathleen as she became more limited in her physical ability, though she was alert and cheerful in demeanour throughout the remainder of her life.

Over the first year of full retirement I made no significant trips away from Sidney, my primary occupation being that of caregiver. I took Cathleen to her numerous medical appointments and adjustments of the machinery of her breathing-assistance devices, shopping at the co-op for groceries and at nurseries for garden plants. There were drives and excursions around Victoria, concerts and films. We socialized as a couple with many old friends, and there was a constant flow of daughters and grandkids coming and going to and from our house in Sidney. When home by ourselves, we shared the pleasure of watching classic cinema and listening to classical music and operas and to lectures about art and history.

We found European radio stations on the internet to be a good source of the music we both enjoyed, particularly the Finnish state radio Yle Klassinen. I managed to understand much of the program list but had never considered studying the grammatically complex non-Indo-European Finnish language, though my maternal grandparents were both Finnish-speaking from childhood. Cathleen found the University of Victoria was offering Finnish classes and encouraged me to enroll. So at the end of 2009, again a university student, I began learning Finnish, attending weekly evening classes.

I continued these studies over the following three years, attending university classes and studying privately with a native-born speaker, Hilkka. I purchased a Finnish language bible at the Christian bookstore to assist me in reading familiar material in the language, also finding a Finnish-Spanish dictionary at a downtown used bookstore.

We had Christmas dinner that year at our daughter's modest home and celebrated the New Year on Helsinki time, at this longitude conveniently 2:00 p.m., in mid-afternoon. The next year, 2011, started as the previous had year ended, with more Finnish lessons, workouts at the gym, visits by daughters and grandkids, socializing with biker buddies and short rides on Sunday, meat draws on Friday, and the same level of daily home care for Cathleen.

In the previous year Cathleen had encouraged me to attend a few meetings of a Victoria-based social group for older gay men called Prime Timers, to augment my friendship network. Len Byron, a retired teacher living in Sidney, shared similar interests in music and literature and became a close friend. He came to the house for afternoon coffee one day to meet Cathleen, who by March had physically deteriorated significantly, though she remained alert.

Cathleen's mental status further declined by the end of the month, and she was admitted to the geriatric psychiatric unit at Royal Jubilee Hospital when home care became too difficult for me alone. She was sedated and remained cooperative over the next two weeks. I visited daily, reading stories to her. She was transferred to a private room in the new building, but her condition was soon no longer treatable, and I was asked for permission to discontinue oxygen. She died peacefully the following afternoon on April 15, 2011, after a long and productive life.

Her death was not unexpected, having been anticipated by many years of progressive lung disease and increased oxygen dependence, even before we relocated south from Yukon, but I was still left with a great empty space in my own life that remains. After many years I still think of her every day and mourn her absence. We were together fifty-five years, and although we had some rough spots, we never fought, talking out conflict when it inevitably arose. We shared everything with one another and truly were one another's best friend.

Reviewing options, I decided to sell the Sidney property and move into an apartment near downtown Victoria, not far from the home of my middle daughter and her family. I grew up living in apartments and liked having other people around me, unlike Cathleen, whose parents had always lived in detached houses. Cathleen and I had similarly always chosen to live in houses, but I knew at this phase of my life I'd be happier living among others in a rented suite, not having to worry about upkeep and gardening.

Our daughters sorted through Cathleen's things, and much was given away to charity that wasn't of sentimental value. I found a pleasant two-bedroom, third-floor, sunny southeast corner apartment in the Cook St. Village area, near the city centre, and moved in at the end of October. I resumed physical exercise at different community recreation centres, motorcycling on Sundays with the Ferryriders, socializing with the Prime Timers, and studying Finnish at the university. I downsized my library of books by two-thirds but kept the hundreds of classical music CDs.

By the end of the year I felt satisfied, having made a successful transition to my new life circumstances, albeit as a widower, alone in a world with a permanent empty space left by dear Cathleen, my companion and life partner for over half a century.

9

Warrior Woman

(In Memoriam)

My wife and life partner Cathleen Anna Smith (née Benson) was born in St. Paul, Minnesota, on July 15, 1932, the eldest of two daughters of American Marjorie Buchanan and Alfred Bengtsson, a Swedish immigrant and ironworker. She attended the University of Minnesota after high school, majoring in art history, and spent one year (1952–53) in Paris studying sculpture with Russian artist Ossip Zadkine. She later obtained a graduate degree in early childhood education, contributing to the specialist literature on working with special needs children in their preschool years. She was a founding member of the family day care movement in British Columbia, Canada.

Cathleen and I met at the university in 1954 and were married in a Quaker ceremony in Montevideo, Uruguay, on August 24, 1956. We had three daughters while living in Argentina until 1963 and, following a brief period back in Minnesota, settled in Nelson and then Vancouver, British Columbia, where she taught early childhood education at Douglas College and became known as an international specialist in that field.

Her interest and creativity in fine arts developed into photography and subsequently cinema and beyond visual arts to appreciation of opera and baroque music.

Our children having all pursued their own lives and partners, Cathleen retired from teaching in 1994 when we moved to Whitehorse, Yukon Territory, where she directed an acclaimed film about Indigenous journalist Edith Josie from Old Crow, in the far north of the Territory.

Poliomyelitis contracted in early adolescence during the mid-twentieth century epidemic left her with scoliosis deformity of the spine and reduced lung capacity, eventually causing her to become oxygen dependent. In 2001 we relocated to a more temperate climate on Vancouver Island, close to our three daughters and by then seven grandsons, where she was able to enjoy gardening and sharing with me her interest in music and literature.

Cathleen died in Victoria on April 15, 2011, after a long life of consistent devotion to our family, her art, and to issues of human rights, particularly racial and sexual minorities. Her positive engagement with social enrichment in areas of health and justice left the country a better place, and our three daughters and seven grandchildren manifest their social attitudes thanks to her example. In a celebration of life ceremony, she was characterized by Indigenous friends as a "warrior woman."

I remain thankful that we were together for so long, recognizing that undeniably I became a better person because of my half-century relationship with this extraordinary warrior woman.

10

Notes from the Bear Cave

2011-

Victoria, BC

In January 2012 I settled into a weekly routine to provide social and intellectual involvement for each day. For the latter, this included keeping a daily diary in Finnish. Social contact came in the form of regular luncheons on Mondays with Len and others, tea on Tuesday afternoons with Kjerstin, walks on Wednesday with the Prime Timers (a.k.a. Gay Geezers), bridge games Thursday evening, opera telecasts on Saturday with Kjerstin or pub lunches with Al, and Sunday dinners at the Mackies's, (I supplying the meat entrée for the carnivores). Fridays were free. For a while I attended hockey games in Victoria, but never became a fan and eventually quit going. I continued regular exercise at different recreation centres around the city and suburbs. While all had the same basic equipment, the layouts and accessibilities varied.

I made several extended trips away from Victoria, the first in April to accompany my cousin Ann to New York City and Connecticut for the marriage of her nephew Alan to his partner Dan. The marriage was celebrated at a posh country resort in Connecticut by over a hundred guests, including members of both families. A party in the evening featured a dance band with extremely loud pop music, provoking me to seek refuge in my hotel room, where I instead watched a hockey game.

While east for the wedding, I had dinner in New York City with a former UBC professor of psychiatry who had always been supportive of my work to remove the psychiatric diagnosis of mental illness from gay people. Never open about his own sexual orientation at the time, he eventually left his wife in Vancouver and to my surprise was now living with a male partner in Harlem. I wondered whether my efforts had contributed to his decision, but he disclosed nothing of that to me and of course I kept my mouth shut.

The second trip was in late August, staying two weeks in Finland. I was kindly given the use of a suburban Helsinki apartment by the family of my Finnish tutor, Hilkka. I took an overnight train to Rovaniemi in Lapland on the Arctic Circle, where I rented a car and drove another seventy kilometres further north, to a location named Tolonen, the surname of my maternal grandfather. Nothing much was to be seen there, apart from a few farm buildings.

In Helsinki I explored the excellent tram system, visited many museums, and bought a print of the painting *Kullervo's Curse* by Akseli Gallen-Kallela, a Finnish painter known for his illustrations from the Finnish national epic, *Kalevala*. I also went to the Finnish National Opera for a production of Janáček's *Makropulos Affair*, sung in Czech but with surtitles provided in three languages: Finnish, Swedish and English.

I met members of SETA, the main LGBT rights organization in Finland, and they told me of a project underway to produce a documentary film about Finnish seniors of minority sexual status. I described the Prime Timers group for gay seniors in Victoria, promising to return next year for the annual Finnish Pride festival.

A colleague of my old friend Peggy Day, theologian Martti Nissinen showed me around the University of Helsinki. Peggy had been a longtime family friend, ever since she and Kjerstin had met at a Jewish dance class in Vancouver over forty years ago, and eventually became a roommate of Joel's. She received her PhD from Harvard in Semitic languages and was Chair of Religious Studies at the University of Winnipeg for years. Peggy lent me Martti's definitive book on religion and homosexuality in the ancient world.

Finland seemed such an agreeable place that I returned to Helsinki for another week in November, when I attended a hockey game and bought a souvenir jersey of the local team, the Jokers. On another night I saw a production of Verdi's *Don Carlo* at the Finnish National Opera. I explored the possibility of retiring there, not only because of my ancestry and knowledge of the language, but because their level of medical and social services for the elderly is even better than Canada's. While this would have been financially feasible, with all my family and friends in Canada, I decided to stay in Victoria and not relocate.

In December I made a quick trip to New York, attending the Metropolitan Opera's production of the Berlioz opera *Les Troyens*, then spending a weekend with Alan and Dan at their home in Connecticut. They kindly drove me one day to see the art museum at Yale University, and I tagged along to Christmas and Hanukkah parties.

Back in Victoria, at a Prime Timers coffee party, I met Jack Wang, a younger gay Chinese man who had immigrated to Canada the previous year but, sadly, after having been together for less than a year, had lost his sponsor and partner to an unexpected fatal illness. He knew no one else in Victoria and had been directed to our group by a gay couple in the condo building where he lived. At the time he was taking high school upgrading courses and looking for a minimum-wage part-time job.

Unexpectedly, and despite the age difference, we hit it off. We became romantically involved and he was basically adopted into our family. Jack and I consoled one another, both having recently lost our partners. And though the initial romance predictably cooled over time, he has remained a dear and loyal friend and close to our family.

In 2013, being by now the elected vice-president of the Victoria Prime Timers, when the president passed away in the spring, I found myself the de facto president of the club, chairing meetings, arranging varied speakers from charities, government agencies, police constables and even a retired sex worker on health issues, for the monthly gatherings. I also gave talks to other groups in nearby Vancouver and Seattle.

In June I travelled overseas again, first to Wales, joining members of the Ixion UK motorcycle club for their annual excursion on a restored narrow-gauge railway, then on to York, where I stayed with Joel for a few days before flying on to Helsinki. Meanwhile, my cousin Ann and daughter Kjerstin had flown together from Seattle to Reykjavik in Iceland, where they stayed two nights with Kjerstin's cousin Eric, to break the long trip to Finland. They then arrived hours after me at Vantaa Airport outside of Helsinki.

We stayed downtown for one week at the cozy Hotel Anna, and they explored the city. I marched in the annual Pride parade and carried a Canadian flag beside an American consular official carrying his own country's flag. There were delegations from Copenhagen and nearby St.

Petersburg, the latter being prevented by law from open manifestations of gay Pride within Russia. I also met with the filmmaker producing the video about aging in Finnish sexual minorities.

After Helsinki we rented a car and Kjerstin drove Ann and me around southern Finland for another week, visiting Peggy's friend Martti and his wife Leena at their lakeside cabin, where we were treated to a traditional wood-fired sauna, followed by an authentic regional dinner of fish baked within a loaf of bread. We also attended a production of Wagner's opera *Lohengrin* at Savonlinna, a medieval castle on an island in a lake, and visited the home of composer Jean Sibelius before returning home to Victoria via Helsinki.

Jack was accepted into a nine-month program at Camosun College to train as a hospital care aide, and in the fall I began Mandarin language instruction at the University of Victoria, having purchased a Finnish-Chinese dictionary in Helsinki. At Christmas we all had a big family dinner at my daughter's, and Jack knit me a beautiful warm woolly scarf with the Finnish colours of blue and white.

Jack went to driving school, and when he passed his driving test, I bought an older Toyota RAV4 for us to share. American psychiatrist and author Loren Olsen, an officer of Prime Timers International, visited Victoria for a weekend, and we took him on excursions to the Butchart Gardens and the Royal BC Museum. He gave a talk to the Prime Timers about aging and sexuality at our monthly meeting, before returning to his home in Iowa.

Most of the winter of 2015 was spent at home, translating a 275-page Finnish police procedural, *Katumurha* (*Street Murder*), into English. My tutor Hilkka was a useful resource for understanding some of the idiomatic expressions, but I had learned enough of the grammar and vocabulary to do the job. I offered the translation to a publisher of Nordic crime novels and they weren't interested, but I felt satisfied with having mastered enough of this language to complete the translation.

In March our friend and former medical colleague from the Klondyke Medical Clinic in Whitehorse, Ken Quong, was briefly in town with his wife and met Jack and me for coffee one afternoon at the Royal BC Museum, where they had just viewed a photography exhibition.

Jack and I watched two parades in July, one in Sidney on Canada Day and the other the annual Pride parade in Victoria. After the Pride parade we visited various booths and exhibits celebrating diversity, including one of the Prime Timers and another where Kjerstin, being licensed by the province to tie the knots, was drumming up business for marriage services through her Unitarian church.

I began to create more time for rote learning of Chinese characters. Although I knew I would never achieve fluency or travel to China, I wanted to understand how the writing system worked and to better appreciate Tang dynasty poetry, as well as learn a few phrases to amuse Jack. I endeavoured to keep physically fit by attending the gym and was socially active with friends and family, as well as intellectually stimulated by reading, music and language study. Still, a Finnish proverb about aging seemed relevant: "Life is uncertain, eat dessert first!"

After the sale of the condo where he had lived with his late partner, Jack stayed with me for four months in the spring of 2016 while he searched for a place of his own, finally finding a new and conveniently located condo in a recently built building near downtown Victoria, close to public transit. He moved there in July, keeping busy with shifts as a health care assistant at different hospitals and taking further technical courses at the college. Sharing the car seemed to work well for both of us, and meanwhile I had the motorcycle for transportation when Jack had the old Toyota RAV4.

At the end of April, Len died unexpectedly at his home in Victoria. Like many of my friends, such as Peggy with her PhD and Joel with his QBE, Len and I were both well-educated and liked the same kinds of music, literature and lively discussions on ideas. After I moved to Victoria, we continued to have lunch together on Mondays, sometimes with Sidney United Church minister David Drake, and continued doing so after Len moved to a condo in Victoria. He would also stop by for afternoon coffee at my apartment on Thursdays.

Later, David also moved to Victoria from Sidney, into the same building as Len, and joined Prime Timers, officiating at the graveside service. I acquired Len's comfy recliner from his estate, and often think of him after a meal as I drift off to sleep for a sometimes inadvertent nap.

I continued regular exercise at the Esquimalt Recreation Centre, where the equipment and facilities were superior to those at closer facilities, as well as having easier access, with no stairs to climb. Age-related deteriorations were addressed individually: improved hearing with new Swiss hearing aids, clearer vision with new glasses for both reading and distance, and better chewing with new dentures. All of these ameliorated the complaints, but of course none restored a function to its earlier condition as in a younger body. My walking declined with arthritic knee joints, and worsening difficulty with stairs compelled me to accept that long walks would no longer be feasible, let alone mountaineering in Patagonia.

Over the summer there were major renovations to my apartment building, Linden Manor. New double-glazed windows were installed, kitchen cabinets and appliances were replaced, and the balcony was reconstructed. A maximum permitted rise in rent followed as expected, and no doubt will continue yearly until costs are recovered, but the increase is modest, the appearance more sprightly, and the convenience considerable, except for the owners failing to construct a ramp to access the front door, retaining five steep steps.

Ann visited from Seattle in August, and Jack had his first experience with the tradition of pumpkin carving at my daughter's before Halloween. There were two trips over to the mainland this year. My old friend from Yukon, Ken Spotswood, suffered a fatal heart attack in late 2015, and Jack and I attended a memorial celebration in June with friends at the home of his former journalism colleague near Vancouver.

And in November I celebrated the fortieth anniversary of my graduation from UBC medical school in 1976. I made an appearance and stayed with friends in North Vancouver, visiting the annual train show of the West Coast Railway Association on the same weekend. That same weekend my old friend Joel arrived at Vancouver Airport from the UK. He joined us for another week in Victoria, and we attended a baroque music concert and drove to Port Renfrew in atrocious weather, a day with howling wind and sleet. We celebrated our common birthday (his seventieth, my eighty-third) before he returned to Yorkshire.

I maintained a very stable lifestyle throughout 2017. In the morning of nearly every day I would arise around six, make coffee and a nourishing breakfast, and check the (mostly bad) news on a variety of websites, including the BBC, *Guardian*, *Washington Post*, CBC, and our local rag, the *Victoria Times-Colonist.* Following a short postprandial nap in Len's comfy chair, I would write and read.

For lunch most days I would have a large mixed salad with cheese and crackers, or perhaps a sandwich. After lunch and another nap in Len's chair, I would spend afternoons reading non-fiction or journals such as the *Times Literary Supplement* or the *London* or *New York Review of Books.* If I was at home, evenings were reserved for fiction. Bedtime reading was often a detective story by Simenon, but sometimes another light tale in Spanish, French, or German to retain familiarity with other languages.

I often shared an evening meal with Jack, who began a two-year college course in information technology in the fall. Since arriving in Canada in 2011, though he had flown across all southern Canada, to Newfoundland, Nova Scotia, Quebec, and Ontario, he had never been east of

Vancouver by land, so in early summer we took a week-long trip together in our car, all across British Columbia, to Jasper National Park in Alberta, then down through the Rocky Mountains to Banff and over to Calgary.

We drove across the prairie to Drumheller, visited the Dinosaur Museum, and on to Lethbridge, where we had a tasty Alberta steak dinner before returning to the coast by the southern Trans-Canada Highway. We stayed a night in Nelson, where Cathleen and I first lived with our daughters after immigrating to Canada fifty years earlier. Unlike some other towns in the BC Interior, Nelson had changed very little, except for the growth of trees. The railway behind our old house had been abandoned and was now a trail for walkers and joggers.

Back in Victoria, I met with my lawyer to update my will at the beginning of 2018, to assist my executor in allocating any remaining assets, though not because I foresaw any immediate demise. I was beginning to tire of the rote learning of Chinese characters, which began to seem like work made to pass the time. Having no television and eschewing social media, I needed an occupation other than returning to crossword puzzles to fill up those solitary hours when neither reading nor listening to music in the Bear Cave, as my apartment came to be called, would suffice.

I considered composing some kind of memoir or autobiography and began writing a chronological account of my life experiences, from birth in 1933 to the present. Avoiding digressions, I rigidly restricted it to one page per year, about 500 words. I found that my old diary material was helpful, along with a few annual "solstice summaries" and travel reports.

I went about reviewing the daily records that I kept during my professional clinical and academic career, summarizing them, shredding them, and avoiding reference to any specific patients.

The writing process took about three months, totalling 35,000 words over sixty-eight pages and organized in chronological sections. Since this concrete account made little or no reference to abstract thought, I soon embarked on a series of short essays relating to ideas on topics arising from books and articles that interested me. I originally posted these on a blog, which can be found at karhunluola.com. The Finnish word *karhunluola* literally means "bear's cave." These writings will likely be continued indefinitely, as long as I am cognitively intact and have something to say about this world in which we live.

Jack formally became a Canadian citizen in July, and changed his surname from Wang to Christie, honouring his late partner. After his citizenship ceremony, Jack and I went to the wedding of my youngest daughter, Emilie, (now an Anglican priest) to her girlfriend Patti in

Vancouver. We drove up the mainland coast to visit my old friend, nurse Bob, who had conducted the STD screening clinic with me when I was a medical student long ago in the 1970s. We then returned to Victoria via Powell River, Comox and Duncan.

No further travel away from Victoria is envisaged. My Canadian and Argentinian passports have both expired, and I'm resigned to remain in what my fellow Canadian octogenarian Mick Mallon slyly called "Victoria, God's little waiting room by the sea." In a recent review in the *Times Literary Supplement*, Alan Murrin posed a profound question central to our existence: "Persevere despite the absence of hope or give up and forfeit what it means to be human?" The underlying problem is the evident unstoppable rush towards the collapse of social order caused by environmental catastrophe. I for one intend to persevere, one day at a time, but remain pessimistic about civilization, the future of the planet, and the foreseeable likely bleak lives of my descendants and others.

Meanwhile, aside from costly trips to the dentist in Sidney and taking friends and family to the airport or ferry terminal in North Saanich, I only made two trips outside of Victoria in 2019 — a day excursion by motorcycle over to Salt Spring Island to have lunch with friends, and another west of Victoria by car with Joel, during his annual birthday visit to Jordan River to look at Pacific surf and the intrepid surfers.

I finally gave my fifteenth and last motorcycle to my grandson Hugh in early November, and it now sits in his garage until he decides to licence it. I still share the 2007 Toyota SUV with Jack, who completed his coursework and was immediately employed by the college on a temporary basis. We see one another regularly and share a meal. (He also trims my whiskers.) He has since secured a permanent full-time position working in information technology at a local hospital.

I'm home alone most days now, writing or reading literary magazines or books, and listening to music on CBC, Yle (Finland), or NPR from the US. I do follow current events on media websites, though it is a depressing activity. Increased social isolation due to the viral pandemic augments loneliness, though physical exercise at home helps to defer excessive rumination about the future. Jack bought me a stationary bike for my eighty-seventh birthday.

So, I continue to live one day at a time, mostly alone, pedalling my thoughts in short essays as I pedal my new bike. Still, having climbed many mountains, from the real to the metaphorical, the unanswered question remains: Now what? Is there nothing more than to admire the view?

I rather suspect not, but hey, what a view!

Self-Criticism

Self-criticism can be a useful exercise, though when prolonged it is pathological, as my psychiatry professor once averred to his medical students. I tend to agree but would add that motivation ideally should be one's own and not imposed by others.

Of the traditional seven deadly sins, gluttony seems rampant in consumer society. I have not been especially gluttonous as an adult, although as a teenager I once ate thirteen ears of corn in an eating contest, but this event was neither prolonged nor pathological, just stupid.

Sloth, associated with inaction and laziness, is perceived as sinful in the Protestant work ethic, as well as in Bolshevism, although the glorification of exceeding production quotas, combined with pride, led to famine in both the Soviet Union and China. I admit to sloth as a negative mild personal trait and try to resist, sometimes avoiding a comfy recliner because I tend to doze in it. But that feels more like a trait than a sin.

Lust — age-related, particularly in younger males, peaking at nineteen and then gradually declining — may lead some to sexual aggression or compulsive masturbation. Tolstoy famously praised diminished sexual drive in old age, comparing it to no longer feeling like being on a troika pulled by uncontrolled horses. I was inhibited as a youth and subdued in middle life, and sex is but a remote memory now in my late ninth decade.

Though usually possessing excellent self-control, being human I have experienced wrath on two occasions, once at a dinner party in the US, confronting an American war apologist, the other when verbally abusing a psychiatric colleague, who from apparent venal motivation had accused me in a lawsuit of failure to diagnose depression in a patient that sadly had injured himself. These, however, were incidental and not prolonged events, and not considered pathological, except perhaps by the victims of my verbal wrath.

Envy seems to be an almost universal feeling, though seldom openly admitted as a source for undesirable behaviour. I don't particularly envy others, other than to feel that youth, as we all know, is wasted on the young. I readily identify with Faust or von Aschenbach, pining for the delights of being young again, but it hardly seems sinful and more like a common human trait.

The assertion of pride by disparaged minority groups represents a rejection of negative social constructs, but when employed as an excuse for boasting is perceived as distasteful or imprudent, and hubris if blatant. I marched in gay Pride parades in Victoria and Helsinki for political reasons, not as personal bragging, and perceive no sign of sinful activity in this.

Greed, termed "the root of all evil" by St. Paul in 1 Timothy 6:10, is celebrated openly as the great enabler in consumer capitalism, marketing, and financial manipulation. Dictators, in developing "third world" countries, tend to divert money allocated for aid programs into their hidden offshore accounts or a private concealed hoard in Swiss banks. One may deny being greedy if lacking no daily needs, but for those experiencing poverty, amassing wealth seems an understandable reaction to adverse life circumstances.

Doubtless I could be accused of displaying other traits meriting regret, character defects or unpleasant personality features, but these could just be considered features of my personal "original sins," for which psychoanalysis may sometimes grant insight, but never absolution.

So it goes.

MOSAIC

essays

... you are dust and to dust you shall return

Preface

Humanities was the title given by scholars to the study of human beings and the structures, values and writings that differentiate *Homo sapiens* from other members of the animal kingdom. Deriving from the Latin word *humanitatis,* humanities was a departure from the theological concept of humanity associated with Christianity, which dominated thought in Western Europe prior to the Renaissance. When I was an undergraduate at the University of Minnesota from 1951 to 1954, humanities was my formal major, an interdepartmental course of studies that included philosophy, literature, history and political science, among others. These studies became the origin of my lifelong worldview, or *Weltanschauung.*

Marking a surface to represent concrete concepts that can be observed and mutually understood by others is characteristic animal behaviour. Take for example bees dancing back at the hive to indicate a source of nectar, or dogs marking a tree to assert territory. Transmissions of information about food supply or the location of predators abound, but in humans the content may be highly abstract. This leads one to consider the sequence of steps involved in forming ideas and concepts, and how these thoughts are expressed so that they can be shared with others.

In our understanding of the natural world, ordering is an effort to find regularity in chaos. Thus, we discovered the difference in atomic nuclei that accounts for the unique properties of each element in the periodic table, and the differences among living organisms determined by the genetic coding of their nucleic acids. These structural features of order were not invented but discovered by scientists. But we also impose order on collections of disparate items to represent and differentiate between them, like profits and losses for an accountant, or votes cast in an election for a variety of candidates. Throughout history there have been many different options for organizing knowledge, from the scrolls in the now vanished Library of Alexandria to the words listed in a dictionary or maps displayed in an atlas.

The principles of ordering may be hierarchical, geographic, chronological, alphabetic or even theological. Early European lists resisted alphabetization because it was felt to be a dishonour to God, or *Deus*, not to head the list. Alphabetic ordering only became common in Europe as subject headings gradually replaced chronology in governmental records. The concept of an encyclopedia, a recording of the totality of knowledge, first appeared in 1630, and the alphabet then became the organizing principle allowing for the retrieval of knowledge. Dictionaries of languages with non-alphabetic scripts in East Asia, however, were ordered in other ways, such as by the number of brush strokes required to write Chinese characters.

What is important is to recognize our tendency to invent some principle, some method, of sorting. "The human mind works by internalizing such arbitrary and useful tools, as a kind of grid onto which knowledge can be arranged, and from which it can be retrieved," wrote the novelist A.S. Byatt. We think, therefore we sort.

These essays that follow cover a wide range of themes, constituting a collection of recent writings that form a mosaic of thoughts. In selecting which essays to include, it was necessary to retrieve each one from a chronological list and assign it to one of four categories of human endeavour:

Homo scribens (human writing): language, books, reading, writing
Homo cognoscens (human learning): science, medicine, environmentalism
Homo credens (human believing): religion, economics, politics, philosophy
Homo ludens (human playing): music, humour

As humans, we first communicate, then learn, later believe and finally play with acquired knowledge. The conclusion is a postscript, an essay I wrote back in May of 1954, "*Auf dem Wegen zur Eigenen Weltanschauung*," meaning "On the way towards one's own world view."

HOMO SCRIBENS

11 Homo scribens

"In the beginning was the Word" begins the Gospel according to John. In this verse, *Word* implies script, which implies language and therefore meaning and communication. In other words, in the beginning there was information. Consider, then, writing and man writing, or *Homo scribens.*

In high school I enrolled in an introductory course in Latin as an elective, my only motivation seeming to be curiosity. Later as an undergraduate at university, I took two years of German, and before emigrating to Argentina I hired a friend who was studying linguistics to coach me in Spanish grammar. Throughout my adult life I have taken courses in French, Italian, Swedish, and Russian, all before travelling to those lands. These were all Indo-European languages, though, and after I retired, for something different, I have been studying the structures of two unrelated, non-Indo-European tongues: Finnish and Mandarin Chinese.

Each of these two tongues has its own unique challenges. Like English, Finnish is written in Latin script and is easy to pronounce, one only needing to remember that the stress always falls on the first syllable and that doubled vowels and consonants are doubly pronounced. Finnish is technically a cenemic writing system, in which the alphabetic symbols themselves are devoid of meaning.

In comparison, Mandarin is a non-alphabetic pleremic writing system, meaning that the symbols each have their own meanings. The Chinese characters give no major clue about how they are to be vocalized — one must learn the sound in addition to recognizing the shape. Every character has an initial consonant and a terminal vowel; there are less than 500 possible such combinations, and they are further divided by rising or falling tones.

Useful in disentangling the structure of Chinese characters is the book *The Chinese Typewriter: A History* by Thomas S. Mullaney, which addresses the vexing problem of constructing a device to print text written in non-alphabetic symbols. The present-day solution is one of computer input. For example, when using a QWERTY keyboard in the Romanized Pinyin script, rather than "what you see is what you get" (WYSIWYG), the characters appear within a pop-up menu of choices for selection. Typing Chinese is thus a two-step procedure.

In Finnish the main difficulty arises not from the common Roman script but from the complex grammar. In addition to prepositions and postpositions, there are fifteen cases, used as noun and adjectival modifier suffixes indicating number, amount, position, possession, size and/or emphasis. The language is agglutinative, and a series of suffixes may be appended to a noun and to its adjectival modifier. Verbs are also complex, with the declensions of different verb types through four tense forms.

Grammar in Mandarin Chinese, on the other hand, is much simpler. Word order is much as it is in English (subject-verb-object) and is totally non-inflected, with no noun case endings or verb conjugations. Cues are employed to indicate tenses, such as completed actions. One minor complication is the use of many different "measure words" to indicate plurals, like saying a "six-pack" of beer instead of "six cans of beer" or a "bunch" of bananas.

Finnish employs an easy script but has complex grammar, whereas Mandarin enjoys a simple grammar but a complex script. Like Tolstoy's unhappy families, they each differ from English in their own ways. —*June 2020*

12 Bilingualism

Writing on leap day 2020 in his column "Johnson," in that holy writ periodical of neoliberalism, the *Economist*, Stephen Hugh-Jones addressed the issue of bilingualism. Bilingualism is a subject close to the hearts of not only Canadians but also citizens of many other countries in which two languages may be used in official documentation such as tax forms, passports, street signs and the like. One country that comes to mind is Finland, where both Swedish and Finnish are designated as official languages, similar to French and English in Canada. Some countries like Switzerland even have more than two official languages (German, French, Romansh and Italian).

Hugh-Jones notes in his article that the cognitive benefits of bilingualism have been debated at different times as either positive or negative, and that a recent study seemed to indicate that the *frequency* of switching from one language to another was likely beneficial. From infancy, humans in any linguistic environment will master whichever language they are exposed to in early childhood, be it English, Finnish, Korean or any other. Moreover, if the child is raised exclusively in a constructed or invented language, such as Zamenhof's Esperanto, that will become its natural language. The sixteenth-century French essayist Montaigne (1533–1592) was deliberately raised in a Latin-speaking environment, with Latin as a first language. He soon also became familiar with Greek through games, conversation and exercises of solitary meditation.

Most of us are not Montaignes; the probable benefit of knowing other languages is that it enables us to have a world outlook not limited by one single linguistic mode of expression. My seven-year-old great-grand-daughter attends a French-immersion primary school, though English is the language used in her home. For her to attain reasonable fluency, she should have some experience of living in a francophone culture.

My first language was English, but years spent living in Argentina have endowed me with a reasonable fluency in Spanish, though a variety of Spanish devalued by Hispanopurists. Working in astronomy while living in Argentina enabled me to easily communicate with other scientists within this field, but when I later returned to the country after retraining in medicine and was asked to give a talk in Spanish to other doctors on the neuropsychiatry of retroviral disease, I was flummoxed by my ignorance of Spanish medical vocabulary.

Johnson wisely noted in his column that speaking a second language less well than your first provides "a constant practice in humility." — *Mar 2020*

13 Nineteen Ways of Looking at Wang Wei

The Tang dynasty is generally regarded as a high point in Chinese civilization and a golden age of cosmopolitan culture. Writing during the long reign of Emperor Xuanzong (713–756 CE), Wang Wei (700–761 CE) was a poet, musician, painter and statesman, and one of the most famous men of arts and letters of his time.

In 1987 Eliot Weinberger wrote the book *Nineteen Ways of Looking at Wang Wei*, which addresses the difficulty of translating a single quatrain by the eighth-century Chinese poet. Weinberger illustrates the vicissitudes of making available to contemporary readers the thoughts of a 1,200-year-old poet from a culture entirely unrelated to our own. He includes nineteen different possible translations, which are reviewed and analyzed to exhibit alternate versions of communicating mood and content. Most of the translations are in English, though a few are in Spanish, French or German, and the book's 2016 update offers an additional ten translations.

Wang Wei's poem, written on a horizontal landscape scroll, describes the sights near a river. Although the original is lost, copies survived, the earliest being from the seventeenth century, 900 years after the poem was written. Each of the twenty Chinese characters represents a word of a single syllable. The complication arises in that every monosyllable can be pronounced in one of four tones, each with many different possible meanings. Rhyme is inevitable, but meter is impossible, and tones are untranslatable.

Weinberger reproduces the four lines of five characters, along with the Pinyin transliteration for the sounds. This is followed by a character-by-character translation, to show the choices available for would-be translators trying to capture Wang Wei's vision. There is obviously no "best" way of organizing such an equivalence, only a range of possibilities, and Weinberger picks apart each version with a close analysis of each attempt.

Of the many different possibilities presented, Burton Watson's 1971 translation conveys meaning fairly well:

> Empty hills, no one in sight,
> Only the sound of someone talking;
> Late sunlight enters the deep wood,
> Shining over the green moss again.

As an afterword, Mexican poet Octavio Paz contributes an essay further discussing the difficulties of translation. Paz observes that the difficulty with Chinese-to-Spanish translation lies partly in that not only is there a smaller corpus of examples available to compare, but also equivalent lines in Spanish tend to have more syllables than those in English. —*June 2018*

14 Tu Fu

Another celebrated Tang dynasty poet, Tu Fu (712–770 CE), is represented in the 1967 collection *A Little Primer of Tu Fu* by scholar David Hawkes. The Hawkes collection consists of thirty-five different poems by Tu Fu, each with the original Chinese text written in modern Mandarin characters along with the Pinyin transliteration. Accompanying each poem is a commentary on the subject, the historical background, the formal structure of the verse in terms of meter and rhyme, and exegesis of every individual line. At the conclusion of this close examination, Hawkes offers his own colloquial translation of the content.

The Tu Fu poems range in content from reflections on a mountain view; dreams; songs of particular vignettes, such as passing army carts, paintings of horses, images of court officials or dress styles of women; and a range of human emotions. Each poem is a vast word-picture of the culture and values of this sophisticated and wealthy society in East Asia, when the western part of the Eurasian continent was mostly illiterate.

In his introduction, Hawkes comments that he wrote the book "to give some idea of what Chinese poetry is really like and how it works to people who either know no Chinese at all or know only a little . . . . It is my ardent hope that a reader who is patient enough to work his way through to the end of the book will, by the time he reaches it, have learned something about the Chinese language, something about Chinese poetry, and something about the poet Tu Fu."

With a non-alphabetic script and a linguistic tradition extending back continuously some 3,500 years from the present day, *A Little Primer of Tu Fu* represents more than just a selection of ancient poetry from a different culture. Tu Fu's poetry is a vast panoply of human creation, reminiscent of the paintings of Bruegel the Elder, in words and thoughts rather than visual images. Hawkes has done us all a favour in providing this key to unlock a great flowering of human civilization in a society so distant from our own. — *June 2019*

15 Writing as Therapy

In the introduction to a collection of short stories by Graham Greene, the author is quoted saying, "Writing is a form of therapy: sometimes I wonder how all those who do not write, compose, or paint can manage to escape the madness, the melancholia, the panic and fear which is inherent in the human condition."

The passive acquisition of scientific knowledge yields satisfaction in terms of understanding the human condition, but it doesn't console. Knowing about the laws of thermodynamics and entropy hardly provides any comfort. Religions may provide solace for those who accept their doctrines, but not for those who abjure supernatural belief. Great music, however, may engender a sense of peace even though inspired by religious belief. For example, the Ninth Symphony of Anton Bruckner was dedicated to God, and Bach's Mass in B Minor is a celebration of Christian belief. One needn't adhere to the Christian religion to appreciate these profound works.

Those more sensitive to visual input than I may derive benefit from creative arts that involve the ordering of space rather than of time or sound, such as painting and sculpture. These artistic endeavours and others, like cinema, dance, or even opera, involve the creative imposition of order. This brings us to writing, using words or language to create not a concrete object like a painting or a symphony performance, but something more abstract — ideas and feelings.

A poem is not the printed symbols on a page, nor the words read or recited, but an idea, a feeling, something intangible that uses language to convey both information and mood states from the writer to the reader or listener. Chinese poetry from the eighth-century Tang dynasty is a good example of this, especially when combined with music such as is heard in some works by Gustav Mahler. Mahler's source for the German text of his symphonic cycle *Das Lied von der Erde* (*Song of the Earth*) was Hans Bethge's *Die chinesische Flöte* (*The Chinese Flute*). Bethge used prior translations and adaptations of the original Chinese poetry.

The philosopher Ludwig Wittgenstein wrote in his *Tractatus Logico-Philosophicus* that one should speak clearly of that which can be said, but of that which cannot be said, one must remain silent. This aphorism has always troubled me, in that it seems to refer only to the communication of information but not of mood states.

Be that as it may, creative writing focuses one's thinking on specific issues, providing a respite from what Greene laments as the vicissitudes of the human condition. — *Feb 2019*

16 Speaking vs. Writing

Robert Lane Greene, writing in the Johnson column about language for the *Economist*, recently penned *Talk on the Wild Side*, a rant attacking "linguistic purists" who maintain that the English language needs to be "protected" against those who would debase its elegance by using non-standard grammar and usage. An obvious target of Greene's outrage may be found in *The Elements of Style* (1935), the classic guide to writing by Strunk and Tenney, which has been through many editions since that time. The current copy before me is the fourth edition, (2000, 1979) with E.B. White as co-author.

The initial chapters of *The Elements of Style* are straightforward and detail the nuts and bolts of forming possessives, use of punctuation, parenthetic expressions, pronoun usage and so on. The second section is devoted to the "elementary principles of composition," with recommendations on design and structure, formation of paragraphs, summaries and placement of emphasis. The third section addresses "matters of form," such as headings, use of colloquialisms, margins, numeral placement, quotations, references and titles.

It is in the fourth and final section where the authors become concerned with "what is correct" or considered acceptable in the use of English. Here the focus is clearly more restrictive than descriptive, suggesting a matter more of taste than of rigid order. "Correctness" is emphasized with a series of "improper" examples of common "misuse," illustrating the point of Greene's essay, in which he deplores those "fuddy-duddies" who promote the "correct" usage of the English language.

But Greene is also specifying the difference between written and spoken language. English, unlike Latin, is a living language. Speech inevitably insinuates itself into writing, as evident in reading citations of spoken words by politicians and others in the media. For example, future tense may be indicated by new modal verbs such as *wanna* and *gonna*, contractions for *want to* and *going to*, as in "Do you wanna have another beer? I'm gonna have one."

France is notorious for its Académie Française, created to invigilate (and unsuccessfully regulate) the purity of the French language, but we have no such body in English, which will doubtlessly continue to expand as a living language whether language purists like it or not.

I tend to side more with Greene than with the apostles of linguistic purity. Though never a professional writer, apart from a few months working as a journalist for an American news agency in South America over sixty years ago, I once edited a journal for medical students at university, and later for many years as a psychiatrist wrote thousands of case histories, along with journal articles, book reviews and even some attempts at humour. —*May 2019*

17 The Abominable Pronoun

What's Your Pronoun? Beyond He and She by Dennis Baron was the subject of a lengthy review — actually an essay — by Oxford professor of social and political theory Amia Srinivasan in the July 2, 2020, *London Review of Books*. Srinivasan describes the book as "a delightful account of the search for what Baron, a professor of English and linguistics at the University of Illinois, calls 'the missing word': a third person singular, gender-neutral pronoun." A typical occasion of the need for such a word might be a sentence like "Everyone misplaces ______ keys." To say *his or her* seems awkward, *one's* sounds stuffy, and *its* is rude. *Their* sounds okay, but it is a plural of *they*.

This seems to be an issue peculiar to English, as *man* in German or *on* in French are used as non-gendered words, and the problem doesn't arise in Finnish, Hungarian, Malay or other non-gendered languages. (In Mandarin Chinese the sound *ta* is the same but the written characters differ.)

To be polite and tactful with nonbinary people, who don't identify as either "male" or "female," throws a spotlight on this situation. Traditionally *he*, *his* and *hers* have been used as generic pronouns, but the custom is unsuitable in some legal situations, and Srinivasan considers it "a tool of patriarchy." Strunk and White's *Elements of Style*, however, have continued to plump for the generic *he*.

Interestingly, Baron reminds us that English grammar once boasted different pronouns for the second person singular and plural, with *thou* being the second person singular until the eighteenth century, when the plural *you* gradually replaced it. Now we employ *you* for both the singular and plural second person, inferring from context both number and gender (perhaps excepting the American Southern *y'all*). Historically, there is also a first person usage of the plural *we* replacing the singular *I*, once used by monarchs, such as in Queen Victoria's alleged riposte "We are not amused."

Many attempts were made to invent an appropriate word to fulfill the need for a suitable third person singular pronoun in the nineteenth century and more recently with the LGBTQ movement. None seem to have caught on, but we are beginning to see some individuals employing the third person plural *they* to refer to themselves, a usage parallel to *thou* being replaced by *you* in the second person singular.

Srinivasan described "doing the pronoun round" with a new class of students, asking them how they preferred to be addressed in class, but admits that it didn't work well. Instead, Srinivasan adopted the procedure of just calling new students by their first name and asking them to email if they preferred something else. "We can choose to respect people's pronouns not only because there is no simple sex or binary but also just to be kind to others."

A sentiment I can agree with, but it still grates to see third person plural employed as singular, habituated as I am to employing the generic *he* for over eighty years. I can try not to be grumpy about it, but still feel annoyed. — *July 2020*

18 The Emoji Code

Vyvyan Evans's latest book, *The Emoji Code* (2017), examines the brief history of the emoji's recent addition to digital communication. Writing in an accessible and non-technical style, Evans describes the word's origin from the combination of *picture* + *character* in Japanese, and then notes the distinction between codes and languages: the former is a system of rules to convert information from one form to another, and the latter is a system for the expression of thoughts and feelings using sounds or conventional symbols.

Emoji lack grammar, or the rules governing combinations of elemental symbols or glyphs. Not a language themselves, emoji nevertheless can fulfill some of the functions of language, such as the replacement of posture, gesture, intonation and other nonverbal cues. Shades of meaning in spoken or written language can be replaced by emoji, modifying digital textspeak by indicating doubt, irony, sarcasm or some other feature. The primary function of emoji is thus not to replace language but to enhance it by supplying these nonverbal cues.

Emoji are not ideographs, or abstract representations established through convention. Instead they are pictographs, each one having an iconic relationship with what it represents, and being meaningful, it is termed pleremic. Chinese characters also began as pictographs, identified in ancient "oracle bones" dating from the second millennium BCE, but over the centuries have evolved into essentially ideographs. I wonder whether the practice of combining Chinese textspeak with emoji may signify a whiff of retrogression.

Emoji are global in the sense that they are recognizable as cues in whatever language is being used digitally. At the time of writing this essay, there were 1,851 characters available to software developers, according to Unicode, the computing industry standard for the consistent encoding, representation, and handling of text expressed in most of the world's writing systems. New emoji are vetted by Unicode before being judged acceptable, and proposals are rejected if they represent logos, brands, deities or persons either living or dead.

Although some have derided the practice of using emoji as a degradation of language, Evans disagrees. Given that face-to-face language is multimodal and textspeak relatively impoverished, he celebrates Emoji for facilitating nonverbal communication cues. — *Apr 2018*

19 Evolving Usage

One of the consequences of living to a ripe old age is the realization that one's language is also living and constantly undergoing shifts in previously familiar meanings and usages. Among the list of contributors to the January 3, 2019, issue of the *London Review of Books*, the writer Alan Bennett is described as one who "can't tell if he's woke or not." I initially thought this use of the word *woke* must be a spelling error, but on further investigation found it to be a recent neologism — an adjective meaning "alert to racial or social discrimination and injustice," deriving from African American Vernacular English.

It is fascinating to observe language evolve, to note how words are sometimes coined anew or used in ways different from their erstwhile meanings. *Woke* for example suggests awakening from sleep, thus becoming a code word for understanding the attitudes it represents. It obviously arose from the past tense of *wake* to create a new adjective.

Evolving language can also go in the opposite direction. For example the English adjective *gay* — a word once meaning "merry or cheerful" — has now become a noun indicating same-sex erotic attraction. A similar process is also seen in other living languages like Mandarin Chinese, in which the word *tóngzhì* (literally, "thinking the same way") previously meant *comrade* (fellow member of the Communist Party) but now has come to mean *gay* in the current English sense of the word. Two unrelated living languages exhibit the same shift in meaning from an unrelated word to one labelling a newly assertive sexual minority feeling free to define themselves, as have other social groups like racial minorities.

Portmanteau words are another variety of neologism, combining parts of two different words to form a new meaning, such as *breakfast* + *lunch* = *brunch*, or *Britain* + *exit* = *Brexit.* And two recent verb forms now in vogue are *to call out*, meaning "to strongly criticize," and *to double down.* The former usage sounds like a German separable verb *ausrufen.* To *double down* means to insist vehemently, as in, "The president doubles down on building a wall!"

All of the above belong to the area of recreational, not academic, linguistics, but hey, why not have a little fun with words in one's dotage — it keeps you out of the bars. — *Jan 2019*

20 Barfing and Babel

A medical friend asked, "Can you explain to me whether the word *nauseated* exists? Is a patient complaining of nausea *nauseous* or *nauseated*?" *Roget's Thesaurus* gives six sentences illustrating the usage of *nauseated*; say no more. Implicit in the query, however, is the question of prescriptive versus descriptive use of language, and as one ages one appears to lean more towards the prescriptive side of usage, implying that there must be a "correct" way of using words, word order, punctuation, and so on. Thus as an old fogey, I may feel annoyed when a part of speech is "misused," like the road sign Drive Slow (instead of *slowly*), or employs a misplaced apostrophe, as in "used car's for sale."

Language is constantly modifying itself, and the modifications are first seen among the young, who eschew punctuation and capitalization rules in texting messages to each other, sprinkling communications with emoji to season their writing, much like a chef employing spices to improve a culinary masterpiece.

The recent book *Babel*, by Dutch enthusiast of recreational linguistics Gaston Dorren, takes the reader "around the world in twenty languages" and is a collection of short essays about the twenty most spoken living languages, from Vietnamese, with 75 million native speakers, to English, with 1.5 billion. Together these languages amount to three-quarters of the world's population. In between the extremes we find not only the usual suspects like Russian, Mandarin, French, Arabic, German and Spanish, but also less familiar (to us) tongues like Tamil (90 million), Persian (110 million), Malay (275 million) and others.

There are many living languages that are used among fewer speakers, such as Scottish Gaelic, Basque in Europe, minority languages in China, and a multitude of disappearing North American native or First Nations tongues. Not dead yet, but ailing in spite of heroic attempts by some to preserve them. But the struggle for linguistic preservation is fated to fail as the steamroller of living languages rolls over those small enough to be overwhelmed by the giants. I know quite a bit of Finnish grammar and vocabulary and have travelled several times to that country, but speaking Finnish as a second language is a non-starter in Finland, for English is taught to children in school from the beginning, and a question in Finnish by a non-Finn invariably results in an answer in English. Regarding *nauseated*, why not just say you feel like barfing? Or use an idiomatic expression such as "doing the Technicolor yawn"? — *Feb 2020*

21 Invented Languages and Zamenhof

The Polish ophthalmologist Lazarus Ludovic Zamenhof is celebrated as the creator of the artificial language Esperanto in the late nineteenth century. The concept of a planned auxiliary language had been previously mooted, and one called Volapük was actually invented in 1879 by Johann Martin Schleyer, a German priest who lived in Baden. Schleyer claimed the idea for creating an international language was suggested to him by God in a dream. But Volapük was a clumsy and complicated mixture of Latin, German and English and did not prosper after reaching a peak of around 100,000 speakers in 1889. Few now understand it.

Zamenhof's Esperanto, however, was simple in grammar and easy to learn. With an estimated two million speakers worldwide, it is the most widely spoken constructed language in the world. There are Esperanto clubs and associations found in major cities in most countries, including Canada. There is even one in Victoria, British Columbia, which holds monthly meetings. A green-star pin worn on the lapel indicates the wearer is an Esperantist.

Zamenhof's name appears on street signs in many countries and even in space, where the minor planet 1462 Zamenhof is named in his honour. Esperanto was created with the noble idea of promoting harmony among peoples, and Zamenhof was nominated for the Nobel Peace Prize twelve times. In 2015 Unesco supported the celebration of the 100th anniversary of Zamenhof's death, and his birthday on December 15 continues to be observed by Esperantists worldwide.

I first came across the concept of an invented universal language in a book I found in the Buenos Aires bookshop Pigmalion in 1956. *A Planned Auxiliary Language* by H. Jacob was published in 1947, soon after the end of the Second World War. Jacob described in detail four additional models that appeared after Esperanto: Ido, Occidental, Novial and Interlingua.

Each has had its proponents, but only Esperanto caught on. Lì'fya leNa'vi is the constructed language of the Na'vi, the sapient humanoid indigenous inhabitants of the fictional moon Pandora in the 2009 film *Avatar*. There is also the recent creation Uropi, a synthesis of European languages.

More recent developments have spawned further efforts in the field of artificial language creation. In 2011 US linguist Michael Adams wrote *From Elvish to Klingon: Exploring Invented Languages*, a fascinating 294-page book published by Oxford University Press. It deserves to be on the bookshelf of anyone with an interest in recreational linguistics.

These artificial languages are all alphabetic, that is, until we came across a script that is pleremic like Chinese characters, with each symbol having its own special meaning independent of any spoken language — emoji. — *Apr 2018*

22 The Voynich Manuscript and the Code Seraphinianus

The Voynich manuscript is 600 years old, written in a language no one can read and full of diagrams no one understands. Since its discovery in 1912, the manuscript has been a mystery and a cult phenomenon. Two recent attempts to decode it have been publicized in the past few years.

The first claims that it is a form of gynecological medical text. Full of handwriting in an unknown language or code, the manuscript is heavily illustrated with weird pictures of alien plants, naked women, strange objects and zodiac symbols. History researcher and television writer Nicholas Gibbs appears to have cracked the code, claiming that the book is actually a guide to women's health that is mostly plagiarized from other guides of the era.

Another attempt to decode the Voynich manuscript is based on information technology. A paper titled "Decoding Anagrammed Texts Written in an Unknown Language and Script" was published in 2016 and presented at a conference in 2019. In it, computer science professor Greg Kondrak and graduate student Bradley Hauer describe a method for finding the source language of ciphered texts, before turning that method on the manuscript itself. Kondrak and Hauer concluded that the manuscript was originally written in Hebrew before being encoded in its current form. Not all who have tried to decipher the manuscript agree with either of these two attempts, and many maintain that the meaning of the document remains an enigma.

Another peculiar manuscript, of more recent origin, is the *Codex Seraphinianus*, originally published in 1981. The *Codex* is an illustrated encyclopedia of an imaginary world created by the Italian artist, architect and industrial designer Luigi Serafini during thirty months from 1976 to 1978. It is approximately 360 pages long and written in a cipher alphabet in a constructed language.

The *Codex* has been compared to the still-undeciphered Voynich manuscript in that the illustrations are often surreal parodies of things in the real world and the writing system appears modelled on ordinary Western-style writing systems. The curvilinear letters of the alphabet are rope- or thread-like, displaying loops and even knots, somewhat reminiscent of letters of the Sinhalese alphabet.

The *Codex* is divided into eleven chapters, partitioned into two sections. The first appears to describe the natural world, dealing with flora, fauna and physics, while the second deals with the humanities and the various aspects of human life: clothing, history, cuisine, architecture and so on. Each chapter seems to treat a general encyclopedic topic.

The language of the *Codex* has defied complete analysis by linguists for decades. In a talk at the Oxford University Society of Bibliophiles held in 2009, Serafini stated that there is no meaning hidden behind the script. He wanted his alphabet to convey to the reader "the sensation that children feel in front of books they cannot yet understand, although they see that their writing does make sense for grown-ups." — *May 2018*

23 Bibliography

Bibliography is the academic study of books as physical cultural objects, and in this sense a book is defined as a graphic communication used to convey information. While printed texts are now common, there have been other forms throughout history, some very ancient, such as cuneiform writing on clay tablets. Bibliography and the history of books as communication reveal a fascinating story of social and cultural perspectives relating to written texts.

The recently published *What Is the History of the Book?* by James Raven examines this interdisciplinary scholarly endeavour, which explores everything from inscriptions on tortoise shells and ox shoulder-blades in China, dating back to the sixteenth century BCE, to contemporary virtual imaging. One might describe the history of books as one of burial and rediscovery, old forgotten works resurfacing.

Enumerative bibliography is essentially a listing of works, as distinguished from analytical bibliography, which addresses the physical structure of books apart from the specific message content. Catalogues in Western and Asian countries provide a systematic record of books in different languages. We are reminded that while the book itself has a physical existence, the text does not and is characterized as an "unstable cultural object."

Raven cites American communication theorist H.D. Lasswell, who described five essential characteristics of the conveying of information from a source to the recipient: the *who, says what, in which channel, to whom*, and *with what effect*. That is, the originator of the message, its content, the means of transmission, the recipient and the result of the communication. Other theorists have elaborated on Lasswell's model, but it remains a foundational framework in communications theory, as seen in the thinking of Canadian Marshall McLuhan, who famously wrote of the extension of written texts from print to electronic media and the resulting influences on cognition and socialization. Raven examines the originators of texts in both Western and Asian cultures and how the means of expression is addressed in both alphabetic and non-alphabetic scripts. He takes into consideration the channels of communication available to those who wish to produce and transmit a message.

Control of communication is a relevant issue to authorities such as state or religious censors, like the notorious papal *Index Librorum Prohibitorum* (1559–1966). Reading, as the consequence of communication, is examined in detail as behaviour that is not necessarily liberating. At times literacy has been thought of as leading to subversion or depravity. (As late as 1993 I was asked to render a psychiatric opinion by a Canadian government agency attempting to prohibit the importation of gay erotica by the Vancouver bookstore Little Sister's.)

Printed matter in both books and periodicals reflects social attitudes which are constantly evolving, like language itself, and constraints imposed by governments are capable of being eroded, as seen in the Little Sister's bookshop case. — *Jan 2019*

24 A Library Miscellany

A miscellany is a group or collection of different items. The Bodleian Library at Oxford University recently published a small miscellany devoted exclusively to snippets of information about libraries, enticing bibliophiles with the promise of arcane information pertaining to those repositories usually of books or manuscripts but at times of items other than written material. Written by Claire Cock-Starkey, this potpourri is a treasure trove of everything you ever wanted to know about libraries.

The *Library Miscellany* includes a reference to the Osmothèque (from Greek *osmē*, "odour"), the world's largest scent collection and "a leading international research institution tracing the history of perfumery, based in Versailles with conference centers in New York City and Paris." Also included are references to plant and seed libraries, as well as many fine art libraries of paintings, sculptures, photographs and prints.

An unusual cross-border library is located on the US-Canada border between Rock Island, Quebec, and Derby Line, Vermont. A thick black line is painted across the floor of the reading room to indicate the international border. French and English books are co-filed. Because of different language conventions in the direction of printing titles on spines — American English books have titles written top-to-bottom, and French books bottom-to-top — the language of a book can be immediately determined.

Along with short articles about lost libraries, such as the ancient library at Alexandria, established in the third century BCE, and the more recent National Library of Baghdad, is a sad note about the historic Glasgow School of Art Library, first destroyed by fire in 2014 and subsequently restored. Since *A Library Miscellany* was printed in June 2018, the restored building was regrettably again consumed by fire. Is there a curse?

One library that Cock-Starkey omits mentioning is a bar in Helena, Montana, named The Law Library, where thirsty lawyers come for after-trial drinks. It was hoped the unusual name would sound decorous when unexpected callers were advised of the lawyers' temporary unavailability — because they were at the Law Library.

The *Library Miscellany* outlines the varying classification systems and details library fines for overdue books with examples of unusually large sums. It goes on to describe mobile libraries, such as bookmobiles, some of which distribute books by unusual modes of transport, like camels in Kenya, ships in Norway, elephants in Thailand and bicycles in Seattle

Although the historical use of card catalogues is now rendered obsolete by digital replacement, the collection lists the preservation of unusual collections around the world, such as The Nurse Romance Novel Collection at the University of Wisconsin or the Vatican's "Inferno," which is reputed to be the world's largest collection of pornographic material, although its existence is denied by Vatican librarians.

Natural enemies of books include pests, sunlight, humidity, fire, flood and pollution, although at a library in Portugal a colony of bats is allowed to reside to eat book-damaging insects. The banning of books, usually denounced by prudes seeking to "protect" children from sexual content or obscene language, is opposed by the American Library Association in the US. Banned works have included titles by authors such as Mark Twain, John Steinbeck and J.D. Salinger, among others. — Compiled from two essays, "A Library Miscellany" and "Libraries and Museums," *Feb 2019*

25 A Book of Book Lists

In 2017 the British Library published a book of book lists compiled by Alex Johnson. The author quotes novelist Walter Mosley in the introduction as having noted, "A person's bookcase tells you everything you need to know about them." I quite agree with this sentiment when the bookcase is visible, but often it is squirreled away in a bedroom or elsewhere in a home where I've visited.

A Book of Book Lists contains reading lists from a mixed set of individuals, including Osama bin Laden, Charles Darwin, David Bowie, Oscar Wilde (while a prisoner in Reading Gaol) and British and American politicians. It also includes lists such as books left behind in hotel rooms, *Desert Island* books, Queen Mary's Dolls' House library (of miniature postage-stamp sized books), books borrowed by Alan Turing from his school library, books burned by the Nazis, and the most unread books (including James Joyce's *Ulysses*, which still has defeated me, and Herman Melville's *Moby Dick*, which I finally read after many attempts, but only by the ploy of bringing it along on a sea voyage of several days with nothing else to read).

Completing the compendium are imaginary books "written" by Sherlock Holmes, including *Upon Tattoo Marks*, *Upon the Tracing of Footsteps* and similar guides to crime detection. Lists of books that never have been written often have bizarre titles like *Tarzan in Mars* by Burroughs, *The Return of Edwin Drood* by Dickens, or *Road Trips to the Emerald City* by Baum.

I am reminded of the Library of Babel, a bizarre conception from the imaginative mind of Jorge Luis Borges, which consists of an enormous and unending series of hexagonal rooms lined with bookshelves, containing the totality of everything that has ever been written. — *Feb 2019*

26 The Libraries of Alberto Manguel

I have been a bibliophile, one who loves or collects books, all my life. A major problem over the years has been the need to winnow my shelves each time I move, though in this process lies one positive feature: in distilling the collection periodically, the ones that remain are those most meaningful for me.

My fellow Argentine-Canadian bibliophile Alberto Manguel recently wrote of the vexing problem of having to relocate from his home in rural France to North America, in his collection of essays *Packing My Library: An Elegy and Ten Digressions* (2018). He reflects on his lifelong passion for reading and accumulating printed texts as he removes the 35,000 volumes from their shelves and packs them into boxes for shipping.

Manguel became a reader for the great author Jorge Luis Borges, who suffered from blindness as he aged, and who at that time was the director of the National Library in Argentina. While the task of packing his large library is impressive, Manguel's own appointment to the position of director of the National Library in December 2015 made him the conservator of a collection two orders of magnitude greater in size, with over three million volumes. Manguel in his own right became an essayist and novelist, and his bibliography reveals a wide range of literary contributions to contemporary thought and multiple awards and distinctions.

The twenty essays in *Packing My Library* relate how Manguel's personal library expresses his identity as it developed over the years of his maturity, as an "utterly private space," and how packing the books away seemed to him like a "premature burial" experienced as a "self-obituary." Like Manguel I have never been without a personal library, but unlike him I haven't retained the contents each time I moved. Yet to discard a book rather than to move it to a new location involves making a choice, often difficult. I can readily identify with Manguel's sense of loss. In relocating from the US to Argentina in 1955, I took a few, and when returning to North America in 1963, kept a few more. The same process continued with each successive move. Each time many were sold or given away, but always some were retained and still inhabit my shelves, a few seeming to glare at me accusingly, not having been held for a longish time.

I regularly read a number of literary periodicals from the UK and US, and when enticed by a positive review, may order a title from a bookshop. Once in my grubby hands, should the positive opinion of the reviewer not be shared, the regretted purchase is consigned to the recycling shelf.

Books once read and not kept may be given to friends or relations. I may sell them to a dealer for a pittance, donate to an annual local literacy drive or just leave it in one of the "little libraries" that spring up around town on the principle of "take one and leave one."

Reference books in particular are hard to abandon, for it seems like imposing a death sentence upon an author or editor having to choose between existence or disposal of a book containing a collection of knowledge. "Who am I to judge?" I ask myself, confronted with the need to decide whether or not to consign to the flames the many dictionaries I have of other languages, of music, of places, of history, of religion, of science, of biography, of ideas and of time. I know, I know . . . we have it all available to us on the internet, but what happens after civilization collapses and there is no longer any internet? In what caves by the Dead Sea will the works of Shakespeare, Goethe, Wittgenstein, or for that matter of Manguel, be secretly stored, awaiting discovery after millennia by future archaeologists? Perhaps this is why I not only post my writings online but also print a hard copy *por las dudas*, as we Argentine-Canadian bibliophiles like to caution — "just in case."

Friends have tried to inveigle me to take a cruise as a holiday, but the prospect of confinement among strangers in a floating hotel with activities of uncertain attractiveness seemed unappealing. I once booked a three-week passage from New York to Buenos Aires on a Norwegian freighter, but before leaving went to Barnes & Noble on Union Square and bought a bag of books to devour on the voyage. These and the flying fish sufficed for my entertainment, along with learning to savour Norwegian goat cheese at table with the captain and others thrice daily. — Compiled from "Bibliophilia," *Apr 2018*, and "The Libraries of Alberto Manguel," *Feb 2019*

27 The Pigmalion Bookshop and Lyall's Languages of Europe

When working in Buenos Aires as a journalist for United Press in 1956, I often haunted the foreign-language bookshop Pigmalion at Corrientes 515. Eight years later, it was here that a young Manguel had an after-school job and met Jorge Luis Borges. In my day it was the mecca for those Anglophones seeking literary solace in their mother tongue amid the millions of *porteños*, and it was there that I discovered Lyall's *Guide to the Languages of Europe*, a handy and compact English compendium cross-referencing twenty-five tongues of the Continent.

The *Guide* is divided into five sections, each grouping together five languages of similar branches of mostly Indo-European provenance: Romance, Germanic, Slavic, Baltic and Finno-Ugric, and a miscellaneous grab bag of Greek, Albanian, Turkish, Arabic and Esperanto. (No Gaelic, Basque or regional dialects appear.)

Each description of a language includes a brief guide to pronunciation, with useful phrases, notices, numerals, days of the week and months. Thirty sample sentences are followed by a tabulated 1,500-word vocabulary. These are all arranged across a double-page table that cross-references an English word with a word from each language in that section, making it simple to compare words in related languages. One finds *blood* in Finnish is *veri*, and in the distant but related Finno-Ugric Hungarian we find a cognate in *a vér*.

Lyall sensibly notes, "No phrase-book will enable a traveller to exchange ideas with the people he meets in anything but the most primitive way. To do that he must learn the language properly." But it is claimed that with this book in his pocket the English traveller should never find himself at a complete loss, "whether he is trying to explain that he has run out of petrol to a peasant in Portugal or arguing finance with a cabman in Kovno."

The author, Archibald Laurence Lyall (1904–64), was a British travel writer with twenty-seven publications in four languages, including not only the *Guide* but also companion guides to the South of France and Tuscany, among others. Mine is the thirteenth printing of the *Guide*, from 1954. This small book has been a faithful chair-side companion for over sixty years, since I discovered it at the Librería Pigmalion in nostalgic old Buenos Aires back in 1956. — *Apr 2018*

28 Writing about Reading

I write about books because I obviously relish reading, not only the books themselves but also the writing about books in the literary journals to which I subscribe. The *Times Literary Supplement* (*TLS*) is the most venerable. I first found the October 22, 1999, issue in the lobby of the Domus Medica rooms of the Royal Society of Medicine in London, with an article written by Andrew Porter about composer Alexander Zemlinsky. After reading the entire issue, I subscribed to the weekly and continue to do so now after more than two decades. *TLS* recently published its six thousandth issue since the first in 1902. The "Nota Bene" back-page feature is a recurrent delightful tradition of odd and erudite miscellany relating to authors, literary prizes, books and bookshops.

A recent glitch in overseas delivery this past winter led to missing issues and long delays, but after remonstrating, I was supplied by the dispatch of all those I lacked. Regular service is now again restored, leaving me with catch-up reading to do. Old issues are not discarded but passed on to a friend, a retired bookshop owner living in my apartment building.

The *London Review of Books* appears semimonthly, now in its fortieth year of publication, covering much the same territory as does its elder sibling. A free introductory offer of a year's subscription makes a welcome holiday gift for friends and family members. Its regular two-page "Diary," a constant delight, features essays by writers like Alan Bennett and the late Jenny Diski.

The *New York Review of Books* provides a transatlantic counterweight to the others, all from the UK, and it is primarily but not exclusively devoted to American culture and books. It is published twenty times a year, and after reading I give each issue to a constipated retired local clergyman who tells me he reads it regularly perched on the throne in the smallest room of his home.

Books that I read about and decide to purchase are usually ordered through independent local bookshops, like Ivy's in Victoria. If the book is not available there, the Guardian Bookshop in the UK has proved reliable, though also often with a lengthy delay in the post. Abe Books is a reliable Canadian source, especially for finding out-of-print items, and Amazon is the last resort (but not ignored because they also sell my own scribblings). — *Apr 2018*

29 Reading

Having no TV, I do not watch television programs, and I rarely go to the cinema. I do not listen to "podcasts" or radio programs. I also avoid video clips and only rarely listen to or watch recommended material forwarded from others. I read.

When visiting the home of a friend or acquaintance, I always like to examine the bookshelves to become familiar with the interests of my host. This can be an instructive exercise, but it sometimes reveals crass pretension. I once visited a residence that had a bookcase of works by famed writers, all beautifully bound in matching bindings but apparently never having been opened. More gratifying is to find someone's bookshelves overflowing with well-thumbed works, particularly when displaying worn bindings and other signs of use.

A good friend, knowing I was a bibliophile, once offered to buy me an electronic reading device on which one could upload a variety of texts to read wherever one wished. But I declined the offer, finding it tiresome to read on backlit screens. Moreover, I enjoy the sensual pleasure of holding a book in my hands, feeling the texture of the printed sheets and smelling the odour of the pages, whether newly printed, crisp and fresh, or musty with the stale scent of a well-used edition.

Annotations are sometimes noted in used books. I am prone to writing in new books at times. For example, on the back flyleaf I may note the page number of a passage of interest with a brief phrase facilitating future retrieval. I sometimes underline text, particularly if the subject is either amusing or considered worthy of recall, but even then, usually only one significant phrase or sentence of a more densely argued paragraph.

I find rereading of both fiction and non-fiction is often rewarding. Speed-reading, however, serves only for the superficial transfer of information and does nothing for the appreciation of the writing itself. Choice of vocabulary, word order, sound and grammatical structure are characteristics of a text quite apart from the information content. To speed-read a short story by Nabokov or Borges would be like walking through a museum without stopping to look at the exhibits or playing Beethoven quartets as background music.

Prose is at times poetic and capable of being savoured by the reader like a tasty morsel of food by a gourmand. Poetry specifically concentrates emotional content, beyond any information transfer, and is lost when read quickly.

When poetry is set to music, the conveyed emotional impact can be powerfully augmented, like Schiller's "Ode to Joy" combined with the music from Beethoven's Ninth Symphony, each celebrating the positive emotions of the other and making it a suitable anthem of European unity after centuries of conflict. — *Jan 2019*

30 Slow Time and Broad Horizons

The April 3, 2020, edition of my weekly dose of literature reviews arrived from the UK the other day, after a full forty days in transit, literally quarantined (and possibly disinfected) by Canada Post. This particular issue of the *Times Literary Supplement* was produced by staff all working from home. Editor Stig Abell announced, "We will restrict ourselves to direct reference (to coronavirus) when the writing merits it, to just a couple of pieces every issue." A sensible compromise.

This issue, then, is the first one to adhere to this restriction, and it leads off with "Slow Time and Broad Horizons," a symposium of twelve short commentaries by different contributors, each a well-known writer describing their own isolation milieu and how they occupy their time. Lee Child, now a Booker judge, is holed up in a remote area in Wyoming, reading assiduously but also able to access streaming video for non-printed entertainment. Lisa Hilton is locked down in Venice, reading about, among other topics, boredom. Everyone's reaction is unique, unsurprisingly, in both milieu and activities.

Although not locked down on Vancouver Island off the Pacific coast of Canada's British Columbia, we are all practising social distancing as recommended by the provincial health officer, and though outbreaks of coronavirus occur, they are not rampant, as in Seattle, just across the now-closed border with the US.

Though never (yet!) a contributor to *TLS*, I continue reading about books reviewed and order items that I fancy from the Guardian Bookshop online, and they normally arrive in my box after an average of twenty days. The reviews often lead to writing one myself and posting it to my online collection of literary essays. — *May 2020*

31 The Man Who Liked Dickens

"The Man Who Liked Dickens" is a 1933 short story by English writer Evelyn Waugh that describes an exhausted and famished traveller lost in the Amazonian wilderness who comes across the home of a solitary man of mixed racial parentage. The traveller is taken in and nursed back to health with herbal remedies, and when recovered, asked to read aloud to his rescuer from the latter's book collection. The collection consists exclusively of the complete novels of Charles Dickens and nothing else.

As the horror story unfolds, the unfortunate traveller realizes he is trapped and condemned to continue until he finishes reading the entire collection, at which time he will have to start over again. And again. And again . . .

A bibliophilic friend of mine who lives nearby also loves Dickens, and has more than one set of the complete novels, including a prized first edition of *Bleak House.* I have read some of Dickens's novels, but not all. And I never anticipated owning the entire set, until I found a small hard-bound copy of 245 pages, measuring only 7 cm by 8.5 cm and but 2.2 cm in thickness. It was compiled by Joelle Herr and published by Running Press in 2012, and the tiny tome was printed in (where else?) China.

In the introduction, following a sketch of the life of Charles Dickens, the author writes, "Let's face it, not many of us have the time — no matter how intrigued we are — to read all of Dickens's novels. Several of them clock in at around a thousand pages! That's where this book comes in handy — whether you want to get to know his collection of classics in a hurry or you're in search of a refresher course." She continues, "Don't let its diminutive size deceive you. In this compact format, you'll find summaries of all twenty of Charles Dickens's novels, along with illustrations and opening lines, a list of major characters, and a short summary of the plots."

While the tiny tome could be read in one sitting, it contains a great deal of information and is probably best ingested one chapter at a time to avoid conversational *faux pas*, like transposing Pip from *Great Expectations* to say, Little Dorrit, or Scrooge to *Bleak House.*

I eventually gave the miniature masterpiece to my grandson Hugh when he moved from the West Coast to distant Toronto, as it was easy to carry in his pocket. Perhaps it will tempt him to begin reading the complete novels someday.

Should I ever find myself in the unenviable situation of the lost traveller in Waugh's story, the same fate might occur, perhaps, though, with a different author, such as Proust.

This horrid fantasy in turn reminded me of the Monty Python sketch of a "summarize Proust" contest: The hapless contestant began, "Well, I was having tea and eating this biscuit—" *Bzzz!* sounded a buzzer, followed by the stern admonition of "Time's up!" by the emcee. —*June 2018*

32 A Bedtime Story: First a Murder, Then to Sleep

When at home during the day, I usually read literary journals or non-fiction. In the evenings after supper, I read mostly memoirs or fiction, like short stories, until it's time to do my ablutions and retire, usually before eleven o'clock. But before falling asleep, I turn to crime fiction. Oddly enough, fictional mayhem and bloody murder are a relaxing change from the incessant daily global accounts about what is really going on in the world.

A regular source of murder these days is one of a series of novellas chronicling the exploits of Jules Maigret of the Parisian *Police Judiciaire*. A street plan of Paris and a road map of France at my side, I visualize Maigret's travels around the capital as he investigates the social and interpersonal circumstances necessary to understand what led to the crime. These are not your run-of-the-mill whodunits but carefully crafted psychological portraits of individuals and families caught up in curious and convoluted relationships that culminate in murder. The Maigret novels conjure the atmosphere of Paris and elsewhere in France (as well as a few other countries).

The author of the *Police Judiciare* series (in itself an impressive seventy novels and twenty-eight short stories) is Belgian author Georges Simenon (1903–89), who has published altogether some 391 novels and numerous shorter works. Simenon was admired for his nuanced powers of description by many other writers, including William Faulkner, who compared him to Anton Chekhov. André Gide called him "The greatest of all, the most genuine novelist we have had in literature," and P.D. James praised his talent as a crime novelist.

Simenon denied modelling his protagonist after himself, but just as Maigret is addicted to pipe-smoking, the author himself is seldom seen in photographs without a pipe either clenched between his teeth or held in his hand. Then there is the issue of alcohol consumption, for every novel contains many instances in which Maigret drinks, either alone or with members of his team, suspects or informants. Maigret has been described as a "functioning alcoholic," in that he continues to be successful at his job in spite of repeatedly drinking beer, wine and spirits. In this he also resembles his creator, for Simenon similarly was known to drink while writing.

A lengthy review article by Julian Barnes appeared in the May 26, 2014, issue of the *Times Literary Supplement*, indicating that Penguin was reissuing the complete series of Maigret novels with new translations.

They were to publish them at the rate of one every month. At my local bookshop I had a standing order for each new one as it arrived. There is nothing quite like the investigation of a gruesome murder to settle one's mind for sleep.

Another set of novels that facilitates sleep by redirecting one's attention away from the usually unsettling climate of current events are the Jack Reacher thrillers, written by the English author Lee Child, though set in the US. Different from the police procedurals of Maigret, they relate the contemporary adventures of the improbable knight-errant Reacher, a retired military policeman who, having no fixed address or relationship, travels around the country hitchhiking or by bus. He invariably becomes involved in helping others at risk and in untangling sinister plots of criminal gangs, corrupted policemen, greedy businessmen and politicians. There is plenty of physical violence, bloodshed and killing, but in the end virtue prevails. Having sorted things out, Reacher leaves town to resume his restless wandering.

Like Simenon, Child's powers of description are impressive, and his plots are intricately constructed. But he is no Chekhov, and psychological subtlety is not prominent within his works. Child churns out one novel every year with the same format. Although initially I ignored them, after reading positive critiques in a variety of publications, such as the *London Review of Books* and the *New Yorker*, I worked my way through the series of twenty-four novels from the beginning.

Apart from Simenon and Child, I also read other fiction in this genre, like the Ian Rankin novels set in Edinburgh with Inspector Rebus and the North Yorkshire police procedurals of Peter Robinson featuring Detective Superintendent Alan Banks, as well as translations of European, Argentinian, Asian and other crime fiction. I find a good source of reviews in the blog *Mrs. Peabody Investigates.*

Not a violent person myself, I have always avoided physical conflict in real-life situations and will walk away from any possible involvement. But like other basically pacific persons, I must admit to a certain fascination with this subject, probably reflecting a common human trait and not just a sad characteristic of the age in which we live. After all, one of the bloodiest and most violent of all stories was Homer's *Iliad*, written circa 750 BCE. — Compiled from the essays "A Bedtime Story: First a Murder, Then to Sleep," *Jan 2019*, and "Simenon and Maigret," *May 2018*

33 Finnish Crime Novels

"Nordic noir" crime novels are primarily based in the Scandinavian countries of Sweden, Norway, Denmark and Iceland. But this is also a lively genre in Finland, a Nordic but not Scandinavian land, with a unique language unrelated to those of most other European countries.

Jarkko Sipilä is a Finnish author and journalist who has reported on the Helsinki crime scene in both TV and print. He has also written a series of novels featuring Detective Lieutenant Kari Takamäki of the Helsinki Police Violent Crimes Unit. The books inspired a local Finnish TV series, and some have been translated into English. His *Seinää Vasten* (*Against the Wall*) was the winner of the Best Finnish Crime Novel in 2009. "A no-nonsense gritty police procedural that gives equal time to the crooks and the cops," wrote one reviewer.

Members of Takamäki's team — such as the hard-boiled undercover cop Suhonen, who specializes in infiltrating criminal gangs — recur in all the novels, and the setting is realistically based in the capital city of Helsinki and its surrounding area. Social and psychological issues colour the otherwise grim milieu. Sipilä's 2010 book *Katumurha* (*Street Murder*) begins with the brazen shooting of a businessman in the midst of rush hour traffic and develops into a rat's nest of sleazy white-collar crime, leading to more murders and undercover work by Suhonen. With the regular appearance of Takamäki and individual members of his squad, the series of novels resembles Simenon's Maigret and his Parisian investigating crew.

We find something completely different in Minna Lindgren's Lavender Ladies Detective Agency tale *Death in Sunset Grove*, described as a "devilishly funny and suspenseful story about old age, friendship and life in a relatively ordinary Finnish retirement home." Two octogenarian ladies investigate a suspicious death in the assisted-living community where they live and are drawn into a nasty scheme involving the board of directors of the private establishment. It resembles the Miss Marple novels by Agatha Christie, with a similar sly whiff of clever inquiry by an aged female sleuth.

An unusual murder mystery set in Helsinki, with a serial killer associating each of his attacks with music of Sibelius, is *The Seven Symphonies* by Simon Boswell, a British film score composer, conductor, producer and musician. Though written in English, the Finnish locale is fairly realistic and the tie-in with a musical analysis of each of Sibelius' seven symphonies creates an offbeat and fascinating structure.

Brutal murders and bloody crime scenes aren't what Finland is famous for – except in the world of fiction. With Nordic crime novels surging in popularity internationally, Finland's contribution is unique. A hint of Russia seasons the exotic setting, for Finland was once part of that country, and to enhance relaxation, there is usually a scene set in a sauna. — *May 2018*

34 Aleksis Kivi and the Seven Brothers

Not to be confused with the American chain of hamburger joints of the same name (described by one food reviewer as a "high quality burger place"), *Seven Brothers* is the first and only novel by Aleksis Kivi, the now esteemed national author of Finland. Published in 1870, it is widely regarded as the first significant novel written in the Finnish language by a Finnish-speaking author. Indeed, some regard it today as the greatest Finnish novel ever written. During the nineteenth century, Finland changed from a region of near illiteracy to a highly literate country, and the novel *Seven Brothers* represents a turning point in this transition.

The plot is simple. At first, in their rural small town the brothers are not a particularly peaceful lot and end up quarreling with the local constable, juryman, vicar, churchwarden and teachers — not to mention their fellow neighbours in the village. Young girls' mothers do not regard them as good suitors, and when the brothers are required to learn to read before they can receive church confirmation and therefore enter official adulthood and marriage, they decide to run away together.

Eventually the brothers end up moving to a distant region in relative wilderness, but their first efforts to survive on their own are shoddy — one Christmas Eve they end up burning down their sauna. The next spring, they try again but are forced to kill a nearby lord's herd of bulls and pay the family back with wheat. After ten years of hard work clearing the forest for fields, and in spite of one brother's hard drinking and alcoholic hallucinations, they eventually mature, learn to read on their own, and finally return to their village, where most of the brothers become pillars of the community and family men.

Still, the tone of the tale is not particularly moralistic. What is unusual, though, is that when this work was written, early reviewers reviled it as contrary to good taste as understood in the nineteenth century, because though addressing ordinary human concerns of good and evil, life and death, and the existence of God, *Seven Brothers* was realistic in terms of respect for the common people and the use of vernacular language, often in a comic vein.

Aleksis Kivi was born in into a tailor's family in a rural area. In 1846 he left for school in Helsinki and in 1859 was accepted into the University of Helsinki, where he studied literature and developed an interest in the theatre. His first play was *Kullervo*, based on a tragic tale from the Finnish epic *Kalevala*. Although Kivi was among the very earliest authors of prose and lyrics in Finnish, he is still considered one of the greatest. Unfortunately, he died alone in a mental hospital at the age of thirty-eight. Finnish composer Rautavaara wrote an opera about Kivi's life and works in 1996.

When learning Finnish, I read part of the novel and listened to a reading of it available on CD. I thought of trying to translate the novel into English but found that a good translation was of course already available and so lowered my sights to a detective novel that hadn't been translated yet. I do continue to wonder, though, if the American hamburger chain Seven Brothers has any connection with the Kivi novel, or in England, the Se7en Brothers Brewing Co., owner of two beer houses in Manchester. — *June 2018*

35 Kalevala

The *Kalevala* is a collection of epic poetry in the Finnish language, compiled by the physician and ethnographer Elias Lönnrot in the 1830s and '40s, assembled from oral traditions of Karelia, in what is now eastern Finland, and the nearby region of north-western Russia. (Finland at that time was a Russian possession, not an independent country.)

The *Kalevala* was published in its final form in 1849, and in the second half of the nineteenth century it became widely known among the Finnish-speaking population, inspiring cultural works of music and art. Many paintings and music by Finnish artists and composers, such as Jean Sibelius, owe their inspiration to poetry from the *Kalevala*. The stories themselves relate to the creation of the world; the exploits of heroes and wonder-workers; the building of boats and musical instruments; the forging of the *sampo*, a magical device; conflicts and wars; and incest and suicide. The whole gamut of epic poetry is arrayed in a language unrelated to almost all others in Europe, aside from nearby Estonian and distant Hungarian.

Lönnrot collected the songs that he used in composing the *Kalevala* by writing them down on field trips to Karelia from the dictation of singers of the epics. Homer's *Iliad* and *Odyssey* were written down by scribes in the same way in ancient Greece. Oral traditions of epic poetry can be found closer to home, too, from First Nations communities in Canada.

Akseli Gallen-Kallela was a late nineteenth–early twentieth century Finnish painter in the Romantic tradition who is best known for his illustrations of the *Kalevala*. Many of his paintings can be seen at the Ateneum Museum, located in the centre of Helsinki, close to the majestic railway station. There is also a bespoke museum of his works in the neighbouring town of Espoo.

Finland's best known musician was Sibelius. His first major success was the symphonic cantata *Kullervo,* the tragic story known to all Finns of a cursed youth with magical powers who falls on his sword and dies when he realizes that he has seduced his own sister. Gallen-Kallela produced a more-than-life-sized image of Kullervo standing in the forest cursing his destiny, and I bought a print of this painting, which now hangs on my wall in the Bear Cave.

J.R.R. Tolkien wrote a prose adaptation of the story of Kullervo. *Kullervo* is also a contemporary opera in two acts, composed by Aulis Sallinen to his own libretto. The opera premiered in February 1992 at the Los Angeles Music Center and opened the new Helsinki opera house in 1993. From its premiere to 2014, it has been performed over seventy times, in six countries and in three languages.

February 28 is *Kalevala* Day in Finland, and flags are raised to commemorate the publication of the first edition. A wreath is placed at Emil Wikström's statue of Elias Lönnrot in Helsinki, and it is an occasion for celebrating not just the *Kalevala* but Finnish culture as a whole. — *May 2018*

36 Karamazovshchina

Sixty-five years ago, as an undergraduate university student, I first read Dostoevsky's final great novel, *The Brothers Karamazov* (1880), translated by Constance Garnett. It opened a window onto a world I'd never imagined, that of late-nineteenth-century Russia, and was the first book I remember having provoked me to read all night, unable to sleep. An acclaimed new translation by Richard Pevear and Larissa Volokhonsky led me to reread the work and discover it anew, though it had surfaced throughout my life at different times, including once when I saw it displayed upon the writing desk of Leo Tolstoy when visiting his estate south of Moscow in the early 1990s.

The Russian suffix *-shchina* appended to the name Karamazov is pejorative and suggests a deplorable state of affairs among a group, as Maxim Gorky described it a century ago. The story is well known, that of an apparent parricide by the eldest of three brothers, Dmitri, following domestic conflicts involving money and sex. The murder and subsequent trial is but a literary scaffolding upon which were built fundamental thoughts about life, religion and morality reflected in, but not limited to, Russian Orthodox Christianity.

Karamazov family members exhibited familiar personality traits characteristic of us all, although amplified to the extent of unrestrained libertine behaviour, as seen in Dmitri, the eldest, a manic sensualist, and in the hallucinatory delusions of the tortured intellectual middle brother, Ivan. The youngest sibling, Alyosha, sought a religious career as a monk and was a stable anchor, giving the final word after Dmitri's trial. And at the funeral of a classmate, Alyosha exhorted young schoolboys to be kind to one another.

Perhaps the most celebrated episode is the chapter devoted to Ivan's story of a dream, describing an imagined encounter in fifteenth-century Spain between the Grand Inquisitor and a revisiting Jesus. After the latter performs a miraculous restoration to life of a deceased child, to the wonder of a crowd, the Grand Inquisitor arrests him, explaining how his return impairs the holy mission of the Church, and commands him to leave and never return. The text displayed on Tolstoy's desk upon my visit was opened to this chapter.

While Dostoevsky describes extreme personality traits of the fictional brothers in his novel, we all contain facets of them, with our own conflicting features of Dmitri's sensuality, Ivan's rationality and Alyosha's piety.

I must admit I do miss the old Garnett translation, with the "rainbow coloured roubles" now having become only "iridescent" in the new version by Pevear and Volokhonsky, and I can't forgive them for placing a character's house on a town's "Main Street," evoking more of a North American setting than a provincial Russian community. Regrettably, in this new edition all explanatory notes are lumped in the back, many only referring to each other, requiring annoying back-and-forthing. —*Apr 2019*

37 Russian Memories

Short fiction by Gogol, Chekhov and other nineteenth-century writers occupies a distinguished shelf in any collection of traditional literature by Russian authors from before the Bolshevik Revolution. Less well known are many stories by those who left the country following 1917 and continued to write and publish as exiles in Europe. Newspapers and periodicals in Russian flourished in Berlin and Paris, printing short stories not only by famous authors such as Ivan Bunin and Vladimir Nabokov, but also from a multitude of lesser-known writers.

Penguin Classics recently published *Russian Émigré Short Stories from Bunin to Yanovsky*, an anthology of over 400 pages of English translations of thirty-five examples of this little-known literature. The stories themselves are preceded by a detailed chronology of events from 1914 to 1940, a sixteen-page introduction to the world of exile experienced by the authors and suggestions for further reading. They are followed by a list of Russian émigré newspapers and periodicals, author biographies and detailed footnotes.

The lengthy introduction notes that "by 1921 over 130 Russian newspapers had been established worldwide, as well as journals filled with poetry, short stories and excerpts from novels and reviews, as well as political, social and philosophical essays and criticism." This flourishing was brief, however, for with the rise of fascism and the Second World War, the hothouse culture of Russian writing withered and was mostly forgotten. Exceptionally, Bunin was awarded the Nobel Prize in Literature in 1933 and is represented with four stories in this collection. The early work of Nabokov only became resurrected and translated after he became famous as a writer in English with the notorious *Lolita* (1955). His Borgesian story "The Visit to the Museum" (1939) was first published in English in *Esquire* in 1963.

Other émigré Russian writers, such as Teffi, Lukash and Gazdanov, reveal the sensibility of the exile, creating visions in one's first language while surrounded by an alien culture. A sense of nostalgia seasoned by regretfulness, and at times horror, creates a powerful mood, associated with a sense of loss, the disappearance of a vanished past now embedded in a disparate culture. The new availability of these texts reveals to the English reader a lesser-known chapter of world literature.

Summing up, the editor writes, "These works represent some of the most talented Russian writing of the last century, and moreover a unique confluence of European and Russian literary traditions. Their primary vehicle, born of necessity, was the short story, and it is for this reason that we present them here, with the aim of giving them a new lease on life, a new journey under foreign skies, in a new language." —*Jan 2019*

38 An Act of Kindness

The gripping novel *Berlin Finale* by Heinz Rein was first published in German in 1947, and an English translation by Shaun Whiteside appeared seventy-two years later, in 2019, published by Penguin Modern Classics. The novel is described by Lee Child as "A wonderful rediscovery, . . . human, suspenseful, shot through with hard-earned wisdom." Among fellow thriller authors, Child's view matters, and I can only concur with his opinion.

The story takes place in the German capital during the last nineteen days of what is known in Western countries as the Second World War, from April 14 to May 3 in 1945. It relates the actions of a handful of dedicated Nazi resisters amid the ruins and chaos of bombing and artillery fire as the Soviet army relentlessly crushed the city, eliminating the remaining vestiges of the Wehrmacht and Gestapo. The resisters, ordinary Germans, distributed pamphlets and engaged in sabotage to promote the collapse of the regime, narrowly evading capture and certain execution by the few remaining fanatic Nazis, as the civilian population cowered in subway tunnels, basements and other air raid shelters.

There are many vignettes of betrayal, loss and survival among those not directly involved in combat. One of the most powerful accounts that remains with me is that of Joachim Lassehn, a young former classical pianist and a deserter from the Wehrmacht. Lassehn despaired of doctrinaire military cruelty and had fallen in with the resisters. He was en route to meet a fellow conspirator during the incessant shelling from the victorious Red Army as it entered the city. Abruptly Lassehn came across the dreadful scene of a dying cart horse, whose belly had been torn open by shrapnel, bleating in mortal pain and surrounded by a group of starving civilian men and women carving out meat from the still-living animal. Taking out his weapon he shot the poor beast in the head, then continued on his errand.

As we and our descendants approach ever closer to oncoming social collapse, comparable situations may arise and lead to considering similar acts of kindness, not necessarily limited to animal species other than *Homo "sapiens."* —*Jan 2020*

39 Berlin Airlifted

Philosopher Isaiah Berlin (1917–97) wrote "The Hedgehog and the Fox" in 1951, a celebrated essay describing contrasting lifestyles, inspired by the ancient Greek poet Archilochus, who wrote, "The fox knows many things, but the hedgehog knows one big thing."

The latest rumblings of discontent over the intellectual status of Berlin appeared not long ago in the pages of the *Times Literary Supplement*, in a commentary by American theologian David Bentley Hart of Notre Dame University in South Bend, Indiana, who called Berlin a "fraudulent scholar." This disparaging remark was subsequently withdrawn by Hart, who then proceeded to amend the adjective from *fraudulent* to *superficial*, describing Berlin as "a man whose learning was broad(-ish) but rarely deep, intellectually lazy," and damning him with faint praise by comparison to the popular American history writer Will Durant, who explained past events for the general reader rather than for professional academic historians.

This entertaining invective is characteristic of Hart's writing. His latest work was described by one reviewer as "no longer countering unbelief — as in *Atheist Delusions* (2010) — but … now in all-out war with fellow Christian believers who hold to traditional views on heaven and hell. The title states the thesis: all creatures who have sinned against God will finally be saved." That this type of medieval controversy should continue to engage otherwise intelligent academics in the twenty-first century seems absurd, and Berlin likely would have waded into the discussion with relish were he still around to comment.

Berlin was called "the non-philosophers' philosopher" by a reviewer in the May 15, 2020, issue of *TLS*, which covered books by Nikhil Krishnan about this "historian of ideas" who separated himself from analytically oriented academic philosophers like A.J. Ayer and adherents of the Vienna Circle.

Though I consider myself aligned to the empirically based philosophy of science of Feigl and others of that group, at the same time I eschew the strict logical positivism of Ayer and his lot. I feel comfortable with Berlin's approach to the history of ideas, whether different academic schools of thought consider him a philosopher or not. The controversy appears to arise from Hart's hedgehoggery as an academic specialist in the arcane discipline of Christian theology.

Berlin, on the other hand, was an urbane and vulpine historian of ideas. — *July 2020*

40 Borges and Eco

In his concluding chapter of *The Lure of the Arcane*, Theodore Ziolkowski observes that the fear of conspiracy has been a factor in politics from the start and has continued unabated down to the present. After summarizing a historical review of the literature associated with secret societies, Ziolkowski contends that each at first "began to be regarded as a conspiracy, and later, conspiracy fiction evolved into satire, parody, and sheer playfulness."

For example, in 1940 Jorge Luis Borges wrote the fantasy tale "Tlön, Uqbar, Orbis Tertius," which depicts an imaginary world with a secret society based on Rosicrucian manifestos that ultimately evolves into a utopian final structure. Ziolkowski reviews several other examples of late-twentieth-century American novels that exhibit this development, beginning in 1966 with *The Crying of Lot 49* by Thomas Pynchon.

Mumbo Jumbo (1972) by Ishmael Reed is another example of the genre, with inventive use of language and competing secret societies, associated with the decadence of civilization. *The Illuminatus Trilogy* (1975), coauthored by Robert Shea and Robert Anton Wilson, is described as an "obviously contrived literary construct," but it again demonstrates features characteristic of fictional works involving secret societies.

The most impressive and best-known contemporary novel of this genre is the acclaimed masterpiece by Umberto Eco *Foucault's Pendulum* (1988). The text is replete with references to a host of secret societies, including the Knights Templar, Madame Blavatsky's Theosophists, the Rosicrucians, Freemasons, Jesuits and even the Elders of Zion. Ziolkowski lauds Eco as a "brilliant semiotician with authentic learning as a scholar of medieval literature and culture" and the novel as "a magisterial summation that recapitulates the history of conspiracy literature from Euripides to the present."

In his conclusion, Ziolkowski describes the pattern from the ancient works of Euripides and Apuleius to the contemporary novels of Eco and Dan Brown, that of a *quest* attracted by some *arcane lore* possessed by a *secret group*. Alienation within a society tends to provoke popular interest in secret societies, and this particular genre seems well suited to times of great uncertainty.

But then it is usually the quest itself rather than the specific nature of the hidden knowledge that is sought, as in the search for the Grail, not the Grail itself.

Ziolkowski asks, "Is it, in the last analysis, a melancholy commentary on our own society and its belief, or lack thereof, that so many millions of us lie in bed each evening perusing conspiracy thrillers that revolve around what Eco called 'a secret without content'?" —*June 2018*

41 Fabulous Monsters

In *Fabulous Monsters*, my fellow Argentinian-Canadian Alberto Manguel shares language and sketches of thirty-seven individual literary figures, revealing his mental image of each fabulous monster and inviting readers to reflect on theirs. Rarely have I treasured such a compendium of short, delicious essays as is found in this rich collection of associations.

We all can find monsters of fable in our own minds if we look for them, and comparing our images with Manguel's is an engaging exercise. Some we may even consider to be literary friends, as suggested by the author on the title page of his book, for the opposing leaf is blank, inviting readers to insert their own.

Most of us are familiar with figures like Superman and Dracula, perhaps less so with Hsing-chen and the Tyrant Banderas, but we all differ in our reading histories and how we accumulate our own images of monsters (or saints). Some of Manguel's thirty-seven can be compared and contrasted with how we imagine the fruit of meta-creations like Dr. Frankenstein's creature or Crusoe's Friday, or by provoking associations with not only fabulous but real monsters: who would be the van Helsing for today's Donald J. Trump? Or indeed my own personal Faustian Mephistopheles? And where lies the ancient monster Humbaba these days, slain many millennia ago by Gil and his sidekick N. Kidoo? Who will guard the Cedar Forest in his absence? Perhaps no one, as we despairingly hear anti-environmentalist woodsmen cry out, "Log 'em to the beach!"

The extermination of a monster doesn't always leave the world a better place. Our personal fabulous monsters may shift over time in their attributes of monstrosity, as the original Humbert Humbert evolves from a witty but inappropriate dirty old man to a horrid embodiment of perversity, universally condemned and shamed.

I fantasize about Manguel on a book tour, giving readings and signing copies of this book at the Pigmalion, but alas, it is no more. Perhaps someday he'll come back to Munro's bookshop in Victoria before our surrounding cedar forests disappear forever, devoured by the monster of greed. —*Feb 2020*

42 Oliver Sacks

I often find biographies and autobiographies more compelling than fiction, for they introduce a whiff of reality into the text instead of a fictional account of an individual, however polished the prose.

On the Move is a memoir by the late neurologist Oliver Sacks (1933–2015), one of my heroes. Physician, author, motorcyclist, athlete and compassionate gay man, Sacks wrote many books and articles about his profession over the course of his long career, and his autobiography chronologically relates his experiences as a child, a medical student, a doctor, a traveller, a friend and a lover, as well as his own experiences as a patient.

Born in Britain and mostly educated there, Sacks spent his career in the United States. He believed that the brain is the "most incredible thing in the universe," and he became widely known for writing best-selling case histories about both his patients' and his own disorders and unusual experiences. Some of his tales were adapted for plays by major playwrights, or for feature films, fine art, dance and opera and other musical works.

His first posthumous book, *River of Consciousness*, an anthology of his essays, was published in October 2017. Sacks specified the order of these essays shortly before he died. Some of the selections focus on repressed memories and other tricks the mind plays on itself. Another posthumous book will be a collection of his letters.

Sacks lived alone for most of his life and declined to share personal details until late in his life. In *On the Move,* he wrote that when his mother, a physician, became aware of his homosexuality in his late adolescence, she initially told him he was an "abomination" and that she wished he had never been born. But that was only an immediate response, and she later wrote thanking him for his letters home after he left and told him she was proud of his achievements.

Sacks received a multitude of honours and awards, including honorary doctorates from twelve universities. In 1996 Sacks became a member of the American Academy of Arts and Letters (Literature); he was a Fellow of the New York Academy of Sciences in 1999 and in the same year was named an Honorary Fellow at the Queen's College, Oxford. Sacks was also a Fellow of the Royal College of Physicians.

Celibate for about thirty-five years, since his forties, in 2008 Sacks began a friendship with writer and *New York Times* contributor Bill Hayes, which slowly evolved into a committed long-term partnership that lasted until Sacks's death. He had earlier noted in a 2001 interview that severe shyness had been a lifelong impediment to his personal interactions. In

2017 Hayes wrote *Insomniac City*, a book about Sacks and the city of New York. It is a wonderful and moving collection of conversations, vignettes, photographs and musings about their seven years together living in New York City.

At the end of *On the Move*, Sacks described himself as "a storyteller, for better and for worse. I suspect that a feeling for stories, for narrative, is a universal human disposition, going with our powers of language, consciousness of self, and autobiographical memory." — *June 2018*

43 Alan Turing: The Enigma

Andrew Hodges's biography of the English mathematician Alan Turing was first published to high acclaim in 1983 and reprinted in 2012 to commemorate the centenary of Turing's birth. In the preface to the new edition, Hodges cites former US President Barack Obama's speech to the UK parliament praising Turing, along with Isaac Newton and Charles Darwin, as a major British contributor to science.

During the Second World War, Turing enabled the cracking of the German Enigma ciphers, as he had already formulated the concept of the "universal machine." In 1945 he produced the first design for a digital computer and is now acknowledged as a founder of computer science. Turing had planned to extend his work into the area of artificial intelligence, but in 1952 he was arrested and charged with having sex with another man. The Criminal Law Amendment Act of 1885 made "gross indecency" a crime in the UK, leading to many convictions against male homosexuals and alleged homosexuals. King George V was quoted as saying, when informed of a homosexual peer, "I thought men like that shot themselves!"

Most famously, Oscar Wilde was convicted and sentenced to two years' hard labour in 1895. Turing was convicted under this same law in 1952 and sentenced to estrogen injections (chemical castration) as an alternative to prison. Despairing, he committed suicide by cyanide poisoning on June 7, 1954, at the age of forty-two.

In August 2009 a petition was started urging the British Government to apologize for Turing's prosecution as a homosexual. It received more than 30,000 signatures. Prime Minister Gordon Brown acknowledged the petition, releasing a statement on September 10, 2009, apologizing and describing the treatment of Turing as "appalling." On December 24,

2013, Queen Elizabeth II signed a pardon for Turing's conviction for gross indecency, with immediate effect. In September 2016 the government announced its intention to expand this retroactive exoneration to other men convicted of similar historical indecency offences in what was described as the "Alan Turing law," an amnesty to retroactively pardon men who were cautioned or convicted under historical legislation that outlawed homosexual acts.

Since 1966 the Turing Award has been given annually by the Association for Computing Machinery for technical or theoretical contributions to the computing community. It is widely considered to be the computing world's highest honour, equivalent to the Nobel Prize.

On May 17, 2014, the world's first work of public art to recognize Turing as gay was commissioned in Bletchley, where his wartime work was carried out. The commission was announced to mark the International Day Against Homophobia and Transphobia. —*June 2018*

44 The Quest for Corvo and Hadrian VII

Frederick William Rolfe (1860–1913), better known as Baron Corvo, was an eccentric English writer and artist. In 1934 A.J.A. Symons published *The Quest for Corvo.* More than just a biography, it is an account of Symons's persistent search for documentation of Rolfe's life. It describes the results of Symons's investigations and reveals the complex life story of the brilliant but flawed and tragic author of *Hadrian VII* and other works.

A contemporary of Oscar Wilde in late Victorian and Edwardian England, Rolfe was apparently not troubled by his homosexual orientation, coyly referred to in Symons's text as "one of those unlucky men in whom the impulses of passion are misdirected." This was undoubtedly a powerful motivation for Rolfe's striving to become a Catholic priest, with its obligation of celibacy. But Rolfe was repeatedly foiled in this hope, becoming bitter and vituperative towards those in the ecclesiastical hierarchy, convinced that he had been cruelly denied his true vocation.

From the documentation collected by Symons from those who had direct contact with Rolfe and from available remaining letters and diaries, it becomes evident that the primary problem was Rolfe's personality, which today we would characterize as narcissistic and paranoid. His sexual orientation would have been a complicating factor in his life adjustment, but his personality traits poisoned all of his attempts to develop friendships and meaningful relationships. He was nevertheless a very intelligent man, an autodidact, with deep knowledge of Renaissance and medieval history. His writing style was idiosyncratic but his vocabulary undeniably eloquent.

Hadrian VII is a thinly veiled autobiographical wish-fulfillment novel in which the protagonist, a poverty-stricken Catholic writer rejected by the Church, is unexpectedly elevated to the papacy. When advised to select a modern papal name, he pompously replies, "The previous English pope was Hadrian IV. The present one is Hadrian VII. It pleases Us, so by Our own impulse, We command." He attempted to make fundamental changes at the Vatican, but the fictionalized papacy did not prosper, and Hadrian VII was eventually assassinated.

Rolfe was never able to sustain himself by his writing and was constantly in debt to all those who had befriended him. His obvious intellect, extraordinary vocabulary and uncanny ability to persuade others to provide support led to a lifelong repeated pattern of failure and subsequent blaming of others for his own misfortunes. At the end of his life, aged only fifty-three, having alienated everyone who had tried to assist him, penniless and living in squalid circumstances in Venice, he died in 1913.

Decades later Symons took an interest in his life and wrote the celebrated work *The Quest for Corvo: An Experiment in Biography*. *Hadrian VII* was eventually made into an award-winning play in 1968 by Peter Luke. — *June 2018*

45 Pampa Grass

This is the story of the adventures in Argentina of a twenty-year-old New Yorker, George Newbery, as written by his son Diego Newbery. George, a recently trained dentist, initially travelled to Buenos Aires as a passenger aboard a sailing ship in 1877 at the urging of his brother, who was already living there and extolled the wonders of the southern republic.

George first travelled to the jungle areas in the north, adjacent to Paraguay, by river steamer, and subsequently by horse cart and rail, up along the route east of the Andes, originally used by the Inca administrators from Peru before attaining independence from Spain. George continued further north to the border with Bolivia before returning to Buenos Aires, and subsequently obtained land in the south of the province. He founded the Media Luna ranch after being paid in a land grant for his services fighting Indigenous people in the "Wild West" milieu of the pampas. George later sold the ranch and married Fanny, a girl from Ohio, and they travelled to the southern region of Patagonia. Together they settled in the area of Lake Nahuel Huapi, nestled in the Andes by the border with Chile, and raised a family. He became the administrator of the first national park in that area of crystalline lakes, dark forests and snow-capped mountains.

Their son, Diego, became a pilot and predeceased his parents. His widowed mother Fanny continued to live at their rustic home in the mountains. In 1962 our family visited her, a feisty and spry ninety-three-year-old, still living there with a daughter as her companion. Fanny treated us with stories of her early years as the first white woman in the region, and of her experience giving a copy of her son's book to US president Eisenhower on a later visit to the country of her birth.

While we were there, she asked me to examine some papers left by her late son, and I was astonished to find a handwritten essay from the mid-1930s, written by Spanish philosopher Miguel de Unamuno. With her permission, I sent it to the director of the National Library in Buenos Aires, at that time Jorge Luis Borges.

In *Pampa Grass*, Diego describes his father's adventures in lands "won from the Indians" matter-of-factly, consistent with social attitudes of his time. A railroad to the town of San Carlos de Bariloche from Buenos Aires was constructed by the British and later named after General Julio A. Roca, best known for directing the "Conquest of the Desert," a series of military campaigns resulting in the extermination of the Indigenous population in Patagonia. An appendix to *Pampa Grass* has a lexicon of about 100 words of the now-vanished Araucanian language, once spoken by victims of successful genocide by the now-honoured General Roca. — *Apr 2018*

46 Guevara and The Motorcycle Diaries

From 1951 to 1952, the twenty-three-year-old Argentinian medical student Ernesto Guevara de la Serna undertook a journey up the west coast of South America with his physician friend Alberto Granado aboard an ancient 500cc Norton motorcycle. He kept a journal recording their experiences and later rewrote the narrative, now archived and published in Havana.

These were formative years for young Ernesto, and the motive of the journey was initially adventure, a young man's quest to expand his horizons and to see how people lived beyond his insular, middle-class society in Argentina. It quickly becomes evident in this narrative that the journey was not only geographical but also cerebral. The degrading quality of lives of workers, subjected to the whims of international corporations, was observed and recorded by the diarist. His awakening understanding of the association of unregulated capitalism with human misery, nurtured by his inherent altruism, produced the psychological basis for his acceptance of Marxism as the solution to the problem of exploitation of man by man.

But it is also a story of adventure, of mechanical breakdowns, spills, punctures, drinking bouts with congenial and some not-so-congenial hosts, football matches with lepers, stowaway passages and encounters with local doctors, some friendly, some not.

Guevara's imagery is a source of earthy delight, as in the passage when he says goodbye to his girlfriend in Argentina as he sets out on his adventure: "The two days I'd planned stretched like elastic into eight, and with the bittersweet taste of the good-bye mingling with my inveterate halitosis, I finally felt myself wafted away on the winds of adventure towards worlds which I fancied stranger than they were, in situations I thought more normal than they were."

His growing resentment of injustice forms a crescendo throughout the narrative, hardly noted at the beginning but becoming louder with his encounters with poverty, as he and his companion proceed northward through Chile and Peru to Venezuela. How could one not embrace a revolutionary attitude, given the system of exploitation described in this journal?

We now know better — or do we?

Guevara was shot in 1967 at age thirty-nine in Bolivia, still trying to foment revolution, still driven by the revolutionary idealism so evident in these diaries. His early death was his personal tragedy; perhaps a greater loss was his idealism. He believed in the altruistic goals of early communism, now absent and replaced by mercantilism, as in modern China's Orwellian newspeak of "socialism with Chinese characteristics."

The motorcycle is preserved in the museum in our hometown of Alta Gracia in Córdoba Province, where Guevara and I both lived in the 1950s. Our paths never crossed, though, for when I arrived in 1955, he had already departed on his historic motorcycle journey. — *Apr 2018*

47 Mao's Little Red Book

Mao's Little Red Book: A Global History is a 2014 title from Cambridge University Press about another book, *Quotations from Chairman Mao Tse-Tung*, initially published in Mandarin in 1964 and with an English translation in the 1966 second edition. At its height of popularity, from 1965 to 1975, there were well over a billion copies of *Quotations* in print worldwide in over thirty languages.

The canonical revised edition of Mao's *Little Red Book* (*LRB*) contains 427 quotations spread across thirty-three thematic chapters, with extracts from Mao Zedong's writings and speeches from 1929 to 1964, ranging in subject matter from philosophy to warfare to art. *Mao's Little Red Book: A Global History* contains fifteen contributions by distinguished academics from the universities of California, New York, San Francisco State, Purdue, Miami, Stanford, Pennsylvania, Singapore, Delhi and Freiburg, as well as Boston and Wellesley Colleges. The majority of the contributors are Americans, with only one (Ban Wang) holding a simultaneous academic appointment in the People's Republic of China (PRC), at the highly respected East China Normal University in Shanghai.

The contributors were specially selected for their unique experiences and expertise, and as a group they are diverse with respect to age, gender, ethnicity and political sympathies. About half of the chapters are written by historians with various regional specializations, while the other half come from historically minded scholars of literature, area studies, political science and sociology.

Bookended with an introduction by editor Alexander C. Cook and a conclusion by Ban Wang are thirteen essays addressing the origins and spread of the *LRB*, popular media recordings, factional battles within the PRC, translation and internationalism, Afro-Asian radicalism from 1966 to 1975, and the *LRB*'s reception and influence in different countries, such as Tanzania, India, Peru, the USSR, Albania, Italy, the former Yugoslavia, West Germany and France.

In the introduction, the editor argues that the *LRB* aimed to explode the Cold War order by exploiting various fissions and fusions within and between the "first world" of American-style capitalism, the "second world" of Soviet-style socialism, and an underdeveloped but emerging "third world." The editor cleverly characterizes the *LRB* as a "weapon of mass instruction."

In Ban Wang's closing summary, he adduces, "the *LRB* is what people made of it, perhaps tempting to think of it as a totalitarian godhead, exerting its numinous power over the mass of enslaved idolaters — or as an ironic accessory for the nonbelievers who know better." He argues that in China the *LRB* — as a fixed text open to interpretation — set in motion a reformation with genuine possibilities for protest, agency, emancipation, and democracy.

Bear in mind, however, that *A Global History* dates from 2014. Since then, developments in the PRC, like amending the constitution to allow extension of presidential power beyond two terms and the centralization of power by Xi Jinping, give pause to predictions of significant change.
— *June 2018*

48 On Writing a Memoir

The English author Blake Morrison was born in Skipton, Yorkshire, in 1950 and has worked in almost every form of literature. His memoir, *And When Did You Last See Your Father?* (1993), is an honest and moving account of his father's life and death that won literary prizes and inspired a film.

A recent issue of the UK's *Guardian Review* featured Morrison's thoughts about the genre of life-writing in a lengthy essay, noting that "it often seems that those writing memoirs, far from being narcissists, need constant encouragement that their story is worth telling, that they're not being self-indulgent, that it's OK to use the word 'I.'" He cites many writers who have wittily commented on this subject, like Mark Twain's "The only reason why God created man is because he was disappointed with the monkey," or George Bernard Shaw's "The man who writes about himself and his own time is the only man who writes about all people and about all time."

Following the long essay by Morrison there are two shorter pieces in the *Review*, one by Will Self describing his earlier addiction to heroin, and another by Alex Clark reflecting on memoirs written by various professionals that have become popular of late, such as those by medical doctors, barristers and even footballers.

Morrison notes, "The best memoirs show self-assertion. But they aren't selfish. They have a unique story to tell — a story that resonates with everyone else's story. . . . Writers can't hope to change the world, but they can (in some small way) influence patterns of thought and structures of feeling."

He offers a few tips for aspiring memoirists, beginning with the instruction to begin with words that will initially grab the reader's attention.

Jan Morris grabbed my attention in her memoir *In My Mind's Eye* (2018), which begins, "I have never before in my life kept a diary of my thoughts, and here at the start of my tenth decade, having for the moment nothing much else to write, I am having a go at it."

Morrison's reflections on the genre were appreciated by this memoirist. — *Mar 2020*

49 Jan Morris in Her Tenth Decade

A prolific writer now for many years, Jan Morris shares with us short reflections about her life in her recent collection, *In My Mind's Eye: A Thought Diary*. These brief vignettes are not individually dated and have no common theme beyond presenting an opinion, a memory, or a thought arising from her daily existence living in retirement with her partner in a quiet rural community in north-west Wales.

Being myself of a similar vintage, I can readily identify with her litany of minor physical and cognitive complaints like poor balance, catarrh, occasional word-finding difficulty, odd aches and pains, cold toes at night . . . and on it goes. But when asked by a friend what was her recipe for a happy old age (assuming she was enjoying one), she wrote, "I could only answer enigmatically, as I always do, 'Be kind.'" Indeed, she writes that for her, kindness is the ultimate virtue.

Morris reflects on companion animals that have been close, specifically mourning the loss of her polydactyl Norwegian cat Ibsen, and inveighs against the cruel animal prisons called zoos. Walking her daily thousand paces along a lane by a small river, she remains acutely aware of her natural surroundings, and in spite of worries both personal and universal, recognizes that she has much to enjoy, too: people to like and love, and seven different kinds of Welsh marmalade to spread on her morning toast, one for each day of the week. A plethora of memories inhabit her mind, of people like Sir Edmond Hillary, whom she accompanied as a journalist to the first ascent of Everest, and places like brash Manhattan in 1945; others are poignant and musty, like Trieste, and even one imaginary, Hav.

Current events are a source of discomfort for her as for those of us of similar senectitude, and she views Brexit as petty squabbling among politicians regarding the consequences of an ignorant decision made by an uninformed electorate two years ago. She expresses a sense of nostalgia not only for her land as it was when she was young but also for the now-often-reviled British Empire and what she remembers of its once-perceived "civilizing effect" on the countries it ruled around the world. Her attitude about men now being accused of sexual abuse because of what was then considered innocent play again reflects values of earlier days, no longer considered appropriate.

Objects at her home trigger memories of trips made, books both written and read. All of us that live long lives end up surrounded by a constellation of objects, each with its own capacity to evoke memory of some trip or event: for her a model ship, for me a replica of Picasso's owl, for her a souvenir of a flight to New York on the Concorde, for me a luggage label from the Intourist Hotel in Irkutsk, Siberia. — *July 2020*

50 On Literary Gratitude

Writing in a recent issue of the *Guardian*, freelance journalist Elle Hunt reflected on the vicissitudes of literary gifts and the motivations of book-giving. The title of her column "I thought you'd like to read this. . ." introduces the idea that books as gifts may reflect a form of well-intentioned but unsolicited advice on the part of the giver — perhaps to kindly cheer up one who is sad or, less benignly, to persuade the recipient to change an opinion.

Sensible advice to the book-giver is quoted, but left unaddressed is the reaction of the recipient. Often the giver hopes for gratitude from the receiver, whether sincere or not. Politics and religion are sensitive areas involving issues of right and wrong, wherein most resist change, even with appeals to logic or compassion.

Aware of the usual beneficent intentions of the giver, a recipient may feel obligated to read it, and at times may be rewarded by discovering a hidden and previously unknown gem. But they may also decide to abandon an attempt to read and regift or otherwise dispose of it. The latter sounds a cautionary note about inscribing the gift of a book, and a sensible recommendation is made to not inscribe but rather include a card that could be used as a bookmark by the reader.

To inscribe a book can be treacherous, particularly when the given tome is found in a used bookshop by the giver, an unpleasant event that has set off more than one literary feud, like that between V.S. Naipaul and Paul Theroux when the latter found a copy of his own book in a used bookshop that he had inscribed and previously given to the former.

Some authors resist giving their own books as gifts, lest they be thought of as self-promoting, but others more attuned to the commercial possibilities of greater sales, and hence royalties, may be unfazed by distributing their work, egged on by agents and publishers to promote wider readership.

I like to give books to friends and relatives on occasions such as birthdays and holidays, often a used book that I have enjoyed, but I may also give a voucher or book token from a local bookshop, to allow the recipient to select what they wish. As a lifelong reader of both fiction and non-fiction, I am saddened to see those whose attention span appears to be limited to less than 280 words, for I know what they are missing. But I am also encouraged by the proliferation of "little libraries" appearing in different neighbourhoods around town, inviting passersby to take one and leave one, and by seeing them used by people of all ages. I use them myself. — *Mar 2020*

HOMO COGNOSCENS

51 Homo cognoscens

To want to know how something works is part of what it means to be human. The present active participle of the Latin verb *cognoscere* means "getting to know," so *Homo cognoscens* represents man the learner, or the one who understands owing to the mental action or process of acquiring knowledge through thought, experience and the senses.

Motivated by hunger, much of animal behaviour can be understood in terms of resource acquisition. Both vertebrates and invertebrates forage for the calories required to sustain life — the honeybee buzzes from blossom to blossom not to admire the flowers but to look for nectar, and the fox will trot from farm to farm not to delight in looking at rural living arrangements but to find an accessible chicken coop replete with fat hens to consume. And while some species of mammals and birds are able to utilize material from their surroundings to perform simple tasks to access food, to enhance security or to obey commands (like teaching a dog to sit), humans are relatively unique in that our learning includes the formation of abstract ideas.

Much human behaviour these days is anything other than food-seeking and is often related to meaningful observation. This is what makes us creative beings. The drive to understand what we perceive with our senses has long been the fuel motivating natural science. While a stargazer may be seen as one who looks at the stars and other celestial objects, an astronomical *observer* is one who not only looks upward and outward but also attributes *meaning* to what is seen. Such is the starting point of all empirical knowledge.

Recognized as the first philosophers and scientists in the Western tradition, the presocratics, such as Thales of Miletus, were sixth- and fifth-century BCE Greek thinkers in Asia Minor who thought of ways of inquiring into the world and the place of human beings within it. Later Greek observers, like Aristarchus of Samos in the early fourth century BCE, conceived of a heliocentric model of the universe long before Copernicus in 1543 CE. After being obscured by more than a millennium of Christian theological fog, with the dawn of the Enlightenment observation led to the gradual understanding of gravity, planetary motion, the solar system, galaxies and beyond.

We humans look at things and study them to find out how they work, and if possible, augment our senses with devices to extend their range of detection. The ability to observe beyond the biological limitations of our senses propelled the construction of instruments permitting the observation of molecular structures with electron microscopy, and of telescopes sensitive to regions of the electromagnetic spectrum that cannot be directly visualized. Yet there appear to still be limits to what can be visualized, both great and small. Subatomic particles can only be described in terms of probability fields in quantum mechanics, and at the other wavelength extreme, the cosmological concepts of dark matter and dark energy remain enigmatic.

The utility of mathematics in predicting both observable subatomic and astronomical events is undeniable, but mathematics is not something observable. It is abstract, a human creation, and a process more akin to aesthetics than to observation. Our inborn abilities to learn how things work are value-free. Many of our achievements have proved beneficial, such as teaching children to read and write, but some of the consequences have led to significant negative outcomes, like global warming and atomic weaponry. With our learning we have developed the means of our own destruction. — Compiled from the essays "*Homo cognoscens*" and "Observation," *May 2020*

52 From Presocratics to Quantum Mechanics

The earliest recorded attempts to explain the nature of the physical world are usually attributed to sixth-century BCE presocratic Greek philosophers like Thales of Miletus, who speculated that all matter was initially formed from water. In the following century, Democritus (c. 460–c. 370 BCE) suggested small indivisible particles, or *atoms*, to be the basis of all matter.

Even earlier than the Greek presocratics, prior to the sixth century BCE, Buddhist atomism in India put forward a very qualitative, Aristotelian-style atomic theory that identified four kinds of atoms, corresponding to the standard elements. Centuries later, seventh-century Indian philosophers developed a very different theory, in which atoms were considered to be point-sized, duration-less and made of energy.

During the "dark ages" of the medieval Latin West, the study of ancient Greek ideas was lost, preserved in Arab libraries until a renewed interest in the nature of the material world and the eventual rebirth of atomism occurred in the twelfth and thirteenth centuries. The works of Aristotle and others were then translated into Latin from the Arabic translations of the original Greek.

By the end of the nineteenth century, classical mechanics as first developed by Isaac Newton appeared to fully describe the known universe with the motion of physical objects, and with Maxwell's equations unifying electricity and magnetism. The atom was found not to be indivisible, and the discovery of subatomic particles, measured in small units, or *quanta*, led to laws governing their behaviour beyond the earlier classical mechanics.

During three decades at the beginning of the twentieth century, the new theory of quantum mechanics was elaborated by Erwin Schrödinger, among others. A great twentieth-century Austrian theoretical physicist, Schrödinger formulated a basic equation that did not describe something tangible but rather a "waveform of probability" that could predict experimental results. But there were conceptual problems, for the logical consequences of Schrödinger's equation led to paradoxical results when applied to systems operating beyond the small distances associated with atoms — for example, Schrödinger's famous thought experiment of a cat in a sealed box being simultaneously both dead and alive until the box is opened.

What works well in analyzing systems at the micro or subatomic level produces absurd results at the macro level within which we live. Over decades, the apparent counterintuitive conflict between classical and quantum mechanics appears to have been resolved by utilizing the concept of quantum coherence and decoherence to derive the former from the more basic latter, like energy seeming to be lost by friction in classical mechanics. Thales of Miletus would no doubt be nonplussed by the suggestion that although matter fundamentally does appear to consist of waves, they are waves not of water but of probability.

For a book helpful in understanding this subject, see *Beyond Weird* (2018) by science writer Philip Ball, who has a knack for making quantum concepts like superposition and entanglement understandable in only 354 pages. For a shorter historical overview of only 25 pages, try *Quantum Mechanics* (2017), a Ladybird Expert Book by theoretical physicist Jim Al-Khalili. — *May 2019*

53 What Is Life?

As living animals capable of abstract thought, this is a fundamental question we seldom ask ourselves, but one which has occupied thinkers throughout recorded history. Schrödinger assembled his thoughts on this question in a series of lectures given in Ireland in 1943, later collecting the material into a small book called simply *What Is Life?*

Do the established laws of quantum mechanics have validity in describing life processes? The difficulty here is that quantum physics works well at the micro level of atoms and molecules, using probability wave formulation, but at the macro level of living organisms it leads to paradoxical results. "An organism must have a comparatively gross structure in order to enjoy the benefit of fairly accurate laws, both for its internal life and for its interplay with the external world." In this assertion, Schrödinger foreshadowed the subsequent discovery of DNA in 1953, which endows an organism with continuity of structure and reveals the mechanism of heredity.

According to Schrödinger, entropy, a measure of the level of disorder or randomness in a closed system, is the key to understanding the persistence of living organisms in a universe governed by the second law of thermodynamics, which asserts that increasing disorder is the ultimate consequence of all energy transfer. For example, a living organism maintains a local negative balance of entropy, in other words, a persistence of order instead of an increase in disorder. This is made possible by the phenomenon of metabolism, wherein the organism acquires order from its environment, either by photosynthesis in the case of vegetation or by feeding in the animal kingdom.

The ultimate local source of this transfer of negative entropy or order is of course the sun, itself the consequence of gravitational attraction following the initial "big bang," followed by local condensation and gravitational compression of matter, leading to heating and thermonuclear reactions within stars, as described by astrophysics.

It appears that the combination of theoretical physics with the elucidation of the structure and processes characteristic of living organisms indicate that the question "What is life?" can be addressed by science without any recourse to ultimate ends, without teleology. — *Feb 2019*

54 Beyond Schrödinger

Physicist Paul Davies takes us beyond Schrödinger's thoughts in his latest book, *The Demon in the Machine* (2019), describing the role of information transfer in biology as analogous to Maxwell's nineteenth-century thought experiment evading the second law of thermodynamics by means of an imaginary "demon" controlling otherwise random thermal distribution, in other words, increasing entropy in a closed system.

This is relevant to living organisms in the fact that the DNA coding of biological information leads to negative entropy, permitting the persistence of life in living creatures, including their reproduction and evolution. In thinking of the molecular genetic substrate of an organism as its hardware, the coded information it contains could then be considered its software.

In an imaginary system such as Turing's universal constructor, encoded information for replication must include instructions for reproduction, otherwise it would be sterile, and this is just what we observe in living organisms. Moreover, Davies suggests epigenetic factors could contribute to a neo-Lamarckian situation, in which acquired characteristics may affect successive generations of descendants.

With the apparent operation of this coded information acting in place of a "ghost in the machine," living organisms maintain a state of negative entropy by virtue of the information pattern encoded in their software, and an answer to Schrödinger's question looks within reach. But what seems to still be missing is the understanding of how it all started. We speculate on the uniqueness of life on our planet, one among many others that we are now discovering with advances in observational astronomy, some perhaps capable of supporting some form of life.

The problem remains unanswered. A physicist like Schrödinger, Davies wonders to what extent quantum features like coherence may be associated with the phenomenon of life — but still the initial spark remains obscure. Vitalism as such is dismissed, and Davies admits, "If there is a life principle at work in nature, then it has yet to be discovered."

A related issue is the phenomenon of our consciousness, arising from the billions of neurons (comparable to the number of stars in a galaxy) and their myriad interconnections in every human's central nervous system. This introduces the age-old philosophical concepts of realism and idealism, the mind–body problem and the illusion of temporal flow arising from our concept of "self" persisting over time. — *Apr 2019*

55 Biophysics

Being interested in issues like cosmology and life, I recently bought two books on the subject, written by academic experts. As a former astronomer, I find considering different possibilities about plausible end states fascinating. That is, if you don't mind reading about inevitable doom and how the totality of everything is bound to come to a final end state.

The End of Everything (Astrophysically Speaking) by theoretical astrophysicist Katie Mack is a beautifully written and clear exposition of contemporary ideas about possible endings of the universe that are debated among cosmologists. Mack appropriately begins with the big bang itself, 13.8 billion years ago, and the events immediately following — the subsequent "soup of particles" condensing into stars, dark matter, the expansion of space, and the formation of galaxies. She lucidly describes how we have only recently come to understand these events in the past century, using theoretical physics and observational astronomy.

Every Life on Fire: How Thermodynamics Explains the Origins of Living Things by theoretical physicist Jeremy England addresses the conundrum that every living thing we know of results from the reproduction of another living thing. Yet at the time of the formation of the solar system about 4.5 billion years ago from a dense cloud of interstellar gas and dust, there was no life. So how did it start? This is a reasonable question that has vexed both scientists and philosophers for millennia. England, who has impressive academic credentials, argues that "the very same forces that tend to tear things apart could also have assembled the first living systems," describing his theory as *dissipative adaptation.*

England goes on to describe recent progress in a branch of thermodynamics called nonequilibrium statistical mechanics, averring that as living things genetically inherit from their ancestors, so too can a collection of physically interacting particles retain patterns "in ways that look an awful lot like living." Writing, "It seems thoroughly necessary to put our examination of the boundary between life and non-life in a suitably rich philosophical context," he confesses to personally finding the best way of approaching the big issues of life is found in interpreting the Hebrew Bible. Working from a "God" revealing himself in a burning bush, England goes on to use other examples from the Book of Exodus to describe the primordial soup from which life apparently emerged.

I recently asked a friend with a PhD in Semitic languages from Harvard, the retired head of Religious Studies at a major Canadian university, for her opinion, and she commented, "I'll let you be the judge of this guy's abilities as a physicist, but he's clearly absolutely naive re the Hebrew Bible, and the only way he could make such statements is by injecting a heavy dose of faith into the text."

Insofar as his work and thought as a physicist is concerned, I believe he clearly not only has expertise but also the capability of describing his work in a clear and understandable manner for interested non-specialists, and though his insights into the borderline between living and non-living provide no ultimate answer, they indicate a possible pathway towards understanding one of the basic questions of life, posed by artist Paul Gauguin: "Where do we come from?"

An Orthodox Jew and a former associate professor of physics at MIT, England identifies himself as a firm believer in a supreme being, the God of Abraham as described in the text of the Hebrew Bible, but his religious beliefs do not conflict with his theoretical physics. He acknowledges encouragement and inspiration from both a rabbi and his colleagues but does not reject Darwinian evolution or resort to simple-minded creationism, and the examples he gives from biblical stories are not intrusive. To me they are more like poetic adornments to the cold, serious physics in the text; the issue of "intelligent design" never arises. — *Oct 2020*

56 Viral Pathogenesis and Vitalism

Common to all forms of life, from the coded information contained in a single strand of nucleic acid to highly complex multicellular organisms, is a will, drive or capacity to exist until the life form has replicated or reproduced itself. This coded information is preserved in a new life form, following replication or reproduction.

Take for example our knowledge of bacterial plague and viral pathogenesis. We know how bacterial plague, or *Yersinia pestis*, causes disease in humans. Viral pathogenesis, however, is something different. Unlike *Yersinia pestis*, the container of the pathogenic nucleic acid is not a bacterium but instead only a protein capsule enveloping the nucleic acid information coding.

Viral pathogenesis occurs in higher organisms when viral replication interferes with the ability of the infected life form to maintain homeostasis. For example, coronaviruses, like the agent of the new pandemic, target cells of the respiratory tract, generating an immune antibody response in the host that will hopefully be controlled by vaccination.

Why do these pathogens do what they do? That's not a question that can be answered by science, which can only answer the question of *how* pathogenesis occurs. We can attempt to understand the how but not the why because the latter implies final cause. The fundamental difference here appears to be linguistic.

French philosopher Henri Bergson postulated that the answer to the question of *why* was an élan vital, or "life force." However, this concept of a life force is illusory, like the Christian soul, for neither is an entity that can be observed or measured. They are both epistemological fallacies invented to create a response in the search for an ultimate reason for existence. Yet this is, in and of itself, an imaginary goal. The science of genetics describes how the mechanics of reproduction function in both a human or a virus in terms of conservation of information in the genetic coding of each, but can offer no explanation of why this should be the case.

The British secular humanist biologist Julian Huxley was said to have dryly remarked that Bergson's élan vital is no better an explanation of life than explaining the operation of a railway engine by its élan locomotif (locomotive driving force). Witty and clever, but then if Isaac Newton's invisible force (gravity) yields observable results predicting planetary motions, why shouldn't Bergson's invisible life force account for growth and reproduction amongst living organisms, like humans and viruses? (Whether a virus should be considered an organism is of course a valid question, given that its only activity is nothing but hijacking the machinery of a host cell to make a copy of itself.)

One can assign blame for infectious diseases on different agents, such as vectors like rats or fleas with the plague, or actions such as coughing and releasing aerosol particles with viruses, but these are only proximate causes. To consider *final causes* introduces teleology, with its whiff of vitalism. Science alone allows us to understand how to resolve the ultimate questions about what constitutes a living thing, be it a virus or a human. Physics, genetics and logic are the keys to knowing *how* things work but not *why* they do so.

Unlike philosophy, science permits us to speak clearly and enjoins us to remain silent about what we cannot say, as advised by Wittgenstein in his *Tractatus Logico-Philosophicus.* To spend one's life searching for an imaginary life force or the "essence of meaning" is a fool's errand. Such preoccupations are best left to philosophers to debate and are unhelpful to those in public health trying to control or at least to ameliorate the consequences of pathogenesis. — Compiled from "Viral Pathogenesis and Vitalism," Apr 2020, and "Vitalism Revisited." *May 2020*

57 Order

At tea with my grandson Hugh today, we ate some fresh cherries, placing the pits on our plates. With typical human curiosity, he noted that he had aligned his pits in neat pairs, rather than just making a random pile of pits as I did, and asked if I had a psychiatric opinion about his doing this. I had no ready reply at the time, but after he left I reflected on his query. My first thought was that imposing order in this way was common behaviour, only considered pathological by the *Diagnostic and Statistical Manual of Mental Disorders* (DSM) when prolonged and repetitive, "causing distress or dysfunction as in obsessional states, interfering with social or occupational functioning."

More generally, I thought of the many ways that we discover and impose order in our lives, at times even leading to general advances in knowledge, such as Mendeleev's periodic table of the elements or the standard model of particle physics. Order in the natural universe was there all the time, awaiting, as it were, discovery by a scientist looking for it. Aesthetic order can be created in space by visual artists, seen in the pictorial representations of line and colour in paintings and sculpture, or in time by composers and musicians, heard in the tonal constructions based on ordering sound vibrations and intervals, imposing beats and rhythms.

Seek and ye shall find, says the adage, for order appears wherever we look: in language we find order in the linguistic classifications of parts of speech and in the visual representations of words, either in varieties of alphabetic scripts or of non-alphabetic representations of objects and concepts, as is seen in Chinese characters.

Relativity theory arose when observational patterns exhibited an order in the universe unaccounted for by classical Newtonian mechanics. But the opposite of order, of course, is chaos, wherein specific patterns are not obvious. Yet even here we have invented ways of describing what appears initially chaotic by using probability theory, as in quantum mechanics. The culmination of the search for order lies in the intangible abstract realm of pure mathematics, wherein patterns may be found to exist among nonphysical concepts like numbers and dimensions. These relationships may turn out to have significance in the physical world, as when non-Euclidean geometry was found to be a useful descriptive of physical reality in relativity theory.

This human characteristic of seeking order, and finding it, whether in the largest or smallest of objects we observe, from galaxies to subatomic particles, is a starting point of understanding this universe in which we dwell. And this characteristic may be seen as profound when asking simple questions, even about arranging cherry pits on a plate.

Thanks, Hugh, for asking, and continue to question what you see. It is what makes us human. — *Aug 2019*

58 Abstract vs. Concrete

As an adjective the word *abstract* suggests the quality of being conceptual, distinct from having physicality, something intangible. Its antonym, *concrete*, on the other hand, indicates physical substance, being an actual object, something tangible. This distinction is blurred when the terms are used metaphorically, but I am one with Wittgenstein in that clarity in discourse is a virtue.

The dichotomy between abstract and concrete is usually just one feature in thinking about thinking, itself not ordinarily the focus of one's reflection. But a recent discussion of information theory by Paul Davies cites the aphorism of Rolf Landauer, "Information is physical!" It was difficult to grasp after having assumed otherwise as lifelong common sense.

Davies argues that information itself is not just an intangible idea or concept but consists of concrete entities. Metaphysical theories like Plato's forms or Berkeley's ideas in the mind of God are non-empirical and unprovable, whereas information is concrete, whether coded in DNA or measurable in atomic weights. Davies's book *The Demon in the Machine* introduces the concept of information as a physical and concrete entity capable of being actualized, transmitted, transformed and understood as a non-abstract substance.

Music may be thought of as one illustration. Take for example, Beethoven's Fifth Symphony. It is not just printed notes on a score sheet instructing players what sounds to make. It is vibrations in air molecules during a performance, or digitized codes on a compact disc. It may even be earworm motifs, such as *da-da-da-dum*, that persist in the mind of one who recently attended a concert. Being myself accustomed lifelong to regard a work of music as an abstract entity, the invitation to consider it instead as concrete information is not just a matter of shifting gears, as it were, but of something more fundamental, like redesigning the engine to operate on a different fuel supply.

Meanwhile, the building adjacent to my residence is being renovated by a local construction company named Abstract Developments, whose motto is "To create iconic spaces that enhance how people live." Cute. I await seeing them pour concrete as part of their project. — *Mar 2019*

59 Art in Science

In his new book, *The Universe Speaks in Numbers: How Modern Math Reveals Nature's Deepest Secrets*, physicist Graham Farmelo examines the history of aesthetics and theoretical physics. An unlikely pairing, aesthetics is the branch of philosophy that deals with the nature of beauty, the arts and artistic creation or appreciation, while theoretical physics employs mathematical models and abstractions of physical objects and systems to understand, explain and predict natural phenomena (such as Newton's laws of motion in classical mechanics or Schrödinger's equation in quantum mechanics).

Farmelo reminds us of the history of how contemporary thought about the nature of matter developed from the first laws of motion, elucidated by Isaac Newton in the seventeenth century, to the subsequent elaborations and extensions by Laplace, Maxwell and Einstein, and finally to quantum mechanics in the twentieth century, by Schrödinger, Heisenberg, Dirac and others, culminating in the current standard model of particle physics. Farmelo then speculates about future developments still hypothetical and awaiting experimental confirmation, but always consistent with the two major theories of the twentieth century: quantum mechanics and special relativity. He states, "Any new idea that has a chance of being correct must be consistent with both theories."

Foreshadowed by Einstein, who was aware early on of the aesthetic beauty of equations relating time and space, English physicist Paul Dirac advanced the principle of mathematical beauty as characteristic of the structures underpinning theories about the natural world in 1939. Aesthetic beauty is found in the Newtonian laws of motion, through Maxwell's electromagnetic field theory, to Einstein's relativity and quantum mechanics. It seemed clear to Dirac that indeed the "universe speaks in numbers," and that future directions of theoretical physics must allow for a sense of abstract beauty to have importance in the scientific understanding of the laws governing matter. A case in point is string theory, characterized by the beauty of mathematical symmetry and felt by some to be a key to understanding the basis of matter, though it lacks any direct experimental evidence and so remains only an attractive conjecture.

A remaining challenge in theoretical physics is to develop a unified theory based on quantum mechanics and relativity that accounts for all four fundamental forces, including gravity. Farmelo observed, "Pure mathematicians and theoretical physicists are now very much in the same world, but it's not clear how much it relates to the real one." He speculates on possible paths lying ahead, challenging both disciplines as they continue to work together, guided by an aesthetic sense of the beauty of abstract mathematics as expressed in the concrete manifestations of nature. — *July 2019*

60 Feigl, Wittgenstein and the Vienna Circle

The Vienna Circle of Logical Empiricism was a group of philosophers and scientists drawn from the natural and social sciences, logic and mathematics who met regularly from 1924 to 1936 at the University of Vienna. Their philosophical position was called logical empiricism, not a formal doctrine so much as a common concern for scientific methodology and the role of science in shaping society. It grew out of the philosophical works of Austrian philosopher Ludwig Wittgenstein, including *Tractatus Logico-Philosophicus.*

Recognized as a significant philosophical conception of the twentieth century, the aim of *Tractatus* was to identify the relationship between language and reality and to define the limits of science. A famous and succinct quotation from *Tractatus* sums up the essence of Wittgenstein's approach to philosophical questions: "Whereof one cannot speak, thereof one must be silent."

During the era of fascism in Austria in the mid-1930s and after the annexation of Austria by Nazi Germany, most members of the Vienna Circle were forced to emigrate. Among those was Herbert Feigl, who had become an active member in the Vienna Circle after training in the natural sciences. One of the few members to have had extensive conversations with Ludwig Wittgenstein, Feigl emigrated to the US and accepted a position as professor of philosophy at the University of Minnesota, where he remained until his retirement in 1971.

Feigl believed that empiricism was the only adequate philosophy for experimental science. And although after training in chemistry he became a philosopher instead of a chemist, Feigl never lost the perspective and common sense of a practical scientist. He was a humanist and a rationalist and was celebrated as a philosopher of science.

As an undergraduate student of philosophy at the University of Minnesota in 1954, I had the good fortune to have Feigl as one of my professors, and my lifelong approach to philosophy has been coloured by what I learned from him and by the approach of the Vienna Circle (and therefore Wittgenstein) to the relationship between language and science. I found a copy of *Tractatus* at the Pigmalion in Buenos Aires in 1957, and it has resided on my bookshelf ever since.

Years later, in 1965, when I returned to the University of Minnesota as a graduate student in astronomy, Feigl and I became friends. Discovering our mutual admiration of the music of Austrian composer Anton Bruckner, we spent evenings listening to recorded performances of his monumental symphonies. Listening to these musical creations together was, for us, comparable to sharing a religious experience, whereof, in the words of Wittgenstein, we remained silent. — *June 2018*

61 Marie Curie and Cecilia Payne-Gaposchkin

A generation separates the lives of Marie Curie and Cecilia Payne-Gaposchkin, both scientists in the early twentieth century. One is famed for her discovery of radioactivity, the other for her identification of hydrogen as the main constituent of stars and as a lesser-known founder of astrophysics.

Marie Curie (1867–1934) is famous for her work in Paris, where she discovered radioactivity and the use of X-rays in medical diagnosis, as well as for discovering and naming the elements radium and polonium, leading to the subsequent development of nuclear physics. Unable to live and work in her native Poland due to widespread misogyny, Curie established her career in France and ultimately received many prestigious honours, including two Nobel Prizes, and is now interred in the Pantheon.

Astronomer Cecilia Payne-Gaposchkin (1900–79) remains relatively unknown to the world at large. Born in England, she studied physics at

Cambridge, though her primary interest was astronomy. Payne-Gaposchkin trained at the renowned Cavendish Laboratory, but like Marie Curie was prevented from furthering her career in her England due to misogyny. Reflecting social values of the time, senior scientists were exclusively male, and although women were employed, it was usually as laboratory assistants or in performing tedious calculations derived from experiments and observations made by their male employers. Curie emigrated to the US, where she studied at Radcliffe, Harvard's college for women, and was awarded a PhD in astronomy in 1925.

Payne-Gaposchkin tirelessly worked in relative poverty on a minuscule salary. Analyzing photographic plates of stellar spectra while training in physics at Cambridge, she later identified the elements represented in starlight. In the 1920s it was thought that the constituents of all celestial objects were similar to those of the Earth, but she challenged that by identifying hydrogen as the overwhelming component of stars. She reported her findings in a 1925 thesis, "Stellar Atmospheres."

Generally dismissed by establishment astronomers, Payne-Gaposchkin was regarded as an uppity graduate student, one of a cohort of women employed by the observatory to work as "computational assistants," decades before the arrival of digital computers. Astronomers at the time were generally all men, who lacked her training in atomic theory, acquired at the Cavendish Laboratory.

Over time her findings were seen as undeniable, and her publication was described by later colleagues as "the most brilliant thesis ever written in astronomy." She became a full professor and chair of the Department of Astronomy at Harvard until her death in 1979.

Payne-Gaposhckin described herself as an astronomer, not a "woman astronomer," and her advice to students resonates with all of us who learn: "Do not undertake a scientific career in quest of fame or money. There are easier and better ways to reach them. Undertake it only if nothing else will satisfy you; for nothing else is probably what you will receive. Your reward will be the widening of the horizon as you climb. And if you achieve that reward you will ask no other."

Her metaphor relating science in general and astronomy in particular to climbing particularly resonated with me, for when in my twenties I was working as an observational astronomer in Argentina, two summers included mountaineering in Patagonia, in the southern Andes. —*Aug 2020*

62 Copernicus and Vesalius

A professor of anatomy in medical school, familiar with my background in astronomy, once asked me what relationship I saw between astronomy and medicine. Thinking quickly, I suggested that perhaps it was related to the achievements of the Polish astronomer Nicolaus Copernicus and the Flemish anatomist Andreas Vesalius.

Copernicus, the sixteenth-century proponent of heliocentrism, placed the sun rather than the earth at the centre of the universe (likely independently of Aristarchus of Samos, who had formulated such a model some eighteen centuries earlier). Copernicus's heliocentric model was a major event in the history of science and was felt to be undermining of the whole system of accepted science at the time. His book, *De revolutionibus orbium coelestium* (*On the Revolutions of the Celestial Spheres*), was initially rejected as a false Pythagorean doctrine contrary to Holy Scripture.

The Roman Catholic Church's Congregation of the Index issued a decree in 1616 suspending *De revolutionibus* until it could be "corrected," that is, made to coincide with the creationist views of scripture. The prohibition was finally dropped in 1835. Meanwhile, the consequences of Copernicus's revolutionary cosmology had led to Galileo, Kepler and Newton's understandings of the structure of the solar system, gravitational theory and the laws of motion.

Andreas Vesalius was a sixteenth-century Flemish anatomist, physician and author of one of the earliest and most influential books on human anatomy, *De humani corporis fabrica* (*On the Fabric of the Human Body*). Vesalius is often referred to as the founder of modern human anatomy.

On the day of his graduation from medical school, Vesalius was immediately offered the chair of surgery and anatomy at Padua, where he performed dissection as the primary teaching tool and urged students to perform dissection themselves. He believed that hands-on direct observation was the only reliable resource for anatomical knowledge, a huge break with medieval practice prohibiting human dissection.

Vesalius took residence in Basel to publish the seven-volume *De humani*. Around the same time he published an abridged edition for students, *Andrea Vesalii suorum de humani corporis fabrica librorum epitome*, and dedicated it to Philip II of Spain, the son of the Holy Roman Emperor. Now collectively referred to as the *Fabrica of Vesalius*, it was groundbreaking in the history of medical publishing and is considered a major step in the development of scientific medicine and the establishment of anatomy as a modern descriptive science.

When I was asked in the dissecting lab about the connection between astronomy and medicine, I suggested Copernicus and Vesalius, because they both published their seminal works in the same year, 1543. The professor nodded solemnly, then replied, "That's a very tenuous connection." — *May 2018*

63 Cosmology, Ufology and the Fermi Paradox

The discrepancy between the expectation that there should be evidence of alien civilizations or visitations and the presumption that no visitations have been observed is known as the Fermi paradox. While it is clear that about 95 percent of reported sightings of unidentified flying objects can be attributed to atmospheric phenomena or mistaken perception of known objects, such as aircraft and weather balloons, according to replies from a survey of 1,356 members of the American Astronomical Society, 4.6 percent reported witnessing or recording "inexplicable aerial phenomena."

US physicist Kevin Knuth, an editor of the peer-reviewed journal *Entropy*, suggested in a recent posting in *The Conversation* that we should consider the "unsettling and refreshing fact we may not be alone." Knuth argues that scientific study of the small number of unidentified flying objects is a reasonable scientific endeavour, and not limited to what he terms "the domain of fringe and pseudoscientists, many of whom litter the field with conspiracy theories and wild speculation."

In the context of what is now reliably becoming understood about the structure of space, the population of stars and possible planetary systems like our own, physicist Enrico Fermi's celebrated question, "Where is everybody?" makes more sense in 2018 than it did sixty years ago upon its asking in 1950, when the ability to reach verifiable information was more limited.

Observational astronomy in the mid-twentieth century was infinitesimal compared to what is now possible with orbital telescopes outside the earth's atmosphere and the ability to examine the entire electromagnetic spectrum in frequencies both above and below the limited range of human visual perception. With the help of digital technology, reliable information is now available that in the past was only speculative.

Studying philosophy, astronomy, medicine and psychiatry left me in a unique position to reflect on our current level of understanding of natural phenomena and the human condition. It sometimes seems both a blessing and a curse to have heightened awareness of these concerns, in that for some people it is satisfying to understand these things, whilst for others who might have preferred to remain unaware, it may be a nightmare.

Given reliable evidence that a small percentage of sightings appear to be of flight characteristics beyond any known human technology, it seems plausible to rationally consider the possibilities of "inexplicable aerial phenomena" other than aircraft and weather balloons. As Knuth notes, "there are simultaneous observations by multiple reliable witnesses along with radar patterns and photographic evidence revealing patterns of activity that are compelling."

I agree with Knuth's suggestion that scientific consideration of these phenomena is warranted, and not to be dismissed peremptorily as only "tin hat nonsense." Unexplained observations merit resolution. —*July 2018*

64 What Is (the) Time?

In English, Spanish, German, Finnish and Mandarin Chinese (and no doubt many other languages), one can easily distinguish between questions about what a clock tells us and questions about the concept of time. In Russian, however, сколько времени (skol'ko vremeni) can mean either "What is time?" or "What is *the* time?" depending on the context.

The response to the question about what a clock tells us is straightforward, and the reply simply reports positions of the hands of the clock (or a digital display of numbers), which represent the conventional divisions of the day into hours, minutes and seconds. The response to the question about the concept of time is more complicated, and the response requires one to think abstractly. The *Oxford Dictionary*, among others, defines time as "the indefinite continued progress of existence and events in the past, present and future regarded as a whole."

And then there is Italian theoretical physicist, philosopher and writer Carlo Rovelli, author of the recent book *The Order of Time.* He suggests, "One after another the characteristic features of time have proven to be approximations, mistakes determined by our perspective, like the flatness of the earth or the revolving of the sun." Rovelli considers the idea of what we call time to be related to the second law of thermodynamics, in which entropy increase is a one-way street, thereby enabling us to conceive of a "before" and an "after."

The nature of time itself, however, is not a concept easily understood. Subjective time seems age-dependent, slowly unfolding in childhood, marching on in youth, accelerating in maturity and flying like an arrow in senescence.

But more complicated than that familiar adage is that what we call time is not really an *object* but an abstract *idea*, once keyed to the movements of celestial phenomena and now to the rate of radioactive decay of a cesium isotope.

From the view of theoretical physics, time neither flows like a stream nor flies like an arrow but is quantized, in other words, discontinuous. What we experience appears continuous because the divisions are so small, as is also the case in cinema, wherein a series of rapidly changing images are perceived as continuous movement. Physical objects are constructed of molecules made of atoms, which are mostly empty space, and the positions of subatomic components only can be described in terms of probability fields.

Time is then an abstract concept, a dimension of the physical universe. It is not scientifically represented in English, Spanish, Russian or other languages but in the symbols of mathematics, the universal poetry not of earthbound Homer, Shakespeare or Pushkin but of the particles, atoms, stars, galaxies and singularity points, like the big bang, that constitute the all-inclusive totality of which we each are ourselves a tiny conscious portion. — Compiled from the essays "Time," June 2018, and "What Is (the) Time," *Mar 2020*

65 Punctuality

"On Being Late," an elegant short essay by Andrew O'Hagan, appeared recently in the *London Review of Books.* O'Hagan noted, "The person who is late and the person who is early have one thing in common: they are equally unlike the person that is just on time."

In Mexico, it is common to say *mañana* (tomorrow) in reference to a planned activity, rather than to a refer to a specific time. And the Argentines are even less punctual, for in Buenos Aires you will often be told *la semana que viene* (next week). Argentina does have a unique expression for being punctual: *hora inglés*, or "English time," probably dating from when the railways were operated by the Brits and, as in fascist Italy, the trains *did* run on time.

The Swiss Federal Railways provide an exemplary and predictable service for making connections, as I discovered once upon arriving at the Zurich airport. I bought a train ticket to Kandersteg, a village in the Alps where I planned to hike, and the agent advised me of the need to change trains at Bern. I queried whether there was enough time to change and was rewarded with the slightly smug reply of "Natürlich." Indeed, the initial train arrived in Bern precisely on time, and on an adjacent platform the connecting train departed exactly five minutes later.

The "Viennese delegation," as Nabokov mockingly called psychoanalysts, would doubtlessly identify psychopathology in the persistently late (hostile!) or too early (fearful of rejection!) arrivers, but then those who are invariably punctual would also be dismissed as "anal." You can't win with those guys.

There is a price to be paid for being punctual, however — being on time assumes one's appointment will take place at the agreed-upon hour, but if this is delayed for any significant amount of time, one is obliged to patiently wait. It is thus desirable to bring reading material to use if needed. Forgetting to do so invariably results in unanticipated waiting around, but once brought, a book often turns out to be unnecessary. Another consequence of being habitually punctual is feeling guilty in circumstances when one is unavoidably delayed. But departing early to avoid delays en route will often just lead to even earlier arrivals, and therefore more waiting about.

We can speculate about synchronizing clocks, but as theoretical physics tells us, this is not possible with different reference frames. While time is not a universal constant, being late to an appointment is unlikely to be forgiven if this explanation is invoked. To blame time itself, though, is silly; you may as well blame gravity for weight. — *Feb 2019*

66 Regret

As a commonly experienced disagreeable emotion, regret is intimately related to the dimension of time, in that it seems logically limited to feelings about past actions or events, although one may also anticipate feeling regretful about something yet to happen. With the return of sunny days in the spring, I may fancy buying another motorcycle but am inhibited by imagining feeling regretful were I to do so, as my sense of balance is less acute than it was in my youth. It's clearly more sensible to stick with the memories of past adventures on two wheels than trying to recreate them as I approach the end of my doddering ninth decade.

Time present is an illusion, for there is no "now," only an imaginary moving point of reference separating time past and the ominous and accelerating time future, whose approach is already beginning to evoke the hell of civilization's collapse and the end of humanity. Considering only time past, then, regret may be associated with either actions done (commission) or not done (omission). We regularly experience regret in both forms, and in each case the question of personal responsibility always arises, and feelings of guilt may linger, subconsciously lowering self-esteem.

Adherents of Roman Catholicism traditionally used the practice of confession to assuage negative emotions about thoughts or deeds. The belief of venial and mortal sins being wiped off the record by priestly absolution was employed to restore a feeling of neutrality about the past. In the last century confession and absolution has declined, and for some was replaced by the practice of psychoanalysis. But that too required belief in the efficacy of the proffered treatment. No doubt some benefit was obtained among those who expected it, but the cost of the procedure, both monetary and temporal, rendered it unsuitable for ordinary human unhappiness associated with regret and guilt.

Therapies other than psychoanalysis have been beneficial for many, particularly intensive group psychodrama, in which the client or patient engages in acting out conflicts before others. As is said, to err is human and to forgive, divine. In the absence of a supreme being or god, acceptance of one's errancy is probably the best that can be expected, and therapy only employed if feelings of guilt are of such intensity as to "adversely affect one's social or occupational functioning," as suggested by the psychiatric nomenclature in the DSM.

There are abundant pithy quotes to be found on the internet about regrets — but it's hardly worth wasting time to read them, for unlike money, time spent cannot be replenished. — *Mar 2020*

67 Carpe Diem

Carpe, an imperative conjugate of the Latin word *carpō*, means "to pick or pluck," while *diem* is the accusative of the Latin word *dies*, or "day." Although the colloquial use of the phrase *carpe diem* has come to mean "seize the day," a more literal translation would be "pluck the day [as it is ripe]" — that is, enjoy the moment. It has been argued by various authors that this interpretation is closer to the Roman poet Horace's original meaning.

This sentiment has been expressed in many forms at different times and in different cultures. What is always implied is the limited human life span and the unpredictability of the future. In Finnish there is a witty adage that expresses this idea: Life is uncertain, eat dessert first.

But then, what does time present mean anyway? Is it logically meaningful to speak of a "now"? Recurrent events are milestones, and each one signals a turning point between past and future. Relativity shows that there is no such thing as a universal now, and that our sense of the present is subjective. To search for lost time is a waste of present time, sorry, Marcel. (But hey, what prose!)

The idea of hope is relevant. The expectation that future events will in some way be more favourable than recent ones is an attitude that allows us to sustain and tolerate life even under adverse conditions. "Enjoy the moment," however, is advice that may be not only inappropriate but at times cruel in the face of suffering. As a physician confronted with a dying patient, one can try to at least provide comfort, but to say *carpe diem* would clearly be counterproductive.

Even in an apparently healthy person, hope is a slippery concept. Youth may not find it very relevant, but for the elderly there is a certain poignancy associated with repetitive events, like seasonal change. Today I observe the birch tree outside my window about to bud with its raiment of greenery for another summer. Will I see another spring? Who knows? Maybe, maybe not.

Yet trying to live one day at a time seems appropriate, as is being kind to others and making an effort to minimize one's carbon footprint by walking or using public transportation. — *Feb 2020*

68 Forgotten, Not Gone

A lead review by social psychologist Carol Tavris of six newly published books on the subject of aging appeared recently in the *Times Literary Supplement*. This elegant and comprehensive summary of writings on the problems associated with old age is pertinent to those societies that are presently experiencing a demographic shift of median age, associated with the combination of decreased birthrate and increased longevity.

Old age once meant over sixty-five and retired, but now refers to those in their ninth decade or more, many living well but with relentlessly decreasing physical and mental abilities. Between a quarter and half of us have signs of cognitive decline by age eighty-five. Signs of physical decline inevitably appear as arthritic pain, reduced mobility and visual and auditory impairment, among other losses. Some of the physical problems can be ameliorated by medical care, but as one author grimly observed, "Health care hasn't slowed the aging process so much as it has slowed the dying process." Paraphrasing Hobbes, "One cannot ignore the evidence that for many of the elderly, life is solitary, poor, nasty, brutish, and long."

Beyond the cognitive and physical concerns, the specific psychological issue of retirement looms large as a major point of stress for many. The psychological issue of defining oneself by one's occupation becomes inoperative for many, who then ask themselves, "Now what?" Tavris also addresses a political issue associated with aging, that of discrimination. She recommends being open and admitting one's age, not always easy in our youth-oriented society, and treating normal aging as something not to be concealed. Cosmetic surgeries and "rejuvenation" clinics exploit the desire to maintain a youthful appearance at all costs for those willing to pay, but as Groucho Marx once noted, "Time wounds all heels."

A stoic approach to the inevitable changes in body and mind that occur, no matter how long we live, seems to Tavris the best way of dealing with the vicissitudes of old age. Hopefully, one is able to age at home, with supportive care as needed; alas, this is not an option for everyone. My own goal is to continue regular physical exercise, to interact with at least one person every day (preferably in person or else by telephone or email), to keep aware of current events no matter how discouraging, to listen to classical music, to read both fiction and non-fiction, and to write brief essays (such as this one) when inspired to do so.

Being sad with the inevitable losses associated with aging is natural, but accepting them and being kind to others is humane. — *Apr 2019*

69 The Way of All Flesh

The Way of All Flesh: A Celebration of Decay is a 1997 book by Dutch biologist and author Midas Dekkers, who reflects on the world we inhabit, including our own bodies, as destined to inevitable decay. Accompanied by many grim illustrations, each chapter reveals different patterns of dissolution, but the overall direction of bodily decay is determined by the inexorable second law of thermodynamics — nothing is permanent, and everything is eventually transformed into dust.

Dekkers begins by recalling the ancient concept of our human "stairway of life," that is, birth followed by ascent to a maximal physical state of functioning, followed in turn by the inevitable descent into death and decomposition. Pictorial representations of this process were at one time common, but the image has since disappeared from our sitting rooms. "Old age is no longer good or bad," he writes, "it's simply denied. There's no place for old people anymore. They dress young, imitate the way young people talk, have their hips replaced, take cruises." Animals have less of a problem. Like us, cats have only one life, but after outgrowing their kittenhood their drives stay much the same until they curl up in your lap and expire. Once an animal has reproduced, in terms of biology there is no further goal mandated by genetic coding, and cognition permitting abstract thinking is itself not immune to the process of aging, as seen in Alzheimer's disease and other types of brain dysfunction.

Our markets are full of decay. What butchers sell isn't fresh meat, it's carrion. Cheese is a way of preserving old milk using bacteria. Wine is nothing more than the rotten juice of raisins. But cheese is never marketed as "rotten," it's called "ripe." And really rotten grape juice is called "wine from a good year." The point is that it is only cultural convention that determines the difference between *rotten* and *ripe*. How age is perceived by younger persons varies among cultures. While signs of aging are described in merchandising as undesirable in urban Western culture, reverence for elders may be found elsewhere, as in Indigenous communities in Canada.

"In the beginning you hardly notice that things are on the verge of getting out of hand. At twenty you are grown up, but from then on you draw on your reserves and signs of aging begin," writes Dekkers. The cosmetics industry thrives on the hopeless desire to maintain a youthful image. Using dentures and hearing aids may be resisted by oldsters who need them, but this is not so with spectacles, which have become accessorized by fashion merchants. Sex resembles eating as one ages, in that although the amount may be less, the pleasures are still enjoyed.

Concern over self-image persists, but then you are never really the same person you once were, for every part of your body is being replaced over and over as you age. Only your brain remains, with memories to link your older with your younger self. Dekkers notes, "What you have become is but a memory of yourself." Dekkers makes an astute observation that in preliterate societies old people were taken care of because they were the keepers of oral traditions. No longer; things are moving too fast. Venerability perhaps suggests an alternate view of decay, but the end result remains unchanged: dissolution into the atomic components and their dispersal. — *June 2018*

70 Can Medicine Be Cured?

Can Medicine Be Cured?, a recent contribution to the medical humanities by Irish physician Seamus O'Mahony (dramatically subtitled *The Corruption of a Profession*), identifies many frustrations in the practice of medicine that arise from current medical care provision and the hopes and needs of those receiving it. Although much of O'Mahony's criticism is related to Ireland and the NHS systems in the UK, it is also relevant to other developed countries.

Unlike in the not-so-distant past, most of the diseases that kill us now are associated with aging, and as the body wears out, much of the work of family physicians is related to helping their patients cope with the stress and distress involved in reconciling this. He writes, "Only in the twentieth century did we (at least those of us living in rich countries) decide that the inevitable vicissitudes of living should be reconfigured as medical problems."

Trained as a gastroenterologist, O'Mahony reviews how the "worried well" respond to perceived threats to their health, leading to the marketing of "free-from" food products, and are willing to pay extra for them because of self-diagnosed food intolerance. The pseudo-disease of "non-celiac gluten sensitivity" is discussed in detail as an example of the commercial exploitation of human gullibility.

Another bugbear of the author is "awareness-raising," a ploy described as dear to the medical-industrial complex. O'Mahony singles out Mental Health Awareness Week as one example: "We should stop the awareness now. In fact, if anything, we might be getting too aware, the ordinary struggles with life problems becoming rebranded as psychopathologies." A huge commercial market in "complementary health services" is provided by non-medical practitioners such as naturopaths, popular in part because they take time to listen to the complaints of hypochondriacs.

Drug companies are always happy to proclaim any possibility of symptom relief and relentlessly promote their products on an individual basis to doctors as well as at exhibitions in medical conferences. As more and more screening programs are initiated for the apparently healthy, frail elderly people may await bed availability in a hospital or a community care facility. Meanwhile, underfunded hospices rely on charity and fund-raising events.

O'Mahony cites philosopher and social critic Ivan Illich, who argued in 1975 that the medicalization in recent decades of many of life's vicissitudes — birth and death, for example — frequently causes more harm than good and renders many people in effect lifelong patients. Illich noted that the more medical services given to a population, the greater becomes their demand for care. Care must be rationed, and rational skepticism is necessary for the practice of medicine to be compassionate.

In sum, "we should simply try to make the conditions of human life more bearable." — *May 2019*

71 Pseudoscience

I recently received a fifty-two-page glossy brochure from an American publishing company, based in a small town in Vermont, featuring a variety of books devoted to arcane subjects such as "healing crystals," "the hermetic science of transformation," "ascending with the higher angelic realms," "sex shamans" and other such topics. Biographical sketches of the authors of these texts make fascinating reading, with claims of expertise by virtue of quasi-academic training, often in some legitimate field of science, represented by their professional credentials, enhancing the assertion of legitimacy by appending PhD, EdD, or MD to their names.

Lesser-known abbreviations like LA MAc, CFMP, CSTeen and CLF are amassed by one author, described as "an internationally recognized authority on autoimmunity, functional blood chemistry analysis, thyroid and gut health, food as medicine, integrating mind, body, and spirit in health care, with more than twenty-two years of experience, education, and wisdom to empower you to heal on all levels."

Another author, allegedly "a medical doctor with a background in physics," was described as "conducting research on the mind-matter continuum, presenting his findings in peer-reviewed scientific papers and at international scientific conferences." Described as a leading expert on the debunked relic known as the Shroud of Turin, he offers a quasi-scientific explanation of its supposed origin to confirm a biblical myth.

Legitimate scientists and physicians see no need to promote themselves by advertising their credentials and find it undignified and unnecessary to do so. Books by Stephen Hawking or Oliver Sacks do not require their authors to be legitimized by appending PhD or MD to their names on the cover.

As P.T. Barnum allegedly observed, "There's a sucker born every minute." Promising relief from the ordinary concerns of living by impressive-sounding practices like those espoused by the authors in these publications has always been a lucrative business. "Nobody ever lost a dollar by underestimating the taste of the American public" was another gem of wisdom from Barnum, revealing of not just an American public but a general human tendency to seek solutions to life's problems from sources promising relief that portray themselves as curative. — *June 2019*

72 Irrationality

In the recent book *Irrationality*, academic philosopher Justin E.H. Smith reviews irrationality, or rejection of reason as associated with Enlightenment values, but ultimately concludes it is "irrational to seek to eliminate irrationality." Citing the mid-twentieth-century work of Adorno and Horkheimer, which illuminated the dialectic inherent in this concept, Smith envisages a "Counter-Enlightenment" appropriate to our age. He exposes sources of irrationality arising from pure logic, dream states (both unconscious, as during REM sleep, and intentional, as with drug-induced states), artistic creation, pseudoscience, religion and myth.

In a brilliant extended discussion of Smith's book in the *New York Review* on May 9, 2019, Kwame Anthony Appiah dissects the historical concept of the Enlightenment as a phenomenon. Initially envisaging modern Europe as "an island of reason in a sea of unreason," in actuality the Enlightenment contained within itself seeds of unreason that have found fertile soil in humanity and are now nurtured by technology, especially the internet.

What then, is rationality? Just as it is difficult to say exactly what we mean by the idea of "intelligence," not only in humans but also in machines and non-humans, so too is it a vexing problem to define rationality. Smith draws attention to "an important asymmetry" between rationality and irrationality: animals and plants always do what they do apparently spontaneously, because they do not deliberate on which path to take. As a result of natural selection, they can only be rational. It is humans that make choices and hence, sometimes choose wrongly. It sounds counterfactual, but Smith concludes, "What makes us human beings unique is our irrationality. We are the irrational animal."

The internet facilitates irrationality in that social media draws together and congeals into groups those who share beliefs, whether these beliefs are objectively right or wrong. This sharing creates bonds of belonging stronger than individual opinions, stronger than demonstrable truth or falsehood. We think we make choices according to what we consider desirable or not, but we are limited in what we can achieve by the constraints of time and aging. Smith reminds us "aging, like death in which it culminates, constitutes a basic parameter of human existence."

Smith stoically concludes that "irrationality is ineliminable" and that "false beliefs are as epidemic as ever," yet he tries to understand his own situation as a living but mortal decision-maker situated, as we all are, like Nabokov said, "between two eternities of darkness." — *July 2019*

73 Freud, Psychoanalysis & Self-Indulgence

On May 6, 1856, Sigmund Freud was born in Freiberg, a town in Moravia, part of the Austrian-Hungarian Empire. With his Jewish parents, he moved to Vienna at the age of four, remaining there until his final year, when he was extricated from Hitler's Third Reich to London, where he died in 1939.

Trained as a medical doctor specializing in neurology, Freud suggested the existence of unconscious mental processes to be the cause of hysterical symptoms, expanding the idea into a complex clinical approach to mental illness involving the so-called talking cure, based upon a presumed structure of the mind. Psychoanalysis, as it came to be called, was more than just a method of treatment, for it grew into a controversial movement, with different schools involving hundreds of practitioners. Psychoanalysis became the predominant orientation of psychiatrists prior to the development of effective clinical psychopharmacology and behavioural therapies in the mid-twentieth century.

Sessions conducted several times weekly, often over a period of years, were required to relieve neurotic symptoms in selected patients, for the cost of the procedure restricted its availability to those who could afford to pay. The highest concentration of psychoanalysts worldwide was said to be in the immediate environs of Central Park in New York City. The image of the analyst's couch, upon which a patient reclined and engaged in free association, remains a persistent feature of every cartoon shrink joke to the present day.

Although Freud himself did not view minority sexual orientation as an illness, the American Psychoanalytic Association (APA) maintained the concept of homosexuality as a mental disorder and strongly campaigned against the efforts of those working to remove this controversial diagnosis from the official psychiatric nomenclature. A rival group to the APA calling itself the American Academy of Psychoanalysis (AAP) begged to differ, supporting the drive to eliminate the diagnosis of homosexuality as a mental disorder from the psychiatric nomenclature.

Psychoanalysis remains an important past approach to the treatment of mental illness, but most contemporary academic psychiatrists now view it as a historical phase in the attempt to understand the cause of neuroses. It continues to be taught in some training programs, and pockets of psychoanalysts persist in Seattle, New York, Montreal and elsewhere. — *May 2018*

74 Astrology and Psychology

Being trained in both astronomy and psychiatry, on occasion I have been obliged to explain that I was neither an astrologer nor a psychologist. Although most people are quick to excuse confounding astronomy with astrology, a pseudoscience based upon personality traits by observation of stars and planets, many are reluctant to think of psychology in similar terms.

Astronomy is an observational science. Although historically *only* an observational science, observations today are no longer limited to telescopes devised to observe the different frequencies of electromagnetic radiation from space, but also include the direct examination of moon rocks or soon perhaps Martian soil samples. But we cannot directly examine a black hole or dark matter, though these entities are deduced from observational astronomy.

Astrophysics, the branch of astronomy dealing with the contents and evolution of stars, is less speculative than cosmology, which uses mathematics to describe the contents and evolution of the universe as a whole in space-time, from the initial big bang to the final extinction of energy dissipation by the second law of thermodynamics. But both derive from observational science, based on intersubjective testability and reproducible measurements.

But what about psychology? Human thinking and behaviours can be measured in many different dimensions, but the interpretation of results is often more subject to speculation in psychology than it is in psychiatry. Though not always a pseudoscience, psychology lacks the ability to construct a unified explanation of what can be observed or inferred, leading to different schools of thought. This is not unexpected, for stars are more predictable than human beings in their developments and behaviours, but knowledge from observations and experiments characterizes both disciplines when the methods of science are employed.

Psychiatry of course is a clinical discipline, a branch of medicine devoted to the study and treatment of thoughts, feelings and behaviours that lead to impairment of personal, social and occupational dysfunctions, characterized as *mental disorders*. It is not a science, observational or otherwise, despite the claims of some psychoanalysts to regard their form of treatment as scientific. The mind–body problem generates much heat among those who devote themselves to explaining the "real" nature of consciousness.

Many years ago, when motorcycling around Northern California on a hot summer's day with a psychologist friend, we stopped at a tavern in a small town for a cold beer. The bartender asked us what we did, and I admitted being a psychiatrist while my companion said he was a psychologist. Wiping a glass, the barkeep asked, "What's the difference?" My pal replied, "About $50 an hour." — *Feb 2020*

75 Lunacy

Asked about a relationship between police involvement and moon phases, a US police commissioner was reported as having said there was definitely a peak in calls related to mental illness issues during a full moon. I have always wondered about that.

From July to December 1980, I was a resident psychiatrist at Vancouver General Hospital and worked in the hospital's emergency room, assessing admissions of new patients. Having worked in astronomy, I was inspired to keep a record of psychiatric admission diagnoses related to moon phase and found no indication of any relationship between them. The police claim was spurious, reflecting a popular false assumption.

My earlier work at the National Observatory in Argentina consisted of using a large reflecting telescope for two-colour photography of stars with a large proper motion (across the line of sight), identifying faint blue stars such as white dwarfs. The observational work itself was limited to a few days every lunar month, before and after each new moon, to avoid diffused moonlight contaminating the photographic plates. I later wrote a thesis on looking for quasars among these faint blue objects.

Interest in lycanthropy, the old European folk tales of werewolves, was fostered by Hollywood and essentially canonized in the public consciousness by the monster films of the '30s and '40s, the genre since then having expanded. One feature of the film werewolf was the involuntary transformation from human to wolf, provoked by exposure to the light of the full moon. An ingenious tale about one such werewolf trapped in the London tube system during a full moon was suggested by Yukon author Steve Parker in a fantastic plot device. To prevent his unwanted transformation, the reluctant protagonist was trapped underground, having to periodically detrain and change before the one he was riding emerged from a tunnel into a night with a full moon.

References to phases of the moon often appear in literature, and sometimes an author reveals a lack of understanding of the astronomical geometry involving the Earth, sun and moon. For example, in Anton Chekov's short story, "The Chemist's Wife," he wrote, "It was close upon daybreak. . . . She could see the eastern horizon growing pale by degrees, then turning crimson as though from a great fire. A big, broad-faced moon peeped out unexpectedly from behind bushes . . ." Chekov was trained as a medical doctor but not as an astronomer, who would have known that a full moon only rises in the east at sunset and never at dawn, when it would be setting in the west.

There is a rare type of mental disorder described in the psychiatric literature as *clinical lycanthropy*, the delusion of being a werewolf, an affliction in which humans are said to physically shape-shift into wolves. This should not be confused with the practice of moonlighting, or taking a secondary job in addition to one's primary occupation, like a fireman working as a bouncer off-duty, or perhaps an astronomer doing psychiatric assessments. — *May 2018*

76 Insomniac Dreams

In the late 1980s I attended a psychiatric meeting at a conference centre in Montreux, Switzerland, on the shores of Lake Geneva. I don't remember much about the presentations, but I shall never forget a banquet for attendees at a nearby château. There were five or six courses of rich food, and the pièce de résistance was an entire roasted wild boar. Each course was accompanied by a different wine of superior vintage, poured by ubiquitous, hovering serving staff. It was a fantastic and unforgettable meal.

However, the first session of the meeting the following morning was devoted to sleep disorders, including both nocturnal insomnia and excessive daytime sleepiness. After the previous evening's formidable banquet and all the wines, the attendance of my colleagues was not exemplary, and of those who managed to show up, many drifted off during the presentation and emitted snores, some soft and mellow, others rasping and more sonorous.

I was reminded of an eminent neighbour who had lived nearby, in a palatial hotel in Montreux, for his last sixteen years and who was interested in dreams. A decade earlier at the luxurious Grand Palace Hotel, their most famous resident, Vladimir Nabokov, resided with his wife Vera from 1961 to his death in 1977, then wealthy from his shocking best-seller *Lolita*. He continued to write unforgettable and idiosyncratic prose, from *Pnin* to *Ada*, over the years in Montreux, and also became fascinated by a possible relation between the phenomena of déjà vu and precognitive dreaming.

Between October 1964 and January 1965, Nabokov kept a record of dreams on file cards by the bedside, with annotations about dream contents. Vera did the same. The recorded observations were collected and published in the book *Insomniac Dreams* by Gennady Barabtarlo. These "experiments in time" were annotated by Barabtarlo and illustrated with photographs of individual cards with handwritten notes by Nabokov.

Nabokov classified dreams into six categories: professional or vocational, intimations of doom, retrieval of remote past memories, immediate preoccupations and impressions, erotic and tender content, and "precognitive" dreams. He reflected on each category at length from a personal perspective and provided examples.

What I found compelling in Barabtarlo's book, besides the dream cards, was the discussion of the role of dreams in Nabokov's oeuvre, with lengthy quotations from many of his works, featuring descriptions of dreams. Nabokov held no truck, though, with the work of Freud and other members of "the Viennese delegation."

Some years ago I was in New York City for several days attending a meeting of the American Psychiatric Association and was kindly offered accommodation by a psychoanalyst friend (AAP, not APA) at his flat on Central Park South, near Columbus Circle. On arrival, he led me to his consulting room, featuring the traditional couch that was to be my bed, warning me to arise in the morning half an hour before his first client and not to leave a warm spot on the couch. When I related this to friends, they would ask about my dreams there, but I always replied, "Just the usual rubbish, no precognitions." — *Apr 2018*

77 Nosology: Psychiatry and Sexual Orientation

Nosology is a branch of medical science that deals with the classification of diseases — not to be confused with rhinology, a subspecialty within the field of otolaryngology (ENT) focused on the treatment of diseases and disorders affecting the nose. *The International Classification of Diseases* (ICD) is the international "standard diagnostic tool for epidemiology, health management and clinical purposes." The *Diagnostic and Statistical Manual of Mental Disorders* (DSM) of the American Psychiatric Association (APA), is often flippantly called "the psychiatrist's bible" by journalists.

The problem with psychiatric nosology, as compared to the nosology of infectious diseases or disorders of particular organs, such as the heart (cardiology), skin (dermatology), ears (otology), eyes (ophthalmology), liver (hepatology) and so on, is that in psychiatry there are no universally agreed-upon criteria for inclusion in a category, such that a patient presenting with a specific complaint associated with thought or behaviour may or may not be included in a diagnostic category, presenting with symptoms of delusions, auditory hallucinations or attempted suicide. This problem does not arise with physical complaints as a rule, but is a bugaboo when it comes to mental disorders.

Classification of gay, lesbian and bisexual sexual orientations in psychiatry underwent major changes in the twentieth century. DSM I (1952) classified these sexual orientations under "paraphilia," and DSM II (1974) listed them under "sexual orientation disturbance." DSM III (1980) further modified this to "ego-dystonic homosexuality," before finally dropping the subject altogether in DSM-III-R (1987) and subsequent editions. These changes were brought about primarily by pressure from

APA members who formed a political group (caucus) of gay and lesbian psychiatrists within the organization to lobby for changes in the nomenclature reflecting current scientific understanding of sexual orientation variations. I was the only Canadian member of this group.

The final stage of deleting the so-called ego-dystonic homosexuality was proposed in a paper I wrote in 1983 and discussed at the New York annual meeting of the APA that same year in a packed session, mischievously titled "Ego-dystonic Nosology." In the discussion, one colleague suggested that removing the diagnosis from the DSM would constitute "a step backwards," and I responded with, "A step backwards would be a step in the right direction if one were initially facing the wrong way!" The witty spontaneous response provoked laughter and applause.

Though the editor of the DSM at the time objected, he was overruled and the diagnosis deleted. He later recanted and decently apologized to the gay community years later on his deathbed for having considered sexual variation to have been designated as a mental disorder.

The ICD, however, retained the diagnosis for a while, until an International Advisory Group was established to review the section associated with sexual development and orientation. The review concluded by explicitly stating, "Sexual orientation by itself is not to be considered a disorder," in line with the DSM and other classifications that then recognized homoerotic thought and behaviour as being a normal variation in human sexuality. The Group reported, "There is no evidence that [these classifications] are clinically useful" and recommended that they be deleted from the ICD. Opposition to the nomenclature change was strongest among some psychoanalytically trained psychiatrists who had been using the now discredited, and in Canada now illegal, "conversion therapy" to reorient sexual desire to the more conventional heterosexuality. —*June 2018*

78 Global Gay

Global Gay is a comprehensive 262-page book by Frederic Martel, the result of a long field survey conducted over some eight years in more than fifty countries. And though a fascinating and well-written journalistic account, it suffers from a sense of being dated, written well before 2016.

Martel reports that, at the time of the book's publication, at least ten countries still retained the death penalty for same-sex activity, and many others had restrictive homophobic laws. He notes that in the

Middle East, India and Africa these restrictive laws were often imposed on peoples colonized by Victorian England, by French settlers, and, even today, by American neo-evangelicals. Positively, however, Martel feels that there appears to be a trend towards the globalization of LGBTQ rights, attributing this worldwide phenomenon to the ubiquity of social media platforms. He affirms that same-sex desire and expression is truly a matter of universal human rights, and not, as asserted by homophobic politicians, a decadence introduced into a nation from elsewhere, as alleged in Russia, Brunei and Uganda, among others at the present time.

Martel's hundreds of interviews across every continent illustrate how LGBTQ persons cope socially within their own communities on group and interpersonal levels, circumventing official limitations where they exist. Revealing interviews from mainland China, Russia, Chile, Cuba, Egypt, India, Singapore, Brazil, Canada, the United States and elsewhere paint a compelling global picture of the state of affairs for people of non-heterosexual erotic desire around the world and their adaptation to local circumstances.

Outside interventions continue to complicate the situation in some countries, particularly in Africa. "An anti-gay law was adopted in Uganda in 2014. Ultimately, a strange American 'culture war' was being carried out, away from the US, by pro-gay and anti-gay groups, evangelicals facing off against gay organizations, both supporting and funding their local allies." This is a prime example of religious and social colonialism. Martel visited an evangelical megachurch on the outskirts of Johannesburg and found it was affiliated with a mother religious organization in Oklahoma City in the US, from which it borrows its charismatic doctrine. Evangelicals have at their disposal, with millions of dollars, books and CDs ready to be shipped abroad, promoting their mission to convert Africa through sectarian persuasion and homophobic sermons.

And it isn't only Christian homophobia. According to a West African lawyer, "The two most dramatic new things homosexuals face in Africa are, first, Christian neo-evangelicalism, which is often inspired by the US, and, second, political Islam, modelled on Iran or Saudi Arabia."

Martel, however, had a sense of cautious optimism, and believes democracy and sexual orientation are coming together as though to support each other. Now five years later it seems more uncertain. — *May 2018*

79 Tongzhi Living

Tongzhi Living: Men Attracted to Men in Postsocialist China is a short book written by Chinese-American anthropologist Tiantian Zheng. The Chinese word *tóngzhì* literally means "same will" and has also been translated as "comrade," in the sense of a fellow member of the Chinese Communist Party. Since the 1990s, however, it has come to self-refer to an "indigenous Chinese same-sex identity distinct from a global gay identity."

Zheng notes that during the ancient and imperial periods in China, same-sex desires were deemed normal and enjoyed by many emperors, upper class scholars and bureaucrats, but the onslaught of Western medicine (and presumably religions) "changed the cultural tradition, and indoctrinated in society heteronormativity and a pathologized and vilified vision of homosexuality." This persists today in media coverage and social attitudes, with the result that *tóngzhì* feel torn between attachment to their own group and to the mainstream world.

Zheng's study was based on eleven months of ethnographic field-work conducted in the metropolitan city of Dalian from 2005 to 2013, phone and email contacts with research subjects since 2005, and archival data of online postings from gay-related internet websites, LGBTQ and *tóngzhì* email lists, and newspaper and magazine articles. The ethnographic fieldwork involved interviews with self-identified gay men in a variety of milieux — parks, gay bars, bathhouses — and in two local grassroots AIDS organizations, as well as interviews with health officials and local residents.

The subjects represented a wide range of social classes and occupations. Zheng's knowledge and understanding of the vicissitudes of being a gay man in mainland China is accurate, according to a recent arrival in Canada of a *tóngzhì* with whom I have discussed the author's findings. Every chapter contains results from individual interviews and follow-ups. Many very moving personal histories bring life to the problems experienced by members of this sexual minority, involving family expectations and conflicts, unhappy heterosexual marriages and suicides.

Individual chapters are devoted to the cultural history of same-sex desire; popular perceptions of homosexuality in post-socialist China; defining, socializing, and specifying gender roles in the *tóngzhì* community; the normal post-socialist subject, class, wealth and money boys; organizing against HIV in China; embracing the heterosexual norm and the double lives of *tóngzhì*; safe sex among men, including condoms, promiscuity and HIV; and speculation about the future for the *tóngzhì* community in mainland China.

State suppression continued, however. The grand final of the 2018 Eurovision Song Contest was not shown in China after performances displaying two men dancing with each other and a rainbow flag image were censored on China's Mango TV. — *May 2018*

80 Psychiatry and Pathogens

Though I wound up in psychiatry as a clinical specialty, as a second-year medical student at the University of British Columbia in 1973, my highest grade in all of the courses was in microbiology. Having worked the previous summer with a health inspector in Nelson, BC, I was eager to learn all about the many pathogens among which we live and die, and actually considered a career in public health as a possibility after completing my medical degree.

In the following year I found time to initiate an anonymous STD screening clinic for gay men at a community centre in Vancouver's West End neighbourhood, there being no dedicated service specifically for this sexual minority at the time. With the help of a nurse, one evening every week we would see a dozen or more clients and draw blood and anogenital swabs to be tested for syphilis and gonorrhea. The specimens would be kept in my family's refrigerator at home overnight, and the following morning on her way to work, my wife would drop them off at the provincial STD clinic at Vancouver General Hospital. Counselling about safe sex practices was provided, along with condoms for anal intercourse. This was ten years before the onset of the AIDS epidemic, and hopefully some lives were spared among those who followed the advice we offered.

This was not my last encounter with clinical microbiology, for after a few years of private psychiatric practice, the epidemic of HIV disease began to unfold, and I became the consultant in psychiatry with the AIDS clinical care team at St. Paul's Hospital in Vancouver, working with patients who all eventually died from complications of their untreatable retroviral disease.

The importance of using condoms became absolutely essential, and when the administration at the community college where my wife was teaching early childhood education refused to install dispensers in the washrooms, she wore a costume identifying herself as "Condom Granny" and publicly handed them out to students until the dispensers were installed.

Before the development of effective antiretroviral drugs in the early 1990s, there was no treatment or preventing transmission of the infection other than condoms, and my clinical interaction with over 800 referred patients was limited to assessment and testing for neuropsychiatric complications from the disease, such as dementia. Our team attended yearly international conferences around the world, meeting colleagues and sharing research findings. I gave lectures and presentations from Argentina to Russia and organized and co-chaired an international conference on neuropsychiatry of HIV in 1994 at the University of British Columbia. When eventually suppressive treatment (required lifelong) was developed, HIV disease became, like diabetes, a chronic and not an acute illness, and the team dissolved.

As a retrovirus with RNA, HIV uses the enzyme reverse transcriptase to generate copies of itself in the host T-cell. It is a disease transmitted sexually or by blood exchange, through sharing contaminated needles. Moreover, the HIV epidemic was limited to marginalized social groups, initially gay men and injection drug users, and is now found among the sexually active of any orientation, but transmission can be prevented by condoms or pre-exposure prophylaxis (PREP). — *Apr 2020*

81 (Recovering) Environmentalist Paul Kingsnorth

A recent collection of essays by acclaimed English writer Paul Kingsnorth, entitled *Confessions of a Recovering Environmentalist*, reviews the degradation of our planet by industrialization, noting that extinction levels are presently the highest they have been in 65 million years. Kingsnorth grimly recognizes that resistance is futile and avers there is "no stopping what we have unleashed."

In the first section, called "Collapse," Kingsnorth describes widespread denial of the impending catastrophe, comparing the glib and reassuring assertions of politicians to "a sermon by a priest who has lost his faith but is desperately trying not to admit it, even to himself." The enemy of the earth is bigness itself, and continual economic growth is environmentally toxic and unsustainable. The fantasy of extraterrestrial colonization is only a fantasy. Mining the moon or asteroids to replace the depleted resources of our planet, were it possible, would only lead to more of the same cycle.

Kingsnorth asserts, and I must agree, that we are all stuck here and there is no way out, including "renewable energy sources." Dams destroying communities are built around the world because of the water or electric needs (or both) of expanding economies, of which we are always slyly told it's for our benefit. We can see what's coming. The infernal machine of the global industrial system is unstoppable, and a mass-extinction event must be the endpoint. What is to be done? Kingsnorth asks and can but reply, "The only thing to do is to keep on keeping on. After all, the alternative must be 'giving up' and watching the world burn."

Disillusioned by environmentalism, which he now believes to be nothing short of hopeless arguing about how best to power industry, Kingsnorth mocks the claim that renewable energy can meet our so-called energy needs: "Our needs for what? More broadband or clean drinking water?" He argues instead we need to cherish a sense of *biophilia*, "a love for the natural world of which we as animals are a part. . . . We have made ourselves caged animals, and all the gadgets in the world cannot compensate for what we have lost."

Unlimited industrialization and explosive population increase, accompanied by worldwide environmental degradation, is proceeding apace, and, he writes, "The Machine" is unstoppable. Kingsnorth maintains that the focus of environmentalism has shifted from the initial concerns of preservation to sustainability, interpreting this as being a euphemism for maintaining the security and comfort level of the wealthiest. He laments the mass destruction of the world's remaining wild places by mining and agriculture in order to feed the economic machine.

Disillusioned by "green politics," which has become "an adjunct to hyper-capitalism," Kingsnorth has chosen to withdraw, to opt out. He celebrates poets like Dylan Thomas, who knew the juggernaut could not be stopped but only lived with, and even though having lost the battle, proclaimed his famous lines "Rage, rage against the dying of the light." Kingsnorth also references writings by the criminal technophobe Ted Kaczynski, foreseeing the collapse of civilization. "None of this is going to save the world — but then there is no saving the world, and the ones who say there is are the ones you need to save it from." This is his grim personal philosophy for a dark time — a dark ecology.

Buddhism teaches us the need to accept that all things perish and that change and transformation is inevitable. The Holocene Extinction is underway and we are the cause. "Much of nature is dying away in order that we might have access to smartphones, takeaway coffee, private cars, aeroplane flights and Facebook." This will not change, it is accelerating. All we can do, as a Zen master said, is to "sit with it."

It is comforting to think of ourselves as being in control of our destiny, but we are not. This does not imply predestination but a projection from past and current human behaviour to the near future. Kingsnorth writes, "The notions that only humans matter, or that humans are in control, even of themselves, are unlikely to outlast this century." The overall tone of *Confessions* resembles a synthesis of Ecclesiastes and Zen Buddhism: "everything is transient" and "so what?" Some have called it defeatism, others say it is realistic. Perhaps it is a mixture of both. I thought of Voltaire's Candide, like Kingsnorth, cultivating his garden as the world outside goes on with its follies. The future will bring discord, uncertainty and loss. To deny this is to deny reality, but that is what most humans do when confronted with the ominous facts. Kingsnorth does admit, "You can spend too much time with thoughts of the future." Other animals don't.

In an epilogue, Kingsnorth sums up his thinking, starting with a trenchant quotation by American essayist and poet Ralph Waldo Emerson: "The end of the human race will be that it will eventually die of civilization." Kingsnorth elaborates on the fragility of civilization and foresees its fall, identifying as an underlying cause the myth of "progress" leading to unlimited economic growth at the expense of the natural world. "Our attempt to separate ourselves from 'nature' has been a grim failure, proof not of our genius but our hubris. Denial is rampant. We are poised at the edge of a massive change, an ecocide we have wrought upon the planet, and there is a reluctance to accept the undeniable truth that the culprit is civilization itself. This is the last taboo."

As a writer, Kingsnorth advances our need to admit this undeniable truth and to detach ourselves from it, employing what he calls the Eight Principles of Uncivilization:

> 1. We must admit to ourselves that we are living in a moment of social, economic and ecological "unraveling." We must face this reality in order to live with it.
> 2. We must reject the notion that the solution to this crisis resides in "technological or political solutions."
> 3. We must challenge the foundational stories of our civilization: "the myth of progress, the myth of human centrality, and the myth of our separation from nature."
> 4. We must begin to tell stories, not for entertainment but for the sharing of knowledge.

5. We must accept the fact that humans are not central to our planet and begin to "reengage with the non-human world."
6. We must celebrate art and literature that grounds us in a "sense of place and time."
7. We must denounce dangerous ideologies with our voices and our words. "We [must] write with dirt under our fingernails."
8. We must appreciate that the "end of the world as we know it is not the end of the world, full stop."

As Kingsnorth notes, "Together, we shall find the hope beyond hope, the paths that lead to the unknown world ahead of us." — *Sept 2020*

82 Book, Bird and Avoidance

The 1964 popular children's book *Pleasant Fieldmouse* by Jan Wahl, with illustrations by Maurice Sendak, has long been a family favourite. It recounts the adventures of a small furry rodent and its companions. I read it to our youngest daughter when she didn't want to hear *Dracula*, the more sophisticated choice of her two elder sisters.

Even today the title has resonance in my vocabulary, representing an icon of non-threatening storytelling, as when being taxed with morbidity in reading French negativistic authors like Mike Wellbeck, I may counter with "Whaddaya want me to do, just stick to *Pleasant Fieldmouse*?" (Wellbeck indeed may be morbid and negativistic, a sex addict who smokes too much, but hey, he writes masterfully with *la plume de ma tante* that comes across even in English translation.)

Then there is the question of the big bird, in fact the largest bird on earth, the ostrich, inaccurately believed to deal with danger by hiding its head in the sand. Nevertheless, it has become a meme for deliberate avoidance of unpleasant consequences, even though to escape detection ostrich chicks as well as adults may only lie on the ground with neck outstretched.

So, what's the connection? To deliberately avoid unhappiness when possible is rational enough, but to prevent knowing about an unpleasant event does not make it disappear, as suggested by pseudo-ostrichy behaviour. Likewise, reading escapist literature allows us to ignore the prospect of anticipated certain extinction, now daily becoming not only unstoppable but increasingly imminent.

In the late nineteenth century, Kurtz could bury himself in the darkest heart of Africa, moaning, "The horror! the horror!," but in the early twenty-first century he can't run and hide in Africa or anywhere else. He can only refuse to look and moan about the coming horrors as he bends over with his head between his knees, to kiss his arse goodbye.

On a railway track somewhere, facing away from the approaching juggernaut of a speeding train, reading *Pleasant Fieldmouse*, he hears the roar of the approaching locomotive and removes his hearing aids, the better to concentrate on his book. —*Jan 2020*

83 Withering

In 2019 Canadian author Michael Christie published his dystopic novel *Greenwood*, whose initial and final segments are set in the not-too-distant future of the year 2038, wherein, apart from a few coastal islands, the world's forests have withered and died as a consequence of anthropogenic climate change. The internal structure of the story consists of an inverted arc, with succeeding sections revealing the complex family history of the protagonist, a trained but underemployed dendrologist, over four preceding generations. Descending first to 2008, then subsequently to 1974, 1934 and finally to 1908 and the origin of great-grandparents, we then retrace our steps through the same time periods, learning of the lives, relationships and fates of the heroine's ancestors.

The setting is almost entirely within Canada, from New Brunswick to Quebec, Ontario, Saskatchewan, Alberta and finally to British Columbia, where on a small island off the west coast of Vancouver Island the tale begins and ends, amid continuing withering.

Reference is made to climate refugees from elsewhere, but that is incidental to the stories of people and trees, of tapping maples for syrup, crafting wooden articles, planting windbreaks on the prairie, logging timber for railway sleeper ties, and finally utilizing the few remaining first-growth Douglas firs as a unique attraction for wealthy city dwellers, protected against the hostile atmosphere in their "climate-controlled towers of glass and steel." Canada became a "global panic room for the elite."

In *Greenwood* forests are conceived as a kind of family, trees as separate members yet connected to one another by bonds promoting survival. The double-page frontispiece of the book is a cross section of a tree trunk, displaying growth rings, each newly laid member supported by those antedating it, as a family member may manifest qualities and values of ancestors. Every section is heralded by a sketch of intersecting lines dramatizing connectivity — roots, railway lines, a highway interchange, a budding branch and finally, a withered one.

Christie clearly knows his trees, living as he does on another island in the Salish Sea, between Vancouver Island and the mainland of British Columbia. While some of the plot developments occasionally hint at being contrived, the stories are all plausible, and it is fascinating to discover how the many pieces fit together to form a satisfying whole. Like Orwell's *1984*, Christie's envisaged future is not only a fable, it is a grim prophecy.
— *Feb 2020*

84 The Wall

A wall suggests a barrier, physical or metaphorical, erected to restrict, control or authorize movement from one side to the other. We can think of a city wall, a living cell wall, a prison wall, a paywall, the Berlin Wall, Trump's wall, the Great Wall of China and others. To be walled off implies restriction, at times positively so, as with during a quarantine in the case of disease control, preventing access to information from internet news sites, or protection from harm for political refugees.

The contemporary British author John Lanchester has written a dystopian novel of the near future called *The Wall*, portraying a Britain that survives an environmental catastrophe by means of enclosing itself within a physical wall, patrolled by conscripts known as Defenders under the control of a national military force.

These young men and women continually patrol the barrier, and it is their duty to kill any of the Others from outside who periodically attempt to penetrate the wall, gaining entry to the land within. Failure by a Defender to prevent such a crossing is subject to draconian punishment, including exile outside the wall, with a resulting anarchic future life among the Others. Should any of the Others remain alive after crossing the wall, they become a state slave, available to residents to assist in tasks as required, and designated accordingly as Help.

Life within the wall continues in a recognizable fashion, with functioning rail and bus transportation, education and medical services, home activity such as watching television programs, sports events, pubs and other familiar features of today's Britain, but with disruptions consequent to the total lack of imports. One is reminded of the *Juche* ideology of North Korea's political, economic and military self-reliance.

The action related in the novel portrays the life vicissitudes of a young man from the time he enters military service as a Defender on the wall and his combat experience fighting against a breach in the wall by a group of Others, not all of whom are killed. His punishment thus becomes that of permanent exile and survival outside the wall, at sea and among Others.

Unlike reading some novels in which one regrets approaching the end of an enjoyable story, in the case of *The Wall* I found myself wishing it would quickly conclude, for the world it conjured was so creepy and distasteful that even present-day society seemed a relief to return to when closing the book. The sour vision remains in one's mind, however, as an unpleasant portent of our possible future, this being no doubt the intention of Lanchester in creating a persuasive dystopic culture that may await us. — *Mar 2019*

85 The Exterminating Angel

Surrealist Spanish director Luis Buñuel's film *The Exterminating Angel* (1962) was a macabre comedy, a troubling representation of human nature suggesting we are but beasts with unspeakable secrets. A recent opera by the English composer Thomas Adès, with a libretto by Tom Cairns, closely follows the film script.

Guests attending a dinner party at the home of a wealthy host find that for an unknown reason they are unable to leave. They resign themselves to remaining overnight, but as the following days continue with them being trapped together in the restricted space, their human courtesies disintegrate. Food becomes unavailable and thirst is only quenched by breaking a water pipe in a wall. Increasingly resentful at being shut off from the world outside, they grow mean and restless, their worst character traits becoming displayed. One elderly and infirm guest dies; two more end up in a joint suicide pact.

Civilized and prosperous dinner guests penned up long enough will turn on one another like rats in an overpopulation study. An early critic suggested the dinner guests must represent the ruling class in Franco's Spain. Having set a banquet table for themselves by defeating the workers in the Spanish Civil War, they sit down for a feast only to find it never ends. This seems to have been an initial interpretation of the hideous outcome of the trapped guests, for filmmaker Buñuel was exiled from his homeland to Mexico after the Spanish Civil War.

There is, however, a more sinister, more general way of reflecting on the possible meaning of this parable: if we think of the site of the dinner party as a microcosm of the planet upon which we dwell, the guests then may represent us, trapped like rats and cannibalizing the weak.

More than just a macabre comedy when seen on first appearance, *The Exterminating Angel* can be a chilling portent of our own future in the twenty-first century, with uncontrolled population growth, dwindling food resources, and hundreds of millions of souls living on coasts less than one metre above sea level and having to relocate inland from the rising seas as the effect of global warming inexorably restricts us all within an increasingly smaller area. With no way to escape, our future is undeniably bleak. Life expectancy will diminish again as viruses and bacterial plagues kill off all who are not victims of wars, provoked by those trying to preserve unsustainable lifestyles egged on by political demagogues.

The Old Testament book of Jeremiah is an appropriate, though not cheerful, text recommended for further reading. Or for something more up to date, try the eerily prognostic poem by William Butler Yeats, "The Second Coming." After that you may wish to have another beer or perhaps a dram of single malt, while you await the arrival of our real exterminating angel. — *May 2018*

86 Cannibalism

Stranded: I've Come from a Plane That Crashed on the Mountains is a 2007 documentary film which tells the story of a rugby team from Uruguay who boarded Uruguayan Air Force Flight 571. The film features interviews with the survivors, who recount their struggle to survive after their plane crashed in the Andes and the survivors cannibalized the deceased to avoid starvation.

There is plenty of documentation throughout history of human cannibalism, and it is seen in many other animal species.

The practice has recently been observed among rats in urban settings who have become accustomed to dining off food waste from restaurants. With enforced closure of food service providers due to the coronavirus pandemic, the usual nutritional supply for the rodents was unavailable, and they turned to cannibalism for sustenance.

Public health authorities worldwide have warned that city rats are displaying unusual or aggressive behaviour amid the pandemic lockdown. Just like the rats, humans will also turn to cannibalism for survival if other sources are unavailable, as did the unfortunate Uruguayan rugby players.

A Yale University nutritionist observed that brain and muscle tissues would be the best options if you had to eat a human, since muscles have protein and brain is rich in fat and glucose, providing slow-burning energy. In the children's tale "Hansel and Gretel," the wicked witch attempted to roast the children she had enticed into her home, though was foiled. But in real life there have been reported criminal cases in recent times in both Germany and the US involving cannibalism, although in the context of mental abnormality, not resource scarcity.

In our "civilized" society, the eating of humans is outlawed. But the veneer of civilization is fragile, and with the foreseen collapse of social norms, recurrence of cannibalism may be anticipated as billions of people are forced to abandon formerly fertile equatorial areas.

Unstoppable global warming causing increasing aridity and lack of water for irrigation, compounded by rising sea levels inundating coastal regions and forcing urban populations to move inland, will create unstoppable migration pressure to resettlement in northern Canada and Russia. Wars will be provoked and the current food supply chain will break down amid social unrest.

Fit young rugby players, if you could catch them, would doubtless be tough and stringy to eat, but slow-moving obese American plutocrats would probably be savoury in a stew, when properly seasoned. — *May 2020*

87 Hawking, Hope and the Curse of Cassandra

A collection of writings by the late astronomer Stephen Hawking was published last year as *Brief Answers to the Big Questions.* In it are responses by an eminent scientist, accessible to everyone who wonders about the ultimate concerns of mankind, as in Gauguin's questions: Who are we? Where do we come from? Where are we going?

The seventh chapter of Hawking's book addresses the question "Will we survive on earth?" His honest opinion is that the threats to survival are too big and too numerous to allow a positive answer.

"As we stand on the brink of a Second Nuclear Age and a period of unprecedented climate change, scientists have a special responsibility, once again, to inform the public and to advise leaders about humanity at the present time. . . . I regard it as almost inevitable that either a nuclear confrontation or environmental catastrophe will cripple the Earth at some point in the next 1,000 years. . . . We are acting with reckless indifference to our future on planet Earth."

The response to this assessment, of course, has been and remains denial by the public and those "leaders" in a position to act on the warning. This is a realistic example of the ancient myth of the Trojan princess Cassandra, who was initially granted the ability to foretell the future by the god Apollo but was subsequently cursed by the burden of disbelief among all those who heard her.

Hawking was unable himself to conceive of a future without hope and viewed the only solution to be leaving the planet and colonizing space: "I am convinced that humans need to leave Earth. If we stay, we risk being annihilated. As the consequence of uncontrolled population growth and depletion of natural resources, if we don't self-destruct by nuclear war, social collapse will lead to the end of civilization, and survivors, if any, will revert to a state of brutalism and barbarity."

It is difficult to share his hopeful vision of extraterrestrial colonization. Once having destroyed our planet, seeking others to destroy would be no kind of improvement. Alas, the real curse is that life itself may be an inherent "disease of the universe." There is no need to follow the advice of Dante about abandoning hope upon entering Hell — we are already there. Hawking would certainly have agreed that there is one absolute certainty we can assert about the future: the second law of thermodynamics. — *July 2019*

88 Extinctions

There are five levels of extinction: individual, social, biological, planetary and universal. Medicine has become increasingly associated with the postponement of extinction on the individual level, beyond just the prevention and cure of disease. We use avoidance to distract ourselves and reproduction to preserve our genetic material, but we can only postpone what is inevitable as the organism wears out and death and decay become unpreventable.

Social extinction will result from unlimited reproduction and exhaustion of the natural resources necessary to maintain civilization. Global warming caused by human activity on the surface of the planet, infectious disease, warfare, and probably radioactive poisoning will destroy social organization as we know it. Governments will collapse and reversion to savagery will unavoidably ensue, as in Hobbes's vision.

On a higher level, biological extinction occurs when a living species can no longer be viable and reproduce. We see this happening all around us, while human activity transforms the planet in ways that inhibit the survival of life. Plant and animal life will contract over time, as an arid and lifeless surface eventually replaces the present variety of living creatures on earth.

What we have learned about stellar evolution from astrophysics also implies planetary extinction, for as the sun exhausts its nuclear fuel and eventually transforms into a red giant star, its radius will expand to a distance greater than that of the earth's orbit, vaporizing what remains long after any organic life has disappeared.

The fifth and final extinction appears to be of the universe itself, with the eventual irreversible conversion of all energy into heat, as implied by the second law of thermodynamics.

How can one deal with this bleak assessment? One approach is that of the Voluntary Human Extinction Movement, which recommends deliberate abstention from reproduction. Theoretically effective, no doubt, but impracticable given the inherent drives to survive and reproduce. Delay the inevitable by minimizing pollution? Commendable, certainly, and engagement fosters a sense of participation by recycling, like using reusable shopping bags. But again, this is only a postponement. Suicide has been thought of as an individual option, but while it no doubt resolves all problems for those that make that choice, it inevitably creates more unhappiness for surviving friends and family members, though assisted death in some cases may be considered desirable when physical pain renders life unbearable.

Stoic acceptance seems to me to be the only reasonable choice. Being kind to others should remain the number one humane goal for all of us, being as we are inexorably trapped in this universe by physical laws we are only now beginning to comprehend. — *Sept 2019*

89 Lucid Melancholy

"Dealing with the Absurdity of Human Existence in the Face of Converging Catastrophes" is a recent posting on *The Conversation* by Canadian biologist Lonnie Aarssen of Queen's University. Referencing evolutionist Theodosius Dobzhansky and others, Aarssen suggests that we are essentially absurd humans trying to convince ourselves that our existence is not absurd but somehow meaningful. His reasoning is convincing, citing Tolstoy's description of two emotional drives, "escape from self" and "extension of self." Each serves to assuage the inevitability of anticipated non-existence and the dispersal of all of what had been meaningful, knowing that the world will go on in our absence as though we had never existed.

Extension of self may exist in the context of our descendants (if any), in the form of our genetic contribution to their own DNA, along with perhaps parental influence on child development. Some exceptional individuals indeed may be remembered for a while for their accomplishments or ideas, but even tombstones and statues eventually crumble, like Shelley's Ozymandias or, more recently, those of American slavers.

Escape from self is ubiquitous, from the trivial to the profound. The entertainment industry, including sports; card games; learning new skills or refining old ones; travelling the world on cruise ships; reading, from classics to thrillers; inebriation and psychedelics; writing essays like this one — we grasp at anything to prevent being transfixed by the prospect of not-being, some to the extent of deciding not to wait and terminating their own existence, but this is unkind, and always creates unhappiness among survivors, especially families.

Mood states associated with reflection on these issues provoke a sense of what I call *lucid melancholy*, and as a psychiatrist I would distinguish it from clinical depressions, a group of mood disorders sometimes treatable by medication, psychotherapy or a combination of both. Lucid melancholy could be described as a rational response to awareness of the temporal limits to life, distinct from (but possibly coeval with) a mood disorder plucked by some algorithm from the DSM. Most unthinking humans employ escapism. Some play Bach, others play bridge, watch television, take adult education courses or write poetry.

The realization of being embedded in a society plunging towards converging catastrophes is a separate issue from existential angst, or *Weltschmerz*, but a fair description of life circumstances that were once considered only apocalyptic fiction but are now recognizably becoming undeniable. I can't recommend any individual response to this, other than perhaps to be nice to others, for we are all caught in the same lethal maelstrom. As with the passengers and crew of the *Titanic*, we are all going down together, and this time there are no lifeboats. — *May 2019*

HOMO CREDENS

90 Homo credens

Homo credens, or man the believer: we read, write, study and learn about ourselves, our society, our world and our future. But this is where it gets murky, and the search for meaning has occupied philosophers from the presocratics of antiquity to logical empiricists of the twenty-first century.

The contrary of belief is doubt. What are the criteria for decision making when there is doubt? Descartes thought, therefore he was; Hamlet wasn't sure; Sartre averred, "The subjective existence of reality precedes and defines its nature"; and Wittgenstein would have sensibly just kept his mouth shut if asked.

The physical world around us seems real enough until you reach the micro level, where what was thought to be solid then dissolves into a field of probability. We are accustomed to agreeing that we live on the surface of an oblate spheroid and that the rising of the sun at dawn is an illusion caused by the rotation of the earth, but while the idea of time as different for every point of reference in the universe may be objectively true, it is contrary to how we subjectively experience events as simultaneously past, present and future.

Absolute truth may be exhibited in mathematical proofs and in formal inductive logic, but these areas are abstract, and their embodiment is concrete, and so approximate. And while uncertainty reigns in what we call the real world, the thirst for absolute knowledge is only quenched in an abstract domain.

So man believes, or tries to believe, enabling religions, political groups, economic systems and other ideologies to arise and promulgate views of the world. And man, being so eager to give up his freedom of individual belief, finds solace in associating with others with whom to share similar worldviews.

But all *isms* are poisonous, and conflict among ideologies promotes great suffering, as observed by Vasily Grossman in his book *Life and Fate*, where two soldiers, one a German Nazi officer and the other a Soviet Communist prisoner, argue about which has a superior ideology. —*June 2020*

91 Faust

I bought my copy of Goethe's *Faust* in 1952, when I was an undergraduate student of humanities. A mid-twentieth-century translation by C.F. MacIntyre, with the original German text displayed on the opposite page for convenient reference, it is the earliest book purchase I still possess and has accompanied me throughout my long life. I thought of it again while rereading an essay I wrote at age twenty in 1954, which summed up my early thinking at the time I received my BA.

Now near the end of my ninth decade, having studied philosophy, astronomy, medicine and alas, psychiatry, like Faust I feel no wiser now than before, just older, realizing and accepting that we are all essentially ignorant. My essay proclaimed the dawn of a world-outlook, and I can now contrast and compare my current views with those I once possessed.

Scientific knowledge, then as now, was celebrated as the sole means of understanding the structure of the universe, with intersubjective testability being the criterion for assessing the truth of propositions about the natural world. The role of language was considered fundamental for conveying this understanding, and my view of that remains strong. Ethical values and social concerns remain much the same now as then, and aesthetic interests, while broader, continue as before. Musical and gustatory tastes are much the same: I didn't like jazz or broccoli then, and I still don't.

My early thoughts about philosophy now seem sterile, with logical empiricism only being useful in dealing with science and epistemology, and of limited benefit in examining value judgments and moral issues. I now incline more towards existentialism, and though having been taught that metaphysics was no more than "a systematic misuse of a terminology, invented only for that purpose," I now reserve judgment, although I continue to agree with Carnap, Wittgenstein and the Vienna Circle on this issue.

In my closing statement from 1954 I wrote, "It would be nobler for mankind if the universe had no preconceived plan, because then we ourselves might endow it with a purpose. For what is man but a very small and yet complex chunk of the universe come alive and conscious? We *are* the universe, and what goals we set for ourselves we set for it also." This remains my credo.

A lifelong theme has been my wide range of interests. I have the breadth of familiarity with many things, like Berlin's fox, and not the learned, specialized wisdom of a hedgehog. Like Faust, I don't presume to be an expert in anything, though learning has always been a source of fulfillment.

Applied reason and competition have enabled the human race to survive and achieve mastery over much of the natural world, but they are destroying us. Compelled by our inborn traits of competitiveness and poisoned by our technology, the Eternal Masculine drags us down.

Freud wins over Goethe. — *July 2018*

92 A View from the Cave of an Urban Hermit

In a Chinese story about a solitary lifestyle, a narrator observes that while anyone can go up a mountain, live in a cave and reflect on the vicissitudes of the human condition, a genuine hermit can still live a satisfying and detached lifestyle in a city. Though surrounded by hundreds, even thousands, of other people, one can elect to remain alone with one's thoughts.

Living in seclusion is often a religious practice for many, yet it is not incompatible with atheism. Solitary prayer and meditation may be an adequate substitute for regular contact with others for those so inclined, but hardly a necessary adjunct to a secluded lifestyle. Seclusion did not always imply loneliness when one's interpersonal life included written material found in books and journals, and now the availability of a wide array of internet resources and social media.

When one's primary companions were books and not the seductive enticements of instant electronic contact, public and private libraries provided access to the minds of others. While to rely on one's own life experiences and what past authors have written may now seem archaic, a personal library allows one to have those that have inspired us as companions in thought: Tolstoy, Voltaire, Wittgenstein, Goethe — the list seems endless. Many remain for me enjoyable companions, like Jan Morris and Alberto Manguel; others less sources of delight, perhaps, but still influential and worthy of attention, like Marx or St. Paul.

The level of direct social contact can be adjusted to reflect one's degree of comfort with others, for a hermit, urban or rural, has the ability to control both psychological and social distancing. Living alone permits one to regulate these levels as needed — one can be cheerful and gregarious with one's neighbours yet retain the option of being alone with one's books when desired.

My family live nearby and two remaining close friends are currently in England and Southeast Asia. I am in periodic contact with them by telephone or email, though I eschew social media like Facebook and the like. Though I have no desire or need for *continual* contact with anyone, it is nevertheless reassuring to retain the ability to do so.

Gazing from the window of my study, I regard a variety of people passing by: some walking their dogs, others jogging or running, geezers and crones shuffling along with their sticks or walkers, children trudging towards or bouncing back from school, and those between puberty and middle age moving along like zombies, ignoring their surroundings, fixedly staring at and fiddling with their little handheld "devices."

The latter remind me of a cartoon from *New Yorker* magazine: the scene was that of a group of primitive "cavemen," unshod and wearing animal hides, strolling aimlessly about a desolate area, each holding in one hand a single rock and staring at it. Perhaps what they needed was an alien monolith, as seen in the first part of Kubrick's *2001: A Space Odyssey*, the confrontation of new and unknown technology inducing a search for meaning. Does not asking why demand an answer? Can we invent a Supreme Being? — *Feb 2019*

93 Confucius

Confucius (551–479 BCE) was a Chinese teacher, editor, politician and philosopher of the Spring and Autumn period of Chinese history. He is widely considered to have been one of the most important and influential individuals affecting the lives of humanity. His 2007 biography, *The Authentic Confucius*, by Yale professor Annping Chin, is a sympathetic and detailed account of Confucius's life in thought and politics. Chin sums up his character as that of a man "distinguished by his learning and a desire to perfect himself, together with an awareness that this life was the only occasion he had to fulfill his wish and promise."

As a public official in 497 BCE, Confucius abruptly quit politics and went travelling for fourteen years, accompanied by a few younger students and admirers, conversing with people and teaching. He described himself as a transmitter of knowledge of the past, not an innovator. Confucius avoided making theories about life and did not believe anything could be beyond doubt or that any rule should be immutable. In so believing, he declined to force his opinions on others as an authority.

The Analects, or "edited conversations," is a collection of sayings and ideas attributed to Confucius, believed to have been compiled and written by his followers. The *Analects* has been one of the most widely read and studied books in China for the last 2,000 years and continues to have a substantial influence on Chinese and East Asian thought and values today.

The importance of education and study is a fundamental theme of the *Analects*. Confucius's primary goal in educating his students was to produce ethically well-cultivated men who would carry themselves with gravity, speak correctly and demonstrate consummate integrity in all things. He regarded moral self-cultivation as his most important subject.

A wonderful and unusual new edition of the *Analects* has been published in the format of a 212-page graphic novel by Chinese illustrator C.C. Tsai, with text in vertical columns in Chinese alongside the drawings and English translations in speech balloons (as used in comic strips). The first forty-three pages of illustrations depict Confucius's early years as a politician and his experiences of wandering before settling back in his native Lu, in modern Shandong province, where he lived and taught students until his death in 479 BCE at the age of seventy-three.

The remaining 166 pages comprise the text of the *Analects*, each page illustrating specific teachings, such as dignity, benevolence, self-criticism and the golden rule, among others. Confucianism is not a religion but rather an attitude or self-discipline, emphasizing personal and governmental morality, correctness of social relationships, justice and sincerity. Chinese cultural institutes around the world today bear his name.

An epitaph by historian Sima Qian reads, "Confucius was a commoner whose teachings have been transmitted for more than ten generations, and there is no intellectual who does not consider him his teacher. Confucius was the greatest of all sages!" —*June 2018*

94 On Being: The Gauguin Questions

On Being: The Gauguin Questions is the title of a small book by Peter Atkins, an English chemist and former professor of chemistry at the University of Oxford and the author of a number of popular science books. In *On Being*, Atkins addresses the fundamental questions of existence as a humanist and a scientist, eschewing religious and other supernatural attempts to provide answers to what we ask about our origin, our identity and our future.

These so-called Gauguin questions refer to the title of a large painting by the late nineteenth-century French post-impressionist artist

Paul Gauguin, now hanging in the Boston Museum of Fine Arts. In his painting of a group of Polynesian people, Gauguin simply wrote on the canvas, "Where do we come from? What are we? Where are we going?"

Atkins has written and spoken on issues of humanism, atheism and the incompatibility of science and religion. While he realizes that many believe that the physical is not all there is, he sees "no objective evidence for the non-physical. . . . We cannot in all intellectual honesty accept its existence as plausible." Atkins regards all supernatural religion as unsound thinking and maintains that the only means of understanding reality is the scientific method.

The origin of the universe from a space-time singularity is a hypothesis that can account for the formation of galaxies, gravitational condensation into stars, stellar synthesis of atoms, and eventual formation of the solar system, including our planet Earth. This is not a creation myth but a plausible account. *This is where we come from.*

The biosphere, with the appearance of organisms surviving and reproducing using genetic coding, has resulted in evolutionary changes leading to natural selection and species differentiation for all the organisms that live on this planet, including humans. *This is who we are.*

But like all organisms, we are not immortal and eventually die. With the end of consciousness, we cease to exist, and our bodies decay back into their constituent atoms. Atkins describes the process of bodily decay or that resulting from cremation: "We need to know that **we are stardust** and are inescapably destined to decay." *This is where we are going.*

Belief in an afterlife is wishful thinking. Atkins wonders how otherwise sensible and educated people cannot come to terms with the fact that death is extinction. Like other stars, our sun has a life cycle, understood now in detail by astrophysicists. After the nuclear fuel is spent, it will first expand and incinerate the earth, then eventually cool to a dense black dwarf.

Moreover, the second law of thermodynamics envisages the eventual fate of the universe, when energy has all been converted into heat and dissipated.

Atkins concludes by referencing his scientific faith: "The scientific method is a distillation of common sense in alliance with honesty, and its discoveries illuminate the world." I share his views and believe his answers to the Gauguin questions to be credible. — *May 2018*

95 Ultimate Questions

Fellow octogenarian Bryan Magee was a British philosopher, broadcaster, politician, author and poet, best known as a popularizer of philosophy. His 2016 book, *Ultimate Questions,* reflected on the human condition as a way of summing up a lifetime of pondering on our situation, of our having no choice but to live the whole of our lives in our own small amount of time. "There is no escaping this. Within the empirical world all time will be taken away from us, and with it everything we have and are in this world," he writes. After death, only the atoms that made up our physical bodies remain to disperse in the environment. Religion, Magee feels, is irrelevant.

The human predicament is that we exist and have a strong instinct for survival, but with the challenge of not understanding the complete picture. The challenge is to tolerate this ignorance, whether we like it or not. What we do know is derived from the five fundamental senses of vision, hearing, touch, taste and smell, and along with the brain and the central nervous system (perhaps enhanced with computers), we use this information to form our constructs of reality.

These constructs, however, are mind dependent, meaning that what can be conceived depends on our powers of conceiving. But that is not necessarily the same as what actually exists.

Magee notes that all living things are limited in their potentialities by what they are. This seems obvious to us as human beings "about any creature other than ourselves." But what is true of other animals must also be true of ourselves. He concludes that not only is most of reality unknowable by us, but it is also "beyond all possibility of apprehension — unconceptualizable."

With regard to moral or aesthetic values, there is no universal or absolute means of choice, and the Latin proverb *de gustibus non est disputandum* (no accounting for taste) sums up his approach to these areas of incessant human contention and conflict. Magee does admit to fearing death and the expectation of permanent oblivion: "It is the destruction of a full-bloodedly alive, conscious being that is so frightening for the conscious being. I find it strange that there are quite a lot of people who do not understand that."

Magee acknowledges that the intensity of his fear is now less than when he was younger, having lived a long life with a good amount of opportunities and successes, but it is accompanied by anticipatory grief of the total loss of everything. He writes, "It is easier to accept the security of a faith, either in the existence of unknowable entities or in their non-existence, than it is to confront the full range and scale of our ignorance and live with that. . . . The only honest way to live and think is in the fullest possible acknowledgment of our ignorance and its consequences." — *June 2018*

96 Atheism

John Gray is an English political philosopher with interests in analytic philosophy and history who held academic posts in the UK and US. Gray has suggested different ways of considering the concept of non-belief in a deity, ranging from simple denial of a creator-god to more elaborate forms of disbelief, such as the common thread among non-believers of invoking "something more," a Whiggish attitude regarding the progression of humanity towards some more perfect state, similar to the myth of progress characteristic of nonreligious belief systems like Marxism.

This idea of human progress was not a feature of classical Greek or Roman civilizations, in which cyclical views were dominant. It was a polytheistic world with gods here and there, and wherein it was ritual rather than belief which reigned supreme. Gray identifies the appearance of Christian New Testament monotheistic eschatology as an ideological shift, replacing the polytheistic classical model with a world promising progression towards a better future, first conceived by early Christians like St. Paul and St. Augustine. He considers secular humanism to be derived from this Christian monotheism, with humanity replacing a deity at the time of the Enlightenment.

Like William James, who wrote of the "varieties of religious experience," so one may also reflect on the varieties of atheist experience. It is not merely a simple black and white issue of whether one believes in a god or not — there are different ways of being a disbeliever. Indeed, some reluctantly identify themselves as agnostics, while others may consider that as but the cowardly evasion of a forthright avowal of disbelief.

A form of atheism that isn't just denial but one that actively condemns a wicked deity is described in the character of Ivan Karamazov in the Dostoevsky novel, in stark contrast to his pious brother Alyosha. Moreover, all religions do not necessarily involve belief in a Supreme Being. For example, Buddhism could be considered an "atheist religion," focusing on meditation and inner states of consciousness rather than on an external deity.

As an outspoken atheist, Gray described feeling most attuned to the more relaxed forms of non-belief that omit any reference to either a god or humanity, identifying writer Joseph Conrad and philosopher George Santayana as acceptable fellow atheists. He also references the "mystical atheism" of Arthur Schopenhauer, transcending human conception, lurking somewhere in the fog of German idealism.

The concept of a universal need to account for meaning in the world within which we live has been proposed by some psychologists. However, being myself more of an empiricist, the deeper I read about quantum mechanics, information theory, and the granulation of time, the more I'm inclined to accept Wittgenstein's view on maintaining silence about the unknown. — *Apr 2019*

97 Battling the Gods

The recently published *Battling the Gods: Atheism in the Ancient World*, by Cambridge professor of Greek culture Tim Whitmarsh, is a close examination of the role of divinities in the ancient Mediterranean, and of the free-thinking voices of antiquity who first denied superhuman intervention.

Disbelief in the supernatural is not a new phenomenon and has persisted for millennia, beginning in ancient Greece. Pre-Christian atheism was controversial, but as a rule, polytheism was much less repressive towards disbelievers than religious monotheism became, and beliefs tended to be a local matter. The principal task of priests was to sacrifice to gods and interpret signs rather to deal with ethical or spiritual issues.

Most importantly, the ancient Greeks had nothing like sacred scripture. Jewish, Christian and Muslim religions are structured around the idea of holy scripture, and therefore are in a position to demand orthodoxy from believers, citing written text. While ancient Greeks did have shared myths or stories about gods, a type of folk wisdom, these stories did not have authority commanding one how to act or what to believe.

When the ancient Greeks thought about the nature of the world, they did so by means of philosophy, seen in the presocratic thinkers of Ionia, who described phenomena in terms of a single substance, such as water or air. They tried to explain the nature of the cosmos and the world they lived in by extrapolating from what they observed. For example, in classical Athens of the fifth century BCE, the historian Thucydides wrote his *History of the Peloponnesian War* without referencing divine explanation. Whitmarsh describes Thucydides's work as "the earliest surviving atheist narrative of human history." Similarly, Protagoras wrote in his *On the Gods*, "I cannot know whether they exist or whether they do not. Or what form they have, for there are many impediments to knowledge, including obscurity and the brevity of human life."

Aside from the question of their existence, gods were represented on the stage of classical drama, as in *The Eumenides* by Aeschylus. In actuality, Socrates was executed by the citizens of Athens for the impiety of not recognizing the gods who oversaw and protected the city.

In the subsequent Hellenistic age, in the third century BCE in Greece, and extending into the early Roman Empire, atheism was widespread, owing to the popularity of Epicureanism, a belief system that considered gods at best remote and uninterested in human affairs, irrelevant to issues of morality and ritual.

After the Christianization of the Roman Empire, beginning with the conversion of Emperor Constantine in 312 CE, Emperor Theodosius I issued a decree in 380 CE that pronounced Christianity the official religion of the empire and ordered all subjects to follow it. This put a decisive end to philosophical atheism for over a millennium. Remaining polytheists were considered atheists by Christian authorities once they achieved power and instituted their own vision and rituals. Atheism could serve no purpose now that the "true Christian message" had been revealed and enforced. — *June 2018*

98 Mortality and the Ancients

Facing Death: Epicurus and his Critics by James Warren (2004) discusses the Epicurean approach to the universal human issue of mortality, derived from the Hellenistic philosopher Epicurus (341–270 BCE), who maintained that death is not bad for the person that dies, even though it is inevitable and is the complete annihilation of that person: "Death is nothing to us, for what is dispersed does not perceive, and what does not perceive is nothing to us." Moreover, to avoid relying on the premise that all goods and evils reside in perception, Epicurus reassuringly wrote that "death is nothing to us, since for the time when we are, death is not present, and for the time death is present, we are not. Therefore, it is nothing either to the living or the dead, since it is not present for the former, and the latter are no longer."

In *Facing Death*, Warren elaborates on the Epicurean approach to life (focused on the present, not the past or future) and death with respect to deprivation, unperceived harms and the so-called symmetry argument, which suggests that there is no relevant difference between prenatal non-existence and postmortem non-existence.

The Epicurean ideal was to ignore fate and to adjust the balance between pleasure and pain such that the former was more important than the latter. They had a negative view of suicide as defeatist, unlike the Stoics, though they admit that rational arguments alone may be insufficient to convince one that life is worth living. Nevertheless, we should accustom ourselves to the fundamental concept that "death is nothing to us."

In comparison, an exploration of the Stoic approach to mortality may be found in the recent small book *How to Die: An Ancient Guide to the End of Life* (2018), a collection of writings selected from letters written by the Roman Stoic philosopher Seneca, edited, translated and introduced by James S. Romm. The Stoic view propounds the desirable attitude towards dying for the individual facing mortality: "The key themes are the universality of death; its importance as life's final and most defining rite of passage; its part in purely natural cycles and processes; and its ability to liberate us, by freeing souls from bodies or, in the case of suicide, from the degradation of enslavement, or from cruel kings and tyrants who might otherwise destroy our moral integrity."

Both Epicureans and Stoics entertained realistic views on mortality. Epicurus writes as an atheist, whereas Seneca refers to "gods" with a whiff of predestination that personally rankles. But it is instructive for us to read what was said on the subject before the Christian takeover of the classical world, the imposition of religious dogma and the suppression of the reasonable teachings and rational advice about mortality from these ancient philosophers. — *June 2018*

99 The Lure of the Arcane

In *The Lure of the Arcane,* Theodore Ziolkowski describes the mysterious cults of antiquity, as portrayed in surviving records and commentary. Broadly defined as "a system of specific ritual and prayers for a single deity or a set of deities," the word *cult* often carries a negative emotional charge, in that it suggests a secondary or inferior status of that particular belief system. A case can be made for viewing the initial source of all major religious sects as cult-like, as in nineteenth-century Mormonism and early Christianity itself.

Although political issues were generally avoided by known writers, accounts of conspiracies in both Greece and Rome were described by early historians. Religious cults were often satirized in drama, as seen in the Greek tragedy *The Baccae* by Euripides, which analyzed in detail the cult of the god Dionysus, a Greek god of fruitfulness and vegetation known more specifically as a god of wine and ecstasy. The occurrence of his name on a Linear B tablet (thirteenth century BCE) is proof that Dionysus was already commonly worshipped by the Mycenaean period, although the cult's exact origins are unknown, though in all the legends he is depicted as having foreign origins. In ancient Rome, the cult of Dionysus was fiercely suppressed, but he was nevertheless popularly celebrated as the god Bacchus.

The cult of Isis, derived from Egyptian culture and assimilated into imperial Rome, is another example of a popular cult of antiquity, though it declined as the cult of Christianity became established. Interestingly, the cult of Isis was resurrected by Freemasonry in the eighteenth century, as seen in Mozart's 1791 opera, *The Magic Flute* (*Die Zauberflöte*).

Subtitled *The Literature of Cult and Conspiracy*, this fascinating book gathers together the common threads associated with paranoid ideation as shared by groups of individuals and seen in literary manifestations from antiquity to the present day. Ziolkowski, a professor emeritus of German and comparative literature at Princeton University, describes "the diachronic appeal to many generations preceding our own of what is known today as 'conspiracy fiction' and its progressive development as a genre."

Popular thrillers often involve secret societies, cults, conspiracies, heroes and heroines; danger and suspense are appealing in that they make sense out of a world that may seem chaotic. Apuleius's second-century works *Metamorphosis* and *The Golden Ass* provide a detailed account of a mystery cult surviving from classical antiquity in North Africa under the Roman Empire. Ziolkowski observes that "both Euripides and Apuleius achieved the popularity of their respective works in part by appealing to precisely that same trait of human nature and cynicism that responds in the twenty-first century to conspiracy theories and to the works of Dan Brown and his fellow conspiracy-novelists."

Ziolkowski also introduces the concept of romantic socialism, which recalls the words of Friedrich Engels to distinguish it from the materialistic Marxist version of socialism proclaimed in the *Communist Manifesto* of 1848.

Not a formal theory, romantic socialism is described as an "amalgam of ideologies arising from the early German Romanticism of Christian values" embedded in a stable society. Although not threatening established values, these newly formed ideologies nevertheless led to suspicion and at times were opposed by more conservative authorities. Those sharing these new views banded together in existing secret societies or formed new ones.

The French writer George Sand produced what Ziolkowski termed "a feminine, even feminist, *Bildungsroman*" in her novel *Consuelo* and its sequel *La Comtesse de Rudolstadt*. The heroine is initiated into a secret order resembling romantic socialist organizations in rites and rituals. Other similar novels include the conspiracy thriller *Underground Rome* (*Rome souterraine*) by Charles Didier and *The Wandering Jew* (*Le Juif errant*) by Eugene Sue in the 1840s. The secret society of the latter was the Jesuits, who had been suppressed since 1767 but restored by the pope in 1814. Entangled in the devilish schemes of the sinister followers of Loyola, *The Wandering Jew* was an early example of today's conspiracy thrillers.

Works by widely read novelists, such as Edward Bulwer-Lytton in England, German Karl Gutzkow and Croatian Eduard Breier, also fall into this category, with their bizarre and melodramatic plots that were immensely popular at the time. The contents and plot devices of these sometimes-lurid tales illustrate the appearance in each of a secret society in which the protagonist participates. They hint at hidden knowledge of traditions, occult orders and elaborate initiation rituals from ancient civilizations, demonstrating how over time secret societies tend to evolve into conspiracies, employing nefarious schemes to destroy traditional structures of church and state.

"These novels represent both the positive and negative views of secret societies: from the evil machinations of Sue's Jesuits and the incompetence of Breier's Rosicrucians to the political activism of Didier's Carbonari and the idealizing visions of Sand's Invisibles, Bulwer-Lytton's master race, and Gurzkow's Knights of the Spirit." Overall, this literature illustrates the pros and cons of these groups from the mid-nineteenth century, in which all facets of contemporary thrillers can be found.

Trivial-appearing popular paperback novels, marketed in airport bookstores to entertain those passengers not wanting to watch movies during long flights, illustrate the human fascination for the lure of the arcane. There is nothing new under the sun. — Compiled from the essays "The Lure of the Arcane," May 2018, and "The Secret Societies of Romantic Socialism," *June 2018*

100 The Order of Knights Templar

In *The Lure of the Arcane*, Ziolkowski explores the history of the Knights Templar through the story of Percival's quest in the epic poem *Parzival*, of which the titular protagonist is seen as a medieval parallel to Lucius, the narrator of Apuleius's *Golden Ass*, who quests for initiation into the cult of Isis. The idea of a secret society emerges as a recurring concept in literature, with a ripple effect extending all the way to Wagnerian musical drama centuries later.

The Knights Templar, or Templars, were a Catholic military order founded in 1119 and active from about 1129 to 1312. Initially formed to provide protection to pilgrims travelling overland to Jerusalem, the Templars became a synthesis of monk and knight, mysticism and chivalry. Templar knights, in their distinctive white mantles with a red cross, were among the most skilled fighting units of the Crusades. The red cross was a symbol of martyrdom, and to die in combat was considered a great honour, assuring the deceased a place in heaven. Because the Templars were so closely tied to the Crusades, when the Holy Land was lost, support for the order faded.

Rumours about the Templars' secret initiation ceremony created distrust, and King Philip IV of France — deeply in debt to the order — took advantage of the situation to gain control over them. The Templars were prominent in banking and were accused by Philip of corruption. In 1307 he had many of the order's members in France arrested, tortured into giving false confessions and burned at the stake. Pope Clement V officially disbanded the Templars in 1312 under pressure from Philip IV.

The story of the persecution and sudden dissolution of the secretive yet powerful medieval Templars has drawn many other groups to claim connections with them as a way of enhancing their own image and mystery, such as Templar Knights Canada, a motorcycle club that is active in communities by doing charitable work. There is, however, no clear historical connection between the Templars and any modern organization.

The legacy of the Templars continues today with legends concerning secrets and mysteries handed down to the select few from ancient times. Rumours of these well-kept secrets even circulated during the time of the Templars themselves. Masonic writers added their own speculations in the eighteenth century, and further fictional embellishments have appeared in popular novels such as *Ivanhoe*, *Foucault's Pendulum*, and *The Da Vinci Code*, as well as in a number of twentieth-century film adaptations.

The first association drawn between the Holy Grail and the Templars occurs in the twelfth-century epic poetry of Wolfram von Eschenbach's *Parzival*, which follows the hero from his boyhood and career as a knight in the court of King Arthur to his ultimate achievement as King of the Temple of the Grail. In the nineteenth century, Richard Wagner based the texts of two of his grandest operas, *Lohengrin* and *Parsifal*, on heroic characters drawn from von Eschenbach's epic. — *May 2018*

101 The Lodges of the Enlightenment

The Freemasons, a secret society promoting freedom, equality, fraternity and tolerance, arose in England with the establishment of the first Grand Lodge in 1717. Participants all shared these common beliefs and Masonic lodges were established rapidly in England and across continental Europe. Although usually feared by absolutist governments and the Vatican, Freemasonry became accepted in Prussia after the initiation of Frederick the Great into a Masonic lodge while he was a crown prince.

A British historian suggested that the panicky attribution of influence given to secret societies was "based not on what they actually accomplish but on what outsiders believe of their intentions." For example, the French Revolution was widely blamed on the conspiratorial schemes of secret societies like the Freemasons and their offshoot, the Illuminati. In *The Lure of the Arcane*, Ziolkowski comments, "The *content* of the mystery mattered less than the *fact of its secrecy*, hence our lack of knowledge about the 'secrets' underlying many secret societies."

The "lodge novel," or *Bundesroman*, from late eighteenth-century Germany exemplifies this fascination with secret societies, as seen in the writings of Schiller and others of the period. "Central to the genre is the idea of a secret society that somehow guides or seeks to control the life of the hero and enlist him in its cause." A particularly vivid and instructive example is observed in the libretto of Mozart's opera *The Magic Flute*, where Act II clearly depicts an initiation ritual. With the glorious music of Mozart and words of librettist Schikaneder, the rituals and symbols of Freemasonry were displayed on stage "in all their Egyptian pomp and splendor."

Ziolkowski notes that these German lodge novels promoted the idea that secret societies were common at that time. While providing entertainment to readers, these novels also document widespread beliefs in hidden mysteries and the arcane, suggesting a progression from cults to conspiracy theorists. Later authors such as Hugo von Hofmannsthal in Austria, André Gide in France, Thornton Wilder in the US, Edward Bulwer-Lytton in England and Hermann Hesse in Germany wrote fiction that modified the traditional lodge novel while retaining the concepts of secret societies and occultism.

The Freemasons are still active around the world, from the esoteric seriousness of the Ancient and Accepted Scottish Rite of Freemasonry to the pseudo-orientalist absurdities of the be-fezzed Shriners. Though claiming not to be a religious organization, to affiliate one must affirm belief in a "Supreme Being." When I once asked an adherent if it were true that Freemasonry was the world's largest secret society, he replied indignantly, "We are not a secret society, we are *a society with secrets*." — *May 2018*

102 The Rosicrucians (Post-Reformation)

Ziolkowski traces the origins of the Rosicrucians to the second half of the sixteenth century in Germany, where as a consequence of the political and religious turmoil associated with the Counter-Reformation, many people were turning to various emerging esoteric and utopian movements. The founding documents of the Rosicrucian movement, consisting of two manifestos dating to 1614 and 1615, are now generally considered by scholars to be fictional, likely a hoax perpetrated by university students. A longer document, *Chymical Wedding*, dated to 1616, is attributed to theology student Johann Valentin Andreae (1586–1654).

Nevertheless, latter-day Rosicrucians, such as Rudolf Steiner, have taken these documents seriously. According to Ziolkowski, "Whether we agree . . . or choose to take them as satires on prevailing alchemistic charlatanry and unrealistic utopian dreams, the fact remains that it was invented and not based on an existing cult." An actual historical group gave rise to the fiction. As psychiatrist C.G. Jung observes, "When no valid secrets really exist, mysteries are invented or contrived to which privileged initiates are admitted."

Initially received with enthusiasm, secret societies self-identifying as Rosicrucian were founded all over Europe. The movement declined in the 1620s due to internal conflicts among followers, as well as the rise of scientific rationalism and the decline of alchemy. But it was revived again in the eighteenth century and survives to this day among those who seek "occult wisdom."

The Ancient and Mystical Order Rosæ Crucis (AMORC), also known as the Rosicrucian Order, is the largest Rosicrucian organization in the world today. It has various lodges, chapters and other affiliated bodies throughout the globe, operating in nineteen different languages. According to their website, "AMORC's teachings cover what may be termed as the *Sacred Sciences*," revealing ideas from all the major philosophers, scientists, and even pseudoscientists — something for everyone.

One might compare the present-day turmoil in the early twenty-first century with that experienced in Europe at the time of the invention of Rosicrucianism. With the rise of irrational suspicion of science, accompanied by the decline of traditional religious systems, belief in magical and mystical movements is understandable. Secret societies promising occult wisdom may seem an attractive and reassuring outlet for the real and imaginary dangers of a world beset by competing ideologies and threats of environmental collapse, if not uncontrolled nuclear warfare in states with irrational leaders. — *May 2018*

103 The Madness of Occultism

In the early twentieth century there was a resurgence of occultism seen not only in Rosicrucianism but also in groups with believers in the Theosophy of Madame Blavatsky, Willam Wescott's Hermetic Order of the Golden Dawn, and the Anthroposophy of Rudolf Steiner. Ziolkowski identifies these as "surrogates for lost religious faith" associated with the rise of applied science and new technology. The search for meaning no longer found in Christian scripture was redirected away from Western materialism towards the "mystical East."

New manifestations of occult threats also surfaced at the beginning of the twentieth century. Ziolkowski's *Lure of the Arcane* devotes a chapter to the analysis of the famous anti-Semitic forgery *The Protocols of the Elders of Zion*, first published in Russia in 1903. The *Protocols* alleged a conspiracy by leaders of international Jewry to achieve world domination by infiltrating governments, controlling the press, acquiring financial control over economies and subverting culture. Although identified as a hoax nearly from the start, the work was nevertheless identified as genuine by anti-Semites such as Henry Ford in the US, who serialized it in printed media he controlled, and by Adolf Hitler, who quoted from it in *Mein Kampf*. In addition, the Nazi ideologue Alfred Rosenberg used it to formulate the official doctrine of the Third Reich, which became required reading in schools after the Nazis attained power in 1933.

Ziolkowski notes a curious similarity between the *Protocols* and the founding manifestos of Rosicrucianism, in that even though identified as elaborations of verified hoaxes, both continue to persist, with believers unwilling to accept evidence of their falsity. Anti-Semites today, still convinced of Jewish people's intentions of world domination, view the document as at least representative, if not authentic.

In the 1930s, the French literary celebrity Céline was a rabid anti-Semite. Working as a physician in poor areas around Paris does not excuse his having plagiarized snippets from the *Protocols*. During the occupation of France, he wrote letters to several collaborationist journals denouncing the Jews. After Germany's defeat in 1945, Céline fled to Denmark. France later claimed his extradition, and while the case was processed, he was imprisoned for more than a year. Named a collaborator, in 1950 he was convicted *in absentia* in France, sentenced to one year of imprisonment and declared a national disgrace. He was subsequently granted amnesty and returned to France in 1951.

Umberto Eco described the tendency for the individual to confound the fictional world as real, because imaginary worlds are often simpler and easier to comprehend than the real one. Eco cited the dreadful results that can occur when fiction is mistaken for truth, and the case of the *Protocols* clearly illustrates the outcome of the madness of occultism in the real world. — *June 2018*

104 Hell

As a psychiatrist, when interviewing a new referral, I always enquired about religious belief as part of the initial assessment, to help me understand how they perceived their world. While reading an essay about hell by Joseph Farrell in a recent issue of the *Times Literary Supplement*, I was reminded of one patient who described himself as being "in recovery" from Roman Catholicism, adding, "It takes more than twelve steps." Farrell's essay describes the effect in later life of being taught as a child about hell as a place of post-mortem retribution by God. In Calvinist and Roman Catholic education, hell is seen as an eternal punishment for sins committed during life.

Among small children, the concept of hell was intended to be literal, as described in the Book of Revelation in the New Testament and seen in later art and literature. Morbid depictions of the suffering of the damned in hell are on display in paintings by Hieronymus Bosch and other old masters, while St. Thomas Aquinas himself was said to have wondered "if the joys of the blessed in heaven would be heightened by the spectacle of the damned getting what they deserved." Part one of Dante's *Divine Comedy* describes detailed tortures inflicted upon varied sinners as appropriate to their individual sins, reminiscent of W.S. Gilbert's lyrics in *The Mikado*, "Let the punishment fit the crime."

Farrell's essay focuses on the literal meaning of hell as a place of divine retribution, and touches upon its lasting effect on those educated in Roman Catholic schools but who, as adults, have lost their faith. He notes that "a lapsed Catholic is someone who cannot altogether shake off a consciousness, if not quite a fear, of Hell and who, knowing they are at death's door, would call a priest, as an insurance policy."

Beyond its literal meaning, the idea of hell is also employed in a metaphorical manner. Jean-Paul Sartre wrote, "*L'enfer, c'est les autres*," in other words, "Hell is other people." More realistically, the cruelties of warfare and genocide are often characterized as hellish, an example of extreme situations meriting extreme terminology. Less intensively, we can all imagine particular situations as personal hells: one of mine might be being trapped in a deafeningly loud pop music concert with no means of escape, while others might feel the same way if subjected to an interminable Bruckner symphony in a closed concert hall with no possibility of leaving.

Purgatory and limbo are fascinating imaginary in-between states where the departed may reside before admission to heaven, like a waiting room for the soul. The Roman Catholic Church once used to sell first-class seats guaranteeing shorter wait times in purgatory, but that was cancelled following the objections of Martin Luther and others. Limbo is another matter (I first thought it was a genre of athletic Brazilian dance).

The word *limbo* derives from the Latin *limbus*, which means "edge or boundary." Limbo is a repository or warehouse for souls contaminated by "original sin," through no fault of their own, and unable to receive absolution. Medieval theologians further refined the concept as consisting of two separate sections. The Limbo of the Patriarchs, also known as the Limbo of the Fathers (*limbus patrum*), was seen as the temporary state for those who, despite the sins they may have committed, died in the friendship of God but could not enter heaven until redemption by Jesus Christ made it possible. The Limbo of Infants (*limbus infantium*) was the permanent status of the unbaptized who died in infancy, too young to have committed actual sins but not having been freed from original sin.

Sin, of course, is a religious concept, thought of as "the basic corrupting agent in the universe," according to theologian James M. Efird of Duke University. In the seventeenth century both Protestants and Catholics utilized the concept of sin in their struggles to account for the vicissitudes of living in an unstable society and in a world filled with death and destruction at every turn.

Although the theological connotations of sin are no longer universal, and primarily limited to religious believers, assigning blame for catastrophic misfortunes continues to persist. Global warming and its consequences increasingly render human society parlous, with the destruction of forests, industrial poisoning of the atmosphere, and the release of bound carbon by burning fossil fuels. These behaviours and their negative consequences are clearly the result of human action and may be thought of as not only androgenic but *peccatogenic*, meaning sin, not against a Christian god, but against nature, or Gaia. In mythology, Gaia is the ancestral mother of all life — the primal Mother Earth goddess. — Compiled from the essays "Peccatogenesis," *May 2020,* "Hell," Jan 2019, and "Limbo," *Jan 2019*

105 Abortion and Neonaticide

The only difference between abortion and neonaticide is that the former occurs before the event of childbirth and the latter afterward. Scientifically, there is no disputing the fact that human life begins with the fertilization of an egg by sperm and proceeds to pregnancy and birth through the process of intrauterine development. While miscarriage or spontaneous abortion may occur, due to chromosomal abnormality or other causes, and is common, the language employed to describe deliberate destruction of a living organism reflects the values of the user.

The ancient classical world commonly practised neonaticide by exposure, continuing this practice until the third century, when it was phased out with the rise of Christianity, whose believers thought an imaginary entity called a soul was possessed at conception by the new organism and supposedly persisted throughout life, only departing at the time of death. Both deliberate abortion and neonaticide were then characterized as sins, or according to Dr. Efird of the Divinity School at Duke University, "behaviours in opposition to God's benevolent purposes for His creation."

Arguments about the concept of *soul* inevitably become entangled with two different perspectives — the factual, or scientific, and the moral, or spiritual — and thus ethical principles are invoked when debating what, if anything, should be the role of society in facilitating or discouraging actions involving therapeutic abortion. Spontaneous abortion is involuntary and, though perceived as a loss if a wanted child fails in its fetal development, is not considered an ethical matter. Neonaticide is often, but not always, rejected as an option for an unwanted live birth, and unwanted infants may find their way to care and eventual adoption.

That leaves therapeutic abortion as a subject of controversy, wherein one side, usually religious, considers it to be a sin tantamount to neonaticide, and the other regarding it as an appropriate medical procedure to preserve the physical or mental health of a woman who, for whatever reason, has an unwanted pregnancy. The difference is one of values, not of science and reason. Unwanted pregnancies can be avoided by means of contraception, but that's another issue. — *Oct 2020*

106 Impure Thoughts

An essay of author Mohsin Hamid with the title "Impure Thoughts" appeared in the *Guardian Review* in early 2018. In Christian moral teachings, impure thoughts are usually identified as arising from erotic fantasies and are characterized as a venial sin in Roman Catholicism. The older Hebrew concept of impurity is primarily associated instead with behaviour, the rites and rituals required to cleanse a person from an impure action. The word itself implies a dichotomy with purity, the latter usually perceived as something positive or desired when compared to a negative or unfavourable alternative. Hamid suggests that one may view impurity differently, indeed, as a desirable and necessary component of ourselves.

Considered as an inborn personal trait, the concept of racial purity contributes to social conflict and political instability. Under the racial laws in the Third Reich, millions died. Combined with xenophobia, the danger to a stable society from proponents of racial purity may be disastrous. Facilitated these days by social media and confounded by appeals to "free speech," populist opportunists in many countries worldwide employ nativism with racial purity to achieve and retain power. However, evolutionary mixing has facilitated adaptation to change, while fixed pure states cannot adjust and are therefore more liable to succumb to environmental variance. Mammals survived the cretaceous extinction — dinosaurs didn't.

This dichotomy of pure/impure is also utilized in commerce. Banal examples of advertising slogans illustrate this: Ivory Soap claims to be 99.44 percent "pure." Of course, this leaves one to wonder what constitutes the remaining 0.56 percent — shit? Or consider the claim that Kokanee beer, or even some bottled water, is "purely of glacial origin." As someone who has observed the disgusting discharge of glacial runoff, the suggestion of glacial water somehow being "pure" is absurd.

Hamid concludes his essay by noting, "We are all impure, but because many of us deny our impurity, those who are most obviously impure among us require allies. And one of their most important allies is literature." Writing. Reading. When we are sitting alone, reading a book, something profoundly strange occurs. We are by ourselves; we are only ourselves. And yet, we contain within us the thoughts of another person — the writer. We become something manifestly impure, a being with the thoughts of two beings inside it. As Hamid notes, "A reader, in the moment of reading, experiences a pooling of consciousness that blurs the painstakingly constructed boundaries of the unitary self." — *May 2018*

107 Slavery, Progress and Human Rights

The Universal Declaration of Human Rights was proclaimed by the United Nations in 1948 as a common standard for all individuals and governments, a commendable wish list, often cited but only intermittently respected. Essentially an abstract social construct reflecting values of a particular age rather than a measurable or observable feature of human beings in general, it is as intangible as the soul (though not based on theology).

The practice of slavery, or ownership of another person, is ancient and was considered a normal feature of both Western classical society and non-Western cultures, such as pre-Columbian Mesoamerica. Slavery is depicted in both the Old and New Testaments. Slaves, usually obtained from those defeated in war, were regarded as chattel, to be bought, sold or indeed inherited, and moral teachings often enjoined masters to be kind to their slaves. Slaves could be freed, and many were, creating a social class of freedmen, a title still being employed today as a surname.

The United States of America was created by slavers, among others, and the fine words of its Declaration of Independence cynically assert a list of "self-evident" human rights. Their terrible nineteenth-century civil war may have been won by abolitionists, but the values of black slavery were never extinguished, and a current fascist government promotes the denial of full equality to non-white racial minorities.

It is a manifestation of the Whiggish belief in steady progress that blinds us to the understanding that oppression of "human rights" has been a usual characteristic of society as far back in history as you like. There is no guarantee that in the future, slavery will not again surface in one form or another. For a dystopic but believable fictional account of a possible future with this social arrangement, one need look no further than Margaret Atwood's *Handmaid's Tale* and its sequel, *The Testaments.* — *Feb 2020*

108 Canadian Museum of Human Rights

We celebrate things that are associated with the values of the society in which we live, like the absence of slavery and the gradual acceptance of sexual and gender minorities among us. Moreover, we disparage historical events like discrimination and genocide that in our society are considered abhorrent by most educated citizens. It seems fitting and proper to formally designate exhibitions and civic holidays that uphold these values.

Atonement or expressions of regret for past behaviour is considered appropriate by many, but not all, citizens, and one can cite examples such as lynching, judicial murder and the deliberate extinction of minorities as a consistent feature of recorded human history from ancient times to the present day. Oppression of racial and religious minorities hasn't been uncommon. Although some adherents of Christianity deplore it, referencing the teachings of Jesus, others who call themselves Christian seemingly endorse it.

As an abstraction, the concept of human rights is difficult to pin down other than in law, wherein specific behaviours are explicitly defined in terms of violation of principles. But difficulty arises when in practice social groups differ on what should be considered a right. Minority groups often complain of repression, appealing to this abstract idea for redress.

The Canadian Museum of Human Rights in Winnipeg, Manitoba, has been controversial from the beginning, with disputes over how much floor space should be allotted among competing groups dealing with real or perceived oppression. The very idea of dedicating a museum to human rights in which the displays are devoted to human wrongs, such as genocide and the oppression of racial, religious and sexual minorities, was bound to elicit conflict about political and cultural issues. The very concept of such an institution can be viewed as a metaphorical can of worms, in which the attempt to improve something actually makes it worse.

In this sense, one can regard the title of the museum as a euphemism: displaying the history of oppression, whether religious, political, economic, racial or sexual, is not a monument to human *rights* but a denouncement of human *wrongs*, facilitating controversy among social groups over who is the more oppressed and more deserving of having the misdeeds against them on display.

Euphemisms are constructed to avoid unpleasant truths. Displaying photographic evidence and other documents exhibiting failures to respect human rights in a museum for the edification of the public may be commendable, and conflicts over display space are understandable, but the institution should logically be called the Canadian Museum of Human Wrongs. — *Aug 2020*

109 Greed

Words written millennia ago in the book Ecclesiastes, from the Hebrew Bible, affirm the futility of human desires. Railing against the universal urge to acquire ever more, then, as now, the despair of one who perceives this endless wanting is scorned contemptuously as useless — the world goes on as always. "There is nothing new under the sun," and desire is "meaningless! Meaningless! . . . Utterly meaningless! Everything is meaningless."

Most of us, of course, are not philosophers, and simply go about our daily routines without reflecting on considerations such as epistemology or ultimate questions about life and death or even our own futures. But the lust after money appears nearly universal among humankind and is described as the "root of all evil" by St. Paul in 1 Timothy 6:10. Greed, an undue desire to acquire or possess more than one needs, appears to be a persistent human trait not limited to issues of political economy. Examples of greed are present throughout history, since at least the eighteenth century BCE, as exemplified in the myth of King Midas, who was magically cursed by all he touched turning into gold.

On May 18, 1986, stockbroker Ivan Boesky famously defended greed in a commencement address at UC Berkeley's School of Business Administration, in which he averred, "Greed is all right, by the way. I want you to know that. I think greed is healthy. You can be greedy and still feel good about yourself." Practising what he preached, Boesky later received a prison sentence of three and a half years and was fined $100 million for illegal marketing of stocks.

Boesky's assertion had its roots in the well-known opinion of the eighteenth-century Scottish philosopher and economist Adam Smith, who described those engaging in selfishness as being led by an "invisible hand" and benefitting others. Even so, Smith admitted that profit-earners "have generally an interest to deceive and even to oppress the public," and noted that government should enact legislation to control profiteering, as was the case of Boesky.

The destabilizing and negative personal consequences of greed are implied in the warning of St. Paul in the New Testament, who wrote in his first letter to Timothy, "Those who desire to be rich fall into temptation, into a snare, into many senseless and hurtful desires that plunge men into ruin and destruction. For the love of money is the root of all evils . . ." In comparison, the influential English historian and Christian socialist Richard Tawney wrote *Religion and the Rise of Capitalism* in 1926, exploring the relationship between the Protestant sects and acquisitive economic action in the seventeenth and eighteenth centuries.

Laura E. Alexander, an American scholar in the field of religious studies, cites theologian Reinhold Niebuhr in positing human anxiety as one possible source of greed, arising from existential anxiety associated with the conscious awareness of limitations inherent in the human condition, which leads to a drive to attain certainty by hoarding. But then we inevitably end up harming others in an insatiable quest to amass more for ourselves.

We see normalization of greed in the proliferation of "business schools," quasi-academic degree-awarding institutions usually associated with legitimate universities and often endowed by wealthy philanthropists. These "MBA mills," devoted to teaching students how to make profits, tend to be intellectually fraudulent and foster a culture of greed. Their message is that capitalism is inevitable and that the technologies for running it are a science.

Adam Smith was well aware that wages tend to be minimized in order to maximize profit and felt that endless growth would be the only alternative to endless poverty. We now realize that the consequence of this will be the destruction of the environment with global warming, accompanied by the collapse of civilization.

The American gospel promoting business has conquered the world, even the former Communist countries, with a vengeance. China's President

Xi pretends that his version of state capitalism is "socialism with Chinese characteristics," but it's the same sun shining on Asia as on Europe and the Americas, under which nothing is new, just the same old promotion of enrichment and greed, gussied up in a different vocabulary.

Even Masonic lodges and service clubs like Rotary International tout their promotion of good works while their adherents attend to advance their business opportunities. Advertisements promoting pharmaceutical products are couched in language suggesting their competitive effectiveness, but the information is inevitably designed primarily to enhance sales, and thus the profits of the manufacturer.

The 1936 book *How to Win Friends and Influence People* by Dale Carnegie remains a best-seller today. There's nothing wrong with making friends, but the implication in the title is that friendship can influence people in such a way as to improve sales, increase profit and lead to greater wealth. You too can have a solid gold toilet for your bottom's line. Cartoonist R. Crumb's sage Mr. Natural was asked by a desperate seeker of truth, "What does it all MEAN?" In the spirit of the writer of Ecclesiastes, he replied, "Don't mean SHEE-IT." — Compiled from the essays "Ecclesiastes and R. Crumb," *May 2018*, and "Greed," *May 2019*

110 The Dismal Science & Its House Organ

"The dismal science" is a derogatory name for economics, or the ups and downs of financial markets, coined by the Victorian historian Thomas Carlyle in the nineteenth century. The *Economist* is an English-language weekly magazine-format newspaper founded in 1843, with a circulation today of some 1.5 million copies, about half of which are sold in the US. It's a neoliberal newsmagazine for intelligent and mainly wealthy readers, like corporate executives and upper level government officials; tellingly, two-thirds of its American readers earn over $100,000 annually.

In the nineteenth century Karl Marx called the *Economist* "the European organ of the aristocracy of finance," and more recently John Ralston Saul termed it "the bible of the corporate executive." Its editorial policy has constantly supported conservative politicians in the UK and US, and American wars in Vietnam and Iraq.

Cajoled by a friend to consider subscribing, I bought and read a copy, finding the lead article by the editor set the tone by identifying the current American president, Donald Trump, as "the leader of the free world" (though noting his many negative traits). This is typical for the magazine, politics being secondary to following the behaviour of the financial markets.

Targeted readership, as suggested by advertising content, included not only the usual luxury cars and pricey watches, but thirteen full-page ads for "wealth management" services, along with educational programs from universities promoting business degrees, promising career advancement, investment seminars and similar schemes of lucrative opportunities.

Among the 146 pages of text, only six were devoted to "culture," seven to "science and technology," and one half-page to climate change. The remaining 132.5 pages were concerned with economic issues and forecasts, a country-by-country review of GDP and discussions on maximizing profits. Negative reporting about economic adversaries such as China were as expected, and rather ominously, there was one full-page display of clear propagandist paean to the dissident Chinese Buddhist sect Falun Gong.

In fairness — throwing a bone to the dog, as it were — there was a full-page essay by the then-leader of the British Labour Party, Jeremy Corbyn, expressing his alternate vision of society. But apart from this single contribution, the entire publication was focused on how to become and remain wealthy.

The organ of the dismal science portends, fittingly, a dismal future for mankind and the planet. The single half-page relating to climate change, buried amid the remainder of the publication, clearly illustrated the frenzied and uncontrollable rush towards social collapse and the impending destruction of the planetary environment motivated by human greed, facilitated by capitalism and promoted by its house organ.

I do not expect to subscribe to the *Economist*. — *Jan 2019*

III Wealth Management

In a recent essay in the *Times Literary Supplement*, Julia Bell described a short visit to the island of Jersey, a UK Crown Dependency in the English Channel off the coast of Normandy. Like a number of other UK possessions, Jersey is known as a tax haven, wherein financial assets may be concealed from tax authorities by wealthy clientele. It is officially designated in the UK as an Offshore Financial Centre and not subject to rules and regulations pertaining to financial entities within the country.

As Bell wandered around the centre of the island's capital of Saint Helier, she saw no signs of the promised picturesque fishing port portrayed in colourful tourist brochures, but rather a range of modern commercial offices "for banks and lawyers and insurance companies and hedge funds and wealth managers." The island was said to house an estimated $5 billion in assets per square mile, "a piggy bank and exchange mechanism, connected to the City of London, yet beyond its reach."

Cited in Bell's essay is the recent book *Capital Without Borders* (2016) by Brooke Harrington of the Copenhagen Business School. Harrington trained as a wealth manager to become familiar with the profession before interviewing wealth managers worldwide. Some were characterized positively as "income defense providers," while others were "clearly criminal." One manager described his role as resembling "social work for the rich."

I have but a limited experience of the profession, with my small amount of savings squirrelled away in a mutual fund administered by a national banking institution to supplement my income from Old Age Security and the Canada Pension Plan. Annual meetings are booked with what was once known modestly as a financial adviser, now ostentatiously as a wealth manager.

A form letter recently appeared in my inbox, supposedly from an individual describing herself as "EVP and Global Chief Marketing, Citizenship and Customer Experience Officer" of a well-known national bank. Obviously composed by someone that doesn't know me personally, it addresses me in boilerplate text with only my first name and middle initial. It quasi-sincerely asks for "feedback," alleging that "we'd love to hear from you," adding mock-caringly, "it means a lot to us."

The first item asked was to rate one's "exceptional experience" associated with the bank on a scale ranging from one (not at all) to ten (strongly agree). I honestly had to rate it as only a one, because I do not consider annual consultations to be exceptional experiences of any sort, more like a necessary duty, perhaps akin to visiting one's accountant or dentist.

I certainly had no complaint about the quality of the service provided by the financial institution and found the provider to be pleasant, friendly and helpful. Nevertheless, using the phrase *wealth management* grates and suggests a whiff of offshore corruption, reflecting the greed and secrecy of our capitalist world so visible in Jersey. — *Apr 2019*

112 Property Is Theft

Pierre-Joseph Proudhon was a nineteenth-century French politician and the founder of mutualist philosophy. He was the first person to declare himself an anarchist and is considered by many to be the father of anarchism. In his book *What Is Property?* Proudhon wrote the phrase "property is theft," referring to the landowner or capitalist class, who he believed stole the profits from labourers. For Proudhon, the capitalist's employee was "subordinated, exploited: his permanent condition is one of obedience."

Proudhon also called himself a socialist, but he opposed state ownership of capital goods in favour of ownership by workers themselves. This makes him one of the first theorists of libertarian socialism. Here lie the roots of the cooperative, or co-op, movement that continues to exist to this day, and to which I belong for the purchase of local food and fuel.

Many live in cooperative apartment buildings, while others may rent as part of a cooperative arrangement. Although some may be tied to the idea of ownership and choose to reside in condominiums, they usually only pretend to own. In reality, they pay monthly fees towards maintenance and upkeep, in addition to taxes and insurance. And if there is a mortgage, the residence could be defined, according to *The Cynic's Dictionary*, as "a private residential unit that re-creates the ambiance of suburban tract housing without the nuisance of private lawns and gardens; a domicile favoured especially by young professionals and retired folks, who apparently don't mind paying substantial monthly fees on property they already own."

For those who dwell in private property they possess through inheritance, there is an apt verse by American poet Carl Sandburg, from his 1936 collection *The People Yes*:

"Get off this estate."
"What for?"
"Because it's mine."
"Where did you get it?"
"From my father."
"Where did he get it?"
"From his father."
"And where did he get it?"
"He fought for it."
"Well, I'll fight you for it." — *Feb 2019*

113 Marx, St. Paul and Human Nature

May 5, 2018, marked the 200th birthday of Karl Marx, whose analysis of capitalism inspired at least two centuries of revolution and millenarian projects for economic reform that ended badly, with the death of millions. The recent book by Yuri Slezkine, *The House of Government*, is basically an account of the history of Bolshevism in Russia, from student revolutionaries in the late nineteenth century through the successful November Revolution of 1917 and the exercise of power up to 1939. It does so through a focus on the residence built across the Moscow River for government functionaries and their families. Slezkine's book is a study in eschatology — the creation of an apocalyptic cult arising from the writings of Marx and his theory of class struggle against the evils of capitalism as key to the formation of a just society.

Writing about history, Marx famously quipped, "History repeats itself, first as tragedy, second as farce." A clever *bon mot* to be sure, and susceptible to a variety of interpretations, one of which seems particularly relevant in the history of the fallout from his theories, beginning with the Bolshevik revolution and followed by Lenin, Stalin, the Chinese Communist victory in 1949 and Mao Zedong, all of whom tried to impose a form of utopia, which led to monopolized dictatorial power, starvation and tragedy. In each case, the farce was realized through the personality cult of a leader, followed by the eventual resurgence of the market, as seen in the uncontrolled crony capitalism of Russia and now mercantilism in China.

Marxism and Christianity are contrasting ideologies, both displaying the limitations of ideologically based attempts to deal with the imperfections of human nature, and both leading to unhappy consequences. Which brings us to St. Paul, who endorsed the apocalyptic eschatological mindset of his age, of a Jewish sect based on the teachings of Jesus of Nazareth. Paul began to preach that Jesus was the Jewish Messiah and the Son of God. Approximately half of the book of Acts deals with Paul's life and works, and thirteen of the twenty-seven books in the New Testament have traditionally been attributed to Paul. Christianity not only prospered in the face of Roman oppression but eventually became the state religion of the empire under Emperor Constantine.

The human propensity to accumulate wealth (i.e., power) seems to be the source of crime and war, and may be seen as the fuel driving competitive behaviour. This is visible today in activities from team sports to the stock market, and manifested in the rampant cheating in the former to achieve first place among rivals to the manipulation of the latter to maximize profit.

The underlying problem, evidently, is not simply a matter of religious belief or economic system but a fundamental characteristic of human nature, the drive to be number one among other teams, or to own the highest building in a city, or to be elected to the highest office in a democracy. Marx wrote sagely, "The past lies like a nightmare upon the present." — *May 2018*

114 Polybius and Anacyclosis

The study of governments is termed political science, though some academics dispute the use of the word *science* in this context and prefer to say political studies. Whatever the terminology, there are many different systems used to organize the structure of society among the many nations that share the planet on which we dwell. The ancient Greek historian Polybius (200–118 BCE) is credited with the suggestion of a cyclical sequence of forms of government, termed *anacyclosis*, described in his *Histories* covering the Hellenistic period (264–146 BCE).

Polybius's sequence of anacyclosis proceeds in the following order: 1) monarchy, 2) kingship, 3) tyranny, 4) aristocracy, 5) oligarchy, 6) democracy and 7) ochlocracy (mob rule). He suggests that the state begins as a form of primitive monarchy and subsequently transitions from monarchy into kingship. Political power will pass by hereditary succession to the children of the king, who will then abuse their authority for their own gain. This represents the degeneration of kingship into tyranny. Some of the more influential and powerful men of the state will then overthrow the tyrant; this is the rise of aristocracy, or rule by the few.

As with the descendants of kings, however, political influence will pass to the descendants of the aristocrats, who will repeat the pattern and begin to abuse their power and influence. This represents the decline of aristocracy and the beginning of oligarchy. By this stage in the political evolution of the state, the people will eventually decide to revolt. At this point in the cycle is the emergence of democracy, the beginning of rule by the many.

In the same way that the descendants of kings and aristocrats abused their political status, so too will the descendants of democrats, vying among themselves to accumulate wealth and power. Accordingly, democracy degenerates into ochlocracy, literally, "mob rule." In an ochlocracy, according to Polybius, the people of the state will become corrupted, and developing a sense of entitlement, become conditioned to accept the pandering of demagogues. Eventually, the state will be engulfed in chaos, and the competing claims of demagogues will culminate in a single (perhaps sometimes virtuous) demagogue claiming absolute power, bringing the state full-circle back to monarchy.

Although Polybius was writing about instability in the Roman Republic in antiquity, his observations resonate with the history of nation states in Europe, and in the modern world one can readily identify systems in these varied stages. The Kim dynasty in North Korea comes to mind, as does the ascendancy of Trump in the US.

No millenarian end is envisaged in this sequence, only continual changes taking place among the constituent societies. We can expect the repeating cycle to continue ad infinitum. Without either utopian expectations or a dystopia, it seems realistic, though bleak. Certainly not the expectation of neoliberalism. — *Sept 2019*

115 Exceptionalism

American exceptionalism, traditionally acclaimed by its citizens, has been a plank of the US Republican Party's platform since 2012. Their current platform, adopted in 2016, defines its exceptionalism as "the notion that our ideas and principles as a nation give us a unique place of moral leadership," affirming that the US therefore must "retake its natural position as leader of the free world."

In German the phrase "leader of the free world" is written *Führer der freien Welt*, which brings to mind the formal title of Adolf Hitler as *der Führer* of the Third Reich. With the American presidency now in the hands of a fascist wannabe dictator, it seems appropriate to call him a leader as well, although in this case not of the so-called free world, but only of the US as it crumbles into the dust of has-been empires.

The phrase *free world* is a leftover from the Cold War of the twentieth century, in which the Americans and their allies waged an ideological battle against Marxist states such as the USSR, China and others, on the grounds of evident human rights abuses but also of different economic systems, specifically capitalism versus socialism. The issue of personal freedoms was thus entangled with economic values; asserting leadership of the former was blended with the latter. Freedom from political persecution became mixed with financial exploitation, as Americans boasted of their freedom to create wealth.

Several years ago in the *Guardian Weekly*, Oliver Burkeman wrote an interesting column whose title, referring to the American president as "the leader of the free world," I found offensive. I wrote to him, and in reply he apologized, and to my relief said he was not responsible for the headline. Fair enough, I thought, but not long afterward, a second opinion piece, this time by American writer Michael D'Antonio, used the phrase in another *Gaurdian Weekly* article. I wrote to the editor politely, strongly objecting to the usage, and received no reply. I haven't seen "leader of the free world" used since in that periodical to describe the American president, so perhaps my complaint had some effect.

"American exceptionalism" has now become a sobriquet of mockery, with a malignant sociopath as the chief executive of a failed state, once admired for its democratic values but now both pitied and reviled by other countries for its racism, xenophobia, official disregard for science, devotion to self-promotion and capitalist pursuit of wealth by gangsters in control of government. America is indeed exceptional. — *May 2020*

116 The Dawn Watch

The Dawn Watch: Joseph Conrad in a Global World, by Harvard history professor Maya Jasanoff, is a recent biography of one of the greatest writers of the twentieth century. With dozens of illustrations and ten maps, it illustrates the voyages made by Conrad during his twenty years at sea before he settled in England and began his literary career (in his third language).

The first quarter of the biography, with the section heading "Nation," explores Conrad's family background and early years in Polish-speaking Eastern Europe. Part two, with the section heading "Ocean," revolves around Conrad's memories of two decades at sea, as portrayed in novels and stories like *The Nigger of the Narcissus* and *Typhoon.*

It is in the third and fourth sections, with headings "Civilization" and "Empire," that our attention is drawn to issues of humanity and geopolitics. We perceive Conrad's creative writing to be not merely of adventure but reflecting fundamental social concerns of his world that remain relevant to our own dysfunctional times. The American Vietnam War film *Apocalypse*

Now has been regarded by cinephiles as paradigmatic of Conrad's novella *Heart of Darkness*, set in nineteenth-century Belgian Congo.

The early-twentieth-century novel *Nostromo*, set in an imaginary Latin American country, eerily anticipates American dominance — "we shall run the world's business whether the world likes it or not" — expressing a sentiment that was feared among those in the British Empire upon considering their future. In *Nostromo*, Conrad not only presents a plot involving commercialism and greed but alludes to the shift of power from Europe to America, predicting, "No war will be waged for an idea. Money was everything." Future prospects for the world were anticipated not in terms of cooperation and harmony but as the inescapable fact that "material interests" would ensure the continuation of imperialism, whether or not it was called an empire.

The twentieth century saw the United States assume a dominant role, as had the UK a century earlier. Now with the collapse of the American state into a fascist kakistocracy led by a narcissistic demagogue, new imperialism is arising in East Asia, manifested in the rise of state mercantilism in China after abandoning the Marxist agenda of Mao Zedong.

In the epilogue, Jasanoff travels to the Congo to experience Conrad's Africa and reflects, "Today's hearts of darkness are to be found in other places where civilizing missions serve as covers for exploitation. . . . The material interests he centered in the United States emanate today as much from China." Marx may have been right about economic materialism, but human greed replaces his concept of class struggle. It's a good time now to reread Conrad, starting perhaps with *Nostromo*. — *June 2018*

117 Patriotism

"Patriotism is the last refuge of a scoundrel," wrote early lexicographer Samuel Johnson. Many more quotes on patriotism can be easily accessed with an internet search, and almost all of them are negativistic and disparaging. This should come as no surprise, however, for the celebration of patriotism seems to be almost universally scorned by those who have reflected on the subject, from the ancients to contemporary writers. This devaluation of patriotism is especially marked in writers who have had personal experience of warfare.

Yet politicians continue to extol the supposed virtues of patriots, commemorating the deeds of valour of a nation's "heroes." Like most

American schoolchildren, I was taught to be patriotic about the country of my birth, but I recognized this as deception after becoming aware of history and politics while an undergraduate at university in my late teens. Some say they would feel uncomfortable to be devoid of allegiance to any government, but for me, having no nationality created an extraordinary sense of freedom and relief. I was choosing my own destiny, refusing to obey the commands of old men sending away youth to kill or be killed in order to preserve their own sense of power.

The American spy Nathan Hale, who was hanged by British troops during the Revolutionary War, famously said on the scaffold, "I only regret that I have but one life to lose for my country." This epitome of patriotism is praised in history classes in the US to this day, but it is never accompanied by the description of those promoting the Revolutionary War, supposedly on behalf of liberty and human rights. Thomas Jefferson and his lot were slave-owning planters, spouting phony praises of equality to induce patriotism among the gullible masses in order to maintain their own status of wealth and ownership of African slaves.

So it has been throughout history. In all wars, abandoning reason in favour of unthinking patriotism leads to military conscription and the death of millions. To not be a patriot is seen by many as shameful and disreputable, but should rather merit praise from anyone understanding the origin and consequences of unthinking obedience to those in power.
— *Mar 2020*

118 What Is to Be Done?

What Is to Be Done? is the title of an 1863 novel by the Russian writer Nikolai Chernyshevsky, who agitated for the revolutionary overthrow of the autocracy. Tolstoy also used the phrase in his pacifist polemics, as did Lenin while formulating his social revolutionary agenda. The phrase also comes to mind when reflecting on the current situation in a neighbouring country, many of whose citizens are appalled by the machinations of their leader, a clinically obvious psychopathic narcissist.

The anticipated general election will either confirm his rule or see him replaced with a contender from a different political party. But his electoral defeat could be avoided by manipulation of voting or spurious accusations of fraudulence. Bound by an eighteenth-century constitution, the majority is unable to legally remove the would-be fascist dictator from office, and the only other branch of government capable of removing him has proven unwilling to do so. As he is surrounded by his sycophants, a palace revolt appears unlikely, and unless he is successfully voted out, the only alternatives seem to be limited to revolution, assassination, or both.

Revolution would require armed force, and only the army is sufficiently organized to mount a coup d'état against their commander-in-chief, as did the Argentinian army in September 1955, when they overthrew the dictatorship of Perón. A transitional government could then be formed to administer the state and hopefully prepare for a democratic election. Risky, because once in power, the generals tend to stay in power.

Assassination would be difficult because of the praetorian guard, or Secret Service, sworn to protect the life of the leader. Claus von Stauffenberg tried to assassinate Adolf Hitler on July 20, 1944, but failed. In any event the Hitler cult or Nazi party would have continued even if he had been successful, as no doubt would the Trump cult if he were assassinated. Nicolae Ceauşescu, who was successfully overthrown and then shot in Romania, is an example of combined revolution and assassination that successfully ended the dictatorial communist regime in Romania in 1989.

These are interesting times, as the old Chinese curse suggests, and it indeed will be interesting to see how the political turmoil in the neighbouring country unfolds in these days of viral pandemic. What is to be done remains to be seen. — *Apr 2020*

119 Swimming in Argentina

On the wall of my study in the Bear Cave I have long displayed a beautiful image of the Islas Malvinas, known outside of the great nation of Argentina as the Falkland Islands. The large colour photograph, from orbiting satellite LANDSAT from a height of 920 km, was provided by the Argentine National Commission of Space Research.

In April 1982 Argentine forces occupied the British Falkland Islands, over which Argentina had long claimed sovereignty. After a brief war, a British task force retook the islands. The conflict lasted seventy-four days and ended with an Argentine surrender on 14 June, returning the islands to British control. In total 649 Argentine military personnel, 255 British military personnel, and three Falkland Islanders died during the hostilities.

Earlier, in 1976, following a coup against Isabel Perón, the armed forces formally exercised power through a junta. These de facto dictators hunted down any kind of suspected political dissident and anyone believed to be associated with socialism or contrary to the plan of neoliberal economic policies. About 30,000 people disappeared, many of whom could not be formally reported as missing due to the nature of state terrorism.

The targets were students, militants, trade unionists, writers, journalists, artists and anyone suspected to be a left-wing activist, including Peronist guerrillas. The "disappeared" (victims of kidnapping, torture and murder, whose bodies were disappeared by the military government) included those thought to be politically or ideologically a threat to the military junta, even vaguely, and they were killed in an attempt by the junta to silence the social and political opposition.

A method generally understood to eliminate those opposing the regime was supplied by the Argentine Air Force: throwing the victims from on high, living or dead, into the waters of the broad Rio de la Plata estuary of the Paraná and Uruguay Rivers. The practice was cynically referred to as "taking them swimming."

Democracy was eventually restored in 1983, but the reputation of the military was significantly debased. Reflecting on this history today, I removed the photograph and replaced it with a print by Yukon artist Jim Robb, showing the skeleton of a dead gold miner in his cabin, surrounded by bags of gold, with the caption "Got 'er made at last." — *Jan 2020*

120 The Herod Solution

The Massacre of the Innocents is the biblical account of infanticide by Herod the Great, the Roman-appointed King of the Jews. According to the Gospel of Matthew, Herod ordered the execution of all young male children in the vicinity of Bethlehem, so as to avoid the loss of his throne to a newborn King of the Jews, whose birth had been announced to him by the Magi.

The story's first appearance in any source other than the Gospel of Matthew is in the apocryphal Protoevangelium of James (c. 150 CE). The first non-Christian reference to the massacre is recorded four centuries later by Macrobius. Contemporary biblical scholars contend that Matthew's purpose was to present Jesus as the Messiah.

In the twenty-first century, violent behaviour by young males guarantees robust media coverage. Whenever there is an outrage, such as an exceedingly rare school shooting by a disaffected youth or a public episode of indiscriminate murderous rage, the assailant is almost always a young male. Following such events and the inevitable prayers and consolations, the question always arises about what to do to prevent these episodes. In the US, with its absurdly permissive constitutional right to own firearms, the answer is usually demands for greater gun control.

But the problem is more general, for in the UK, with restrictive laws about gun possession, violent youth have turned to using knives. Elsewhere, motor vehicles have been used to indiscriminately attack strangers. A recent episode in peaceful Victoria, Canada, featured a youth running amok beating pedestrians with a stick.

Crowds of enraged young men are regularly seen in news reports of political protests in the Middle East. It is inevitably young men, rarely young women. The underlying problem is not so much in access to lethal weapons but in the male brain. The "wiring" of the male brain, however accomplished, perhaps developed as an evolutionary means of asserting dominance ("survival of the fittest"). We don't know the reason and can only speculate about causes, but the effects are obvious and socially destructive: take away their guns and they'll come at you with knives. Take away their knives, they will beat you with clubs.

In the spirit of Jonathan Swift's ironic essay *A Modest Proposal*, one approach to the problem of young male violence might be that of King Herod, but that is hardly realistic. An alternative may be the controlled media in mainland China, where the official news agency, Xinhua, only reports what the Party deems appropriate for the public to know. That is not really a solution, for Uighurs still managed to mount a murderous assault with knives, randomly killing at the railway station in Kunming in 2014, in spite of a managed press. And doesn't a free press necessarily foment increased male violence because of publicity?

If the underlying problem arises from male brain neuroanatomy, the Herod Solution would not eliminate violence any more than a managed press. There may be no solution, but social stability entails finding a balance between the extremes of total state control and absolute freedom of action. Some countries like Finland, or perhaps Canada, seem to have approached this ideal, but the poison of demagoguery persists at both extremes, facilitated and amplified by social media and its glorifications of violence, leading to antisocial behaviour. — *May 2018*

121 Trust and Truth in Journalism

Swedish physician Hans Rosling died last year. His book *Factfulness* was published posthumously, and an edited excerpt was printed recently in the *Guardian Weekly*. He suggests that the generally negative world view fostered by news media should be understood as a function of journalism. Not necessarily "fake news," but selection is always an issue in the mass media, and the pressure to present what sells and captures the attention of readers is undeniably the prime determiner of content.

Crime, disasters — both natural and man-made — and political scandals make the headlines, and headlines sell papers. What is the source of this pressure?

The essential function of newspapers in our capitalist society is to make a profit for the owners, and only secondarily to inform and educate the reading or viewing public. The Bolsheviks understood this well when they named their official newspaper *Pravda* (*Truth*), though here the motive was not financial but ideological. Calling propaganda truth is but Orwellian newspeak.

In any case, the result appears to be tainted either by money or ideology. Social media isn't much different, readily facilitating the diffusion of information, reliable or otherwise, to vast numbers of consumers. And these consumers become customers, with the harvesting of data and its provision to merchants seeking to maximize profit by focusing on the interests of a cohort of potential buyers.

Some would call this cynical, others realistic. But the love of money is the prime motivation, and the result is what Rosling calls "the over dramatic worldview." He reminds us that "the media and activists rely on drama to grab your attention, that negative stories are more dramatic than positive ones, and how simple it is to construct a story of crisis from a temporary dip pulled out of context."

I asked a Chinese friend what he thought of print journalism in his country and he replied, "They only tell you what they want you to know." The official Chinese news agency is called Xinhua, which literally means "newspeak." Like its Soviet predecessor and model, it may as well be called Pravda.

A reliable source of information these days is the *Conversation*, an independent, not-for-profit media outlet that uses content sourced from the academic and research community. Launched in the UK almost five years ago, "with a vision of creating a daily diet of news analysis by academic experts," this was to be a new type of journalism by researchers, supported by a team of professional editors. Not being driven either by financial gain or an official ideology, the *Conversation* appears to be a trustworthy source of information in these days of so-called fake news. — *May 2020*

122 Curses

A friend in the UK wrote me consolingly today: "You need nice things to think about, like how lucky you are to live in a country like Canada. Unlike us, who, along with the US and Russia, are among the biggest economies on earth and are also the countries with the worst death tolls from Covid-19. The UK is now officially the second worst in the world. Why? Because those countries have the worst leaders. And the most developed small countries have the fewest deaths, like New Zealand, Canada and Australia. Why? Because at least two of them have good leaders. Think about it. Humanity is cursed."

Thinking about that opinion provoked reflection on the idea of a curse. Consider the curse of war: Tolstoy's great novel *War and Peace* argued against the "great man" theory of history, and his twentieth-century fellow Russian writer and thinker Vasily Grossman echoed these thoughts in his magisterial *Life and Fate*, a novel based on the battle for Stalingrad in 1942, wherein ideology is singled out as the villain behind the misery of man's inhumanity to man.

Beyond these literary examples we can think more generally of the underlying cause of human misery as arising from a psychological or cultural drive of competition to be number one, be it a matter of political power or simply greed.

It is a biological fact of life, though, this ubiquitous drive to get the most, obvious in the competitive struggle among plants to obtain the greatest amount of sunshine, and in animal predators to secure sufficient food to allow growth and reproduction.

Human competition is found everywhere, most blatantly in athletic games, in the financial marketplace, in political struggles and in academic disputation. The pathological narcissisms of Donald Trump and Boris Johnson reflect this universal tendency among living creatures to become number one among others, slyly disguised in the US constitution as "life, liberty and the pursuit of happiness."

In *Civilization and Its Discontents*, Freud wrote that in the last century, "the inclination to aggression is an original, self-subsisting instinctual disposition in man," affirming the existence of a universal competitive drive as accounting for the personal and social miseries we see around us.

The curse lies not just in poor leadership manifesting inborn human nature; it is an example of a universal biological principle. Life itself could be thought of as a curse suffered by the physical universe. An anarchist friend told me that before he volunteered to work in Africa he was a cynic, but after he returned he realized that he had become a misanthrope. I am not a misanthrope. Some may call me a cynic, but I think of myself as a realist. — *May 2020*

123 Hope

A protestant clergyman friend with whom I shared lunch recently asked about hope, a topic ordinarily not arising in social conversation. His question remained latent after I returned home, and not being a Christian, I consulted the Harper Collins *Bible Dictionary* (ed. P.J. Achtmeier) to see what was written on the subject in scripture. Hope was defined therein as "the expectation of a favourable future under God's direction."

In the Old Testament, the concept is non-eschatological, and words meaning "to wait or expect" (*kawah*) and "to be full of confidence, to trust" (*batah*) are commonly employed to convey a similar meaning to that found in the *Bible Dictionary*. In the New Testament, in the synoptic Gospels and the Gospel of John, the Greek verb meaning *to expect* is employed in the common laic sense, but in the Pauline Letters the concept refers to eschatological belief in final things, including eternal spiritual existence after death for those who are "saved" by virtue of their belief in Jesus Christ.

A secular definition of hope necessarily omits any mention of a deity but retains the meaning of it being a quality or attitude of optimistic expectation. But one may ask, expectation of what? If it's not a blissful afterlife, we could suggest the desire sought: the gambler seeks a monetary gain, the prisoner freedom, the narcissist recognition.

The common thread among them would appear to be an unpredictable pursuit of happiness. *Despair* is the antonym of *hope*, though the absence of hope does not necessarily imply the presence of despair. A stoic resignation, more characteristic of Eastern thought than Christian, suggests a neutral state without either hope or hopelessness.

Excessive preoccupation with these concerns tends to be non-productive, fostering morbid ideation leading to nights of insomnia and days of useless rehashing of ideas, such as writing essays about the larger issues that bedevil us. I personally find a combination of physical exercise and peer socialization, accompanied by a sense of humour, a protective approach to persistence of these vexing issues. While driving across southern British Columbia to Vancouver for the first time in the late 1960s with my colleague Arthur, we left the coastal range and passed through the soggy town of Hope. I asked my companion (who grew up nearby) about the origin of the name. Art dryly explained it was that they hoped it would stop raining someday.

Rather than being overly preoccupied with the vicissitudes of life, the collapse of civilization or even the second law of thermodynamics, it undeniably seems healthier to hope that it will stop raining someday, even though we choose to dwell in a rainforest. — *Jan 2019*

124 Life and Loss

To no longer possess what was once had is a loss. The first loss in the life of a human is called birth, because before birth the fetus enjoyed a perfect environment in which all needs to sustain life were provided by the maternal placenta. Following birth, however, these needs must be provided from the environment. Throughout life, energy intake must be greater than energy lost, sustaining metabolism by means of nutrition. The final loss is that of life itself, with the failure of metabolism.

In between these two losses of birth and death are a series of losses: in childhood, loss of needs being supplied by others, such as weaning from breast milk, followed by a series of other losses associated with increasing independence from caregivers, until gaining adulthood. Following puberty, reproduction may occur, resulting in a new life whose genetic structure is composed of coded information supplied equally by both parents, restarting the cycle.

Throughout adult life, physical losses continue as the result of time and gravity. There are also losses of parents, friends and relations, loss of employment, loss of physical function due to illness or accident, loss of income — the list goes on and on. We can try to protect ourselves physically through healthy behaviour and insurance for unforeseen losses. Medical care can help prevent life-threatening disease and often ameliorate physical disability, delaying death when possible. Financial loss may sometimes be minimized by professional help from an advisor.

Expectation of a life without loss is unrealistic. A stoic attitude will contribute to a sense of acceptance of inevitability, and being kind to others will facilitate one's own ability to tolerate loss. — *Sept 2020*

125 We Were Only Human

The small book *We Were Only Human*, written and illustrated by Peter Ustinov and published in 1961, has particular relevance to the world we inhabit in our current troubled days, wherein the concepts of blame and attitudes of hatred are paramount among minority groups, usually racial but often religious, and sometimes both. Ustinov's book and sketches recall the arguments of the Nazi defendants in the Nuremberg trials in the late 1940s following the Second World War. The title was meant to be satiric, and was understood as such, but now seems factual and appropriate as real and aspiring dictators promote obedience to orders from those in power.

North America, particularly the "United" States, is the focus of much of this discontent, founded as it was by slavers, perpetuated by a minority of white supremacists, egged on by an aspiring fascist government, and facilitated by an eighteenth-century constitution that both prevents majority rule and promotes indiscriminate possession of lethal weaponry.

While the problem was undeniably evident in Nazi Germany and appears to be increasingly so in the US, the very fact of normalizing brutality to others indicates that the origin is more deeply seated than just a matter of politics and constitutions. The underlying nativism and xenophobia that lead to what we see results basically from the human condition, and while those not disposed to cruelty to others may bemoan the situation, they cannot change it.

To think of the human race as cursed by virtue of the fundamental brain structure of its members is disheartening, but to close oneself off to the truth of this proposition is but seeking the comfort of avoidance to ignore the reality of the world in which we are condemned to live and die. Listen to Beethoven's setting of Schiller's "Ode to Joy" or the Mass in B Minor by J.S. Bach. Admire the beauty of great works of art and celebrate the wonders of mankind's creation by all means, but above all else, be kind to other people if you can, for the curse is shared by all of us. — *Sept 2020*

HOMO LUDENS

126 Homo ludens

Immersed as we are in the constant pressures of our social and cultural lives and the fears for our future, at times we understandably seek relief in distraction. The book *Homo Ludens*, originally published in 1938 by Dutch historian and cultural theorist Johan Huizinga, elaborates on the importance of the element of play within culture and society. Although diversion or play is not necessarily cheerful, the activity is always meaningful. It shifts our attention to a different immediacy, whether we are performing in a piano recital, playing a role on stage in a Shakespearean tragedy or participating in a sporting event, such as today's football matches or the funeral games from the *Iliad*.

For many it is play in the form of athletic contests that captivates — the ancient Greeks competed in the Olympic Games, the Romans had their lurid spectacles in the Coliseum, medieval knights jousted, contemporary armies taunt their enemies by war games, and ordinarily peaceful citizens may enjoy watching mayhem at the ice hockey rink, arising to cheer when a fight breaks out. Then there are also computer games, where sometimes simulated violence provides a socially acceptable outlet for teenagers and adults alike.

For those more sedate types there is always the performing arts. While opera has plenty of violence, in the immortal words of Anna Russell, "You can do anything you want in opera, as long as you *sing* it!" And staged drama, from the trivial and ridiculous to the sublime and profound, has entertained us throughout recorded history. For over a century cinema has been playfully consumed by humans, though not ordinarily by domestic animal companions. Similarly, music is playful for both its listeners and players. It can be joyfully infectious, stimulating dancing, or spiritually uplifting, by focusing attention on belief.

To be human is to be playful. When children play it is a rehearsal for adult life, clearly seen also in young animals, such as puppies play-biting or lambs frisking about the meadows in springtime. Huizinga identifies characteristics that all play must have: freedom from everyday constraints; separation from "ordinary" or "real" life, though nevertheless associated with order; and explicit or implicit rules. To not play by the rules is anathema; to cheat or to spoil the pleasure merits punishment. "It's not fair!" seems childish when exclaimed as an adult.

A necessary human and cultural quality of play is that it be enjoyable for spectators, if not always for participants. Structured play in a group promotes bonding with others, making life more tolerable for individuals, though not always beneficial to society as a whole, as in participating in antisocial groups. Yet it is an inescapable characteristic of the human animals that we all are.

To play, to have fun, to enjoy and to laugh are actions protective of life itself. Discovering sources around us that provoke these emotions grants relief from the otherwise inescapable harbingers of doom and our own extinction looming in the future. But today we can find pleasure in discovering humour lurking in unexpected places around us, in literature, in music and in science. Sometimes joyous, at other times serious or even sad, playing or listening to music acts as a powerful distraction from boring or repetitious daily tasks and engages our emotions as a welcome diversion.

127 Music

Armando Giovanni Iannucci is a Scottish satirist, writer, director and radio producer. Born in Glasgow, he studied at the University of Glasgow and the University of Oxford before ultimately abandoning graduate work to pursue a career in comedy. Iannucci rose to national renown in the UK and was awarded an Order of the British Empire for services to broadcasting. He has often appeared on the BBC and was a columnist for the classical music magazine *Gramophone*.

Hear Me Out (2017) is a collection of Iannucci's writings about classical music, containing forty short essays on the world of art in sound and listening to serious music. Iannucci describes his feelings for classical music, with which I strongly identify, as "the single most inspiring, most moving, most magical thread running through my whole cultural experience, the art form in whose presence I feel most comfortable, most myself." He regards music as a wordless expression of the composer's living thoughts and emotions, and emphasizes that active listening requires concentration and practice, paying attention to what is being heard.

Unlike me, Iannucci had musically sophisticated parents and was exposed to opera at home as a child. Yet he didn't begin to appreciate music as an art form until adulthood, although he has admitted to being smitten with the symphonies of Gustav Mahler as a teenager. Throughout his life Iannucci has extended his musical knowledge to include an ever-increasing array of composers and musical forms, and his lifelong, expanding interest in new directions and genres is one shared by me and other lovers of classical music.

Contrasting classical with popular music, Iannucci suggests the latter is more rooted in context — where one first heard it or when it was first recorded. He notes that "its energy and power relates to the particular moment in time when one first hears it," and for that reason popular music tends to echo a particular time of one's life. In contrast, Iannucci offers his own experience of hearing the same symphony in concerts and recordings over many years, always finding something new. "Popular music is very much of the moment; classical music demands an eternity."

Two of the essays in Iannucci's collection are comic masterpieces. "A Life at the Opera" pokes fun at everything associated with an unforgettable operatic performance — the singers, the orchestra, the conductor, the staging and the patrons and their smells and noises, all relentlessly revealed during a production of Wagner's solemn and tragic love story *Tristan und Isolde.*

His other essay, "Mobile Phones Off," is a hilarious account of an orchestral performance in which things go wrong, such as inappropriate applause. Those who violate this custom are admonished with a printed statement in the program notes: "The names and addresses of the troublemakers are passed on to the police, and after the concert they are arrested and taken away for clapping between movements. At their trial, the judge gives them a heavy sentence, saying it's necessary to make an example of scum like them."

I often tend to associate certain musical memories with music heard while driving — the rondo movement from Beethoven's *Emperor* piano concerto is driving in a VW with a friend across the North Cascades highway in Washington State on a sunny early spring morning in the 1970s. Also, unusually for me, a pop number, Elton John's "Rocket Man," is riding my BMW motorcycle north up the I-5 from California to British Columbia on another sunny spring morning many years ago. —*June 2018*

128 Music Criticism

Literary critics can be scornful, but for real snarky-ness, music critics can't be beat. Nicolas Slonimsky has ingeniously assembled *The Lexicon of Musical Invective: Critical Assaults on Composers Since Beethoven's Time*, a choice collection of titillating tirades against new works from an assortment of now-revered classical composers. It is an amusing selection of vituperation, dismissals and innuendos, and merits being shared among all those interested in classical music.

The nineteenth-century German music critic Eduard Hanslick once characterized Bruckner symphonies as "huge, shapeless serpents" and denounced the Tchaikovsky violin concerto as "odorously Russian." Though a big fan of Brahms, Hanslick loathed Wagner, describing *Tristan und Isolde* as a "boneless, tonal mollusc, self-restoring, swimming ever on into the immeasurable." Wagner was a favourite late-nineteenth-century target for the derision of other composers as well. Richard Strauss described *Lohengrin* as "abominable, not a trace of coherent melodies. It would kill a cat and would turn rocks into scrambled eggs from fear of these hideous discords. My ears buzzed from these abortions of chords, if one can still call them such."

New World critics, not to be surpassed by the Europeans, also weighed in. In the *New York Tribune* on November 13, 1886, critic H.E. Krehbiel termed Bruckner's Seventh Symphony "a sort of musical Volapük, cold as a problem in mathematics." And in the *New York Herald Tribune* on October 11, 1940, American composer Virgil Thompson found the Second Symphony of Sibelius to be "vulgar, self-indulgent, and provincial beyond all description."

Even the now-revered Beethoven was not exempt from derogatory criticism when a new work of his was first performed. A Viennese paper described his Second Symphony as "a crass monster, a hideously writhing wounded dragon, that refuses to expire, and though bleeding in the finale, furiously beats about with its tail erect."

The key to understanding all this invective lies in a particular psychological inhibition, described by Slonimsky as "non-acceptance of the unfamiliar," an auditory analogue to racial xenophobia that affirms "to listeners steeped in traditional music, [that] modern works are meaningless." Somewhat less rejecting after hearing a concert of Schoenberg's Three Piano Pieces in 1911, a bemused critic wrote, "It is possible that the music of the future will be like that, but I have no understanding of its beauty." Stravinsky's *Rite of Spring* ballet is a famous example, characterized by critics as "deliberately discordant and ostentatiously cacophonic," and provoking a riot when first performed in Paris on May 29, 1913.

Being human, I am not immune to disliking some contemporary music. I learned to appreciate a few works in the genre of progressive rock late in life, but never liked the syncopated rhythms of jazz, and consider hip-hop to be mere annoying and disagreeable noise — sound, but not "music" to my ears. Yet now that Kendrick Lamar has been awarded the 2018 Pulitzer Prize for music, who am I to judge? In music, beauty is in the ear of the listener, and since there's no accounting for taste, I gave up trying years ago. —*Apr 2018*

129 A Non-lexical Dictionary

My first favourite book was a dictionary, and since then I have remained fascinated by lexicography. My shelves groan with the weight of them, from Latin to Finnish and even the non-alphabetic Chinese pleremic script. There are Russian, Hungarian and Swedish dictionaries, along with some odd separate limited lists, like useful phrases in Araucanian. Then there are bilingual dictionaries, like German to Spanish, presumably for newly arrived Nazis in Argentina in late 1945. I personally have a Mandarin-Finnish specimen that I picked up in Helsinki, for one never knows when a monolingual Finnish tourist may find themselves in Beijing, or a Chinese visitor in Finland, wanting to express an urgent need for a public convenience.

But the strangest of all is a tome by Harold Barlow and Sam Morgenstern, *A Dictionary of Musical Themes*, that I bought in 1954 in Minnesota and brought with me the following year to Argentina. The sections are arranged alphabetically by composer, each with thematic subsections with entries organized by type of composition (concerto, quartet, symphony, etc.). Each musical work is then subdivided into its movements or parts, along with a list of principal themes, illustrated by a few bars of musical notation. For example, we find the famous opening of Beethoven's Fifth Symphony, "da-da-da-dum," under Beethoven > Symphony > No. 5, in C Minor, Op. 67, "Fate" > 1st Movement > 1st Theme > line B948 > page 71, accompanied by an illustration of the first five measures.

But suppose you have an earworm and the theme keeps resounding in your mind and you can't remember from whence it comes? Easy! Pages 527–644 contain a "notation index," in which you first imagine the theme in any key and transpose it to C Major or Minor to obtain the corresponding series of notes. "Da-da-da-dum" thus becomes "G-G-G-E-flat-F-F-F-D," easily referred and readily located in the alphabetized notation index, listed on page 641 in the second column as B948. It is then a simple matter of turning to line B948 on page 71, where you are given the relevant information, starting with the name of composer, type of work and so on. The process is reminiscent of the twofold procedure of using a Chinese dictionary to identify a specific character in the script.

There is also an index of titles and nicknames at the back of the book, which contains for example "Fate," directing you to B948. Ingenious. I bought a companion volume, *A Dictionary of Vocal Themes*, by the same authors at the Pigmalion bookshop in 1956. Both have been well used for well over half a century, and continue to dwell chair-side, worn and tattered but still in use. They have been rendered somewhat superfluous now by websites that allow you to find the wanted tune using a piano keyboard to plunk out the notes, but this lacks additional information about the work itself, such as short notational examples so that users who read musical notation can hum the tune.

To close with a double dactyl nonsense poem (author unknown):

> Higglety pigglety, Ludwig van Beethoven,
> asked by his pals for some music to hum;
> furrowed his brow, replying composedly,
> "Here's my Fifth Symphony, da-da-da-dum!" — *Apr 2018*

130 Earworms

The mental experience of persistently recalling a musical tune or earworm is familiar. My earliest ones from childhood, in the days before the advent of television, were of advertising jingles on the radio, like "I'm Chiquita Banana and I've come to say, bananas must be treated in a special way" or "Pepsi Cola Hits the Spot, twelve full ounces, that's a lot! Twice as much for a nickel too, Pepsi Cola is the drink for you!"

When I became devoted to classical music in adolescence, the eighteenth and nineteenth centuries were rich tonal minefields to plow, adding earworms to my library of personal tonal memories. Eventually, opera became and remains the primary source of new earworms, like tuneful nineteenth-century works such as Verdi's "Va pensiero . . ." from *Nabucco*, the Pilgrim's Chorus from *Tannhäuser*, or the duet for tenor and baritone from Bizet's *Pearl Fishers*. Less persistent are most twentieth-century works, apart from Richard Strauss and Benjamin Britten — and none at all from the great but tuneless Alban Berg.

My grandson Hugh, who is a professional musician working in the pop music genre, drew my attention to a 2016 review in a journal of the

American Psychological Association, "Dissecting an Earworm: Melodic Features and Song Popularity Predict Involuntary Musical Imagery," by a group of authors based in the UK and Denmark. After reviewing initial previous research with a limited number of subjects, they designed a study with a large sample of participants (3,000) and of songs (200), including a larger set of melodic features and utilizing more powerful statistical modelling techniques. They compared tunes that provoked earworms and those that did not and classified them according to their melodic features, such as rhythm and tone intervals.

Concepts of "catchiness" (the degree to which a musical fragment remains memorable after a period of time) and "song hook" (the most salient, easiest-to-recall fragment of a piece of music) were identified as worthy of attention. These predictive variables of hit songs, however, were not impressive, suggesting that "extramusical factors, such as artist popularity and audio features such as timbre, must play a large part in the commercial success of pop music." The actual research led to the unsurprising conclusion that "both features of a melody and the song's relative success in the charts contribute to the likelihood that a tune is reported as involuntary musical imagery," in other words, an earworm.

The research and conclusions refer exclusively to the genre of contemporary pop music, and one can speculate whether deliberate design of melodic features could promote commercial success. That doesn't seem too promising at this stage, but perhaps future refinements may stimulate experimentation in that direction. While it is interesting to read about this type of academic research, personally my regular listening to "Saturday Afternoon at the Opera" with Ben Heppner on CBC Radio seems to provide an adequate and satisfactory constant rotation of earwormery on a weekly basis. (Now if I could only erase last week's blasted Pilgrim's Chorus from *Tannhäuser*...) *— July 2019*

131 Music and Metaphysics

Defined as a branch of philosophy dealing with what is grandiosely called "the fundamental basis of reality" by traditional thinkers and mocked as "a systematic misuse of a terminology invented for that very purpose" by the twentieth-century school of logical positivists, etymologically the word *metaphysics* simply means "beyond physics."

Metaphysics of music can thus refer to the non-physical aspects of music, distinct from the physical sciences of sound production by vibrating objects, transmission by means of a medium, reception by an auditory apparatus, and interpretation by cerebral associations presumably related to neuronal structure.

Apart from these considerations of the science of sound, music can be considered in terms of how it relates to other human activities like literature, learning, believing and playing. Reading and writing are not limited to literature, for a musical score is also a script, constituting a set of written instructions to a musician, with a text not in words but in notes that represent information transmitted from the mind of the composer to that of the listener, via the performer(s). A trained musician can read a score and mentally "hear" the music it represents. Music as metaphor appears in fictional guise in Thomas Mann's late novel *Doctor Faustus*, wherein the composer of new music, Adrian Leverkühn (modelled after Arnold Schoenberg), imagines giving up his soul in exchange for time and inspiration. Mann wrote the book while exiled in California and doesn't specifically name Hitler's Third Reich. Nevertheless, the implicit political metaphor is unavoidable.

We can also think of music in terms of the dimension of time. The universe began with a bang. A big one. And the eighteenth-century Austrian composer Franz Joseph Haydn also gave us one at the beginning of his oratorio *The Creation*, derived from words of the writer(s) of the Book of Genesis. After a brief period of muted instruments and hushed murmurs from the chorus, God calls forth LIGHT!, and a big bang of sound explodes in our ears and minds. Haydn also musically represented the end of time with his "Farewell" Symphony. The last movement begins with a full orchestra but ends as one player after another stops and leaves the stage until all are gone. In between the *Creation* and the Farewell are 106 of his symphonies, along with a multitude of other works, including sonatas, quartets, concertos, operas and religious compositions. Haydn was prolific.

Music can be related to medicine as well as to cosmology, for composers Robert Schumann, Gaetano Donizetti and others had their careers cut short by tertiary syphilis. And then there was philosopher Ludwig Wittgenstein's brother Paul, a pianist who lost his right arm in the First World War, but who continued playing keyboard music written for the left hand, including adaptations of Bach and a brilliant piano concerto for the left hand written especially for him by Maurice Ravel, which is still in the concert repertoire today. Beethoven's hearing loss is quite well known, with his profound late string quartets being composed when deaf, as well as his glorious Ninth Symphony (with the choral setting of Schiller's "Ode to Joy" as the final movement). There were no hearing aids in his time, and some have wondered how Beethoven might have fared had they been available in the early nineteenth century. But the benefit might have been minimal, for while these devices may improve hearing loss, they do not restore natural hearing ability.

Belief systems are commonly associated with music in the Christian tradition (particularly by Johann Sebastian Bach), from the grandiose to the intimate. Works include masses both celebratory and requiem, motets, cantatas, concertos for both keyboards and strings and a multitude of solo pieces for different instruments and majestic works for organ. Other composers have also been inspired by belief, such as Anton Bruckner, who dedicated his final symphony to God; the religious ritual portrayed in opera by Puccini in *Tosca*; Wagner's *Parsifal*; and Poulenc's *Dialogues of the Carmelites*.

Political tensions and historical events can also be displayed musically, seen in Beethoven's *Fidelio*, Mussorgsky's *Boris Godunov* and Verdi's *Nabucco*. Psychological and sexual passions and conflicts suffuse most opera, combining poetry, spectacle, stagecraft and song in *Gesamtkunstwerk* (total art).

We make and listen to music because we are human and music is play, distracting us from the vicissitudes of current events and the parlous prospects of our future. From the grandiose spectacle of Mahler's Eighth Symphony of a Thousand to the intricate cameo of J.S. Bach's Goldberg Variations, music enriches our lives, painting our world in colours of tones. — *Sept 2020*

132 Nibelungenlied and Walhalla

The *Nibelungenlied* (*Song of the Nibelungs*) is an epic poem from around 1200, whose anonymous poet was likely from the region of Passau in Germany. It is based on an oral tradition that spread throughout almost all of Germanic-speaking Europe, which has its origin in historic events and individuals of the fifth and sixth centuries. Parallels to the German poem can also be found in Scandinavia, especially in the heroic lays of the *Poetic Edda* and the *Völsunga* saga. As with the Greek epic poetry of Homer and the Finnish *Kalevala*, the *Nibelungenlied* was written down by one or more scribes following a long oral transmission by storytellers or singers. Similarly to the Finnish epic, once in written form it became the inspiration for both visual arts and music.

The poem was forgotten after around 1500 but was rediscovered in 1755. Sometimes called the German *Iliad*, the *Nibelungenlied* began a new life as the German national epic. It was appropriated and extensively used in anti-democratic, reactionary and Nazi propaganda before and during the Second World War, glorifying the honour and bravery of ancient German warriors to promote nativist German objectives.

The Walhalla, named after the hall of heroes in the *Nibelungenlied*, is a "hall of fame" that honours laudable and distinguished people from throughout German history, including politicians, sovereigns, scientists and artists of the German tongue. The hall itself is a nineteenth-century neoclassical building overlooking the Danube River, east of Regensburg in Bavaria. As successor to the founding king, the government of Bavaria decides on additions to the shrine. Anyone may propose a name, but candidates must have died at least forty years prior to be eligible. Only 31 busts have been added to the hall since its opening, for a total of 191, only 12 of them female. Since the Second World War, a number of new additions are individuals who were opposed to the National Socialists, and an especially prominent place at the end of the series is allotted to Sophie Scholl, a Munich student who was gruesomely executed in 1943 for her nonviolent resistance to Hitler's regime.

The legacy of the *Nibelungenlied* epic is today visible in Richard Wagner's celebrated tetralogy *Der Ring des Nibelungen.* The cycle of four operas is regularly staged around the world in major cities and performed almost yearly within Germany and Austria. The Bavarian city of Bayreuth has produced various cycles at the Wagnerian Festival House, with mixed reviews over time, and indeed the work is such that it remains open to the vivid imagination of contemporary designers, in stagings sometimes mocked as "Eurotrash," like the one set on a starship in outer space. The orchestral music and libretto written by the composer are considered sacrosanct and unaltered in every production.

Many editions of Wagner's text are available in print and online, along with video performances. My favourite lowdown on the story of the four operas is a video recording of the presentation by soprano and comedian Anna Russell, whose unforgettable witty analysis of the four operas is found easily on YouTube. "It begins in the River Rhine, *in it* . . . If it were in New York it would be the Hudson." —*May 2018*

133 Two Words from Kundry

Parsifal, the great last opera by Richard Wagner, is the quest of the hero Parsifal to retrieve the Holy Grail from an evil magician, who compels the voluptuous woman Kundry to seduce him, and concludes with the restoration of the Holy Grail to its guardians by the eponymous "guileless fool" as the chorus solemnly and enigmatically intones *Erlösung dem Erlöser* (redemption to the redeemer). This mysterious phrase has been raked over the coals by explicators since it first appeared in the late nineteenth century. Christians, Marxists, psychoanalysts and even Nietzsche have all had their say, but the best interpretation of the *Erlösung dem Erlöser* that I've heard comes from Michael Tanner's discussion in the May 2020 *Literary Review* of Roger Scruton's *Wagner's Parsifal: The Music of Redemption.* Tanner writes, "The final words of Parsifal, 'Redemption to the Redeemer,' are best left uninterpreted, I feel, but Scruton offers an elaborate exegesis. The central part of this book feels as if it's a reinforcement of its author's beliefs, rather than an exploration of a work by which even its creator was bemused."

In the April 10, 2020, issue of the *Times Literary Supplement*, Robert Zaretsky discusses *The Plague*, the often-cited 1947 novel by Albert Camus, which describes the effects of a fictional epidemic disaster among those living through it. The physician and hero of the tale, Dr. Bernard Rieux, survives, but insists his motivation to continue his medical work in the face of the epidemic was simply because he was "doing his job." Camus reflects on the thoughts and behaviours of those who are forced to adjust to the invisible but omnipresent threat.

Similarly, when in the third act of *Parsifal* the guilt-ridden seductress Kundry is asked why she washes the returning hero's feet, she responds in two words: *Dienen, Dienen* (to serve, to serve). Kundry exhibits behaviour that resonates with the world of the twenty-first century, when expiation of guilt continues to be thought of as a motivation for charitable work, perhaps as simple as donating to a food bank after enjoying a sumptuous meal at home.

Kundry describes her kindness and comfort extended to another as atonement motivated by her past behaviour, while Rieux goes on with his work because he feels it is his duty. Their motivations may be different, but their actions are equally beneficent and selfless. *Dienen, Dienen* conveys the Christian message of doing good works as expiation of past sinful behaviour and resonates with the image of Rieux, who denies heroism in working with his patients, seeing it only as his duty to provide care to the sick and dying.

Those two words need not necessarily be an atonement of perceived sinfulness, but simply a statement of fact, though what Nabokov mockingly called "the Viennese delegation" (psychoanalysts) would no doubt beg to differ. — *June 2020*

134 Fascinating and Unexpected Books and Those Deemed to Be Boring

The Catalogue of Lost Books by Thaddeus F. Tuleja is a fascinating compendium of 100 titles, flogged as "an annotated and seriously addled collection of great books that should have been written but never were." One of these titles is *The Ill-Tempered Clavier.* In the words of "Einrich Walther Stichprober," "This 1674 intricate mystical novel has generally been assigned footnote status in the history of Western culture. It is the book that J.S. Bach humorously acknowledged as the origin of his *Well-Tempered Clavier*, and few musicologists have ever bothered to go further than that."

The story describes the vicissitudes of the suspiciously named Hans Castorp, "a circuit-riding clavier tuner whose work symbolizes the human condition." The unnamed author relates his hero's difficulties, "fighting against the inevitable string-stretching with the same valour and existential grimness that the Greek Sisyphean hero summoned against gravity." Apparently, the book was required reading "in both the Viennese and Leipzig conservatories until the 'prepared piano' revolution of the 1950s, and virtually all the keyboard artists trained in the Swabian corridor between the wars acknowledged its influence, including Adrian Leverkühn."

Tuleja's *Catalogue* is a witty imaginary compendium, whereas another odd tome, *This Book Will Send You to Sleep*, deliberately tries to be dull. Now residing on my shelf of miscellany, *This Book* came to my attention while I was reading a short article in the current *Guardian Weekly*. Marketed as an intentionally boring book, it is deliberately void of anything stimulating or challenging to a reader. Examples of the short and dense chapters listed in the table of contents include information judged to be dull by the compiler, such as "Railway Gauges: An Overview," "Economic Statistics from the First Two Five-Year Plans in the Soviet Union" and "A Few Facts About Roundabouts."

One wonders, however, about how universally dull any of these subjects really are. There are rail fans who take interest in trackage issues, such as the difference in gauge between Russian railways and the rest of Europe (except for Finland!), or economic historians that find the early Soviet five-year plans utterly fascinating. There are even designers of highway roundabouts who have to keep in mind the difference between clockwise and counterclockwise directions as a function of right- or left-hand driving rules in different countries (sometimes even in the same country, as both Sweden and Argentina switched in the 1940s from right-hand — clockwise — to left-hand — counterclockwise).

As H.L. Mencken once remarked, "There are no dull subjects, only dull writers." — *May 2018*

135 Poetastery

The quality of poetry is much a matter of taste. Take for example when the verse of the now-revered nineteenth-century poet Walt Whitman was trashed by no less than W.H. Auden, who thought him one of many American poets who were "formless, windy, banal, and utterly boring." Meaning in poetry can also be elusive. Jean Cocteau commented once, "Poetry is indispensable, but to what I could not say." A writer of inferior poetry has been known as a *poetaster* since the word was coined by Dutch philosopher Erasmus of Rotterdam in 1621. Implicit in the meaning is a judgment of value, for to describe a poet as a poetaster reveals more about the critic than the writer.

The Joy of Bad Verse is an overview of poetastery published in 1988 by British freelance writer Nicholas T. Parsons, who writes in his introduction, "Many persons who appear quite normal in other respects, nevertheless persist in writing poetry, an activity for which they have no discernible talent whatever." Parsons has clearly researched a wide selection of English and American resource material, particularly from the eighteenth and nineteenth centuries, finding examples often imitative of well-known successful poets. He admits that recognizing bad verse is easier than defining it, quoting T.S. Eliot in saying, "The bad poet is usually unconscious where he ought to be conscious, and conscious where he ought to be unconscious."

The first half of the book explores what Parsons terms "the varieties of badness," and consists of eight sections referencing religion, Eros and bathos, politics, medicine and patriotism, along with a chronological account and witty critiques of successive English poet laureates, beginning with the first, John Dryden (1631–1700).

The second half is devoted to close examinations of works by twenty-five poets, ranging from "Scottish Homer" by William McGonagall (c. 1825–1902) to "Wisdom of Wisconsin" by Ella Wheeler Wilcox (1850–1919), that merit, as Auden suggested of Whitman, being called leading examples of poetastery.

Though limited to poetic works written in the English language, *The Joy of Bad Verse* is described on the cover as "a light-hearted Cook's tour of the world of inept poetry — a world characterized by sentimentality, sycophancy, solemn propaganda, sexual embarrassment and charlatanism." This is a fair summary of the author's amusing dismissal of artistic pretension among the writers cited in his compendium, but his judgments reek with a whiff of snobbery, not unlike many of the examples he provides.

To laugh at literary ineptness hints at possibly overestimating one's own proficiency, as well as being unkind to others. But then, versifying may be thought of as a form of play not always engaged in by those adept in the craft, perhaps akin to writing essays in one's dotage to preserve a residual attachment to human intellectual activity becoming increasingly remote, but yet not fully detached. — *Sept 2020*

136 Fictional Linguistics

The Italian author Diego Marani served as the officer in charge of cultural diplomacy for the European Union in Brussels and has published eight novels, including a trilogy in which each one is based on linguistic themes, such as translation or lost and imaginary languages.

The first, *New Finnish Grammar*, is the story of a man found injured in the port of Trieste during the Second World War and taken aboard a German hospital ship, where he is treated by a German physician of Finnish origin. When he emerges from a comatose state and is unable to speak, the sole clue to his nationality is a label on the jacket he is wearing — a Finnish name. His physician undertakes the laborious task of teaching him the complicated non-Indo-European language, and the story unfolds as the man recovers and is repatriated to Finland, where his adventures in Helsinki lead to an astonishing conclusion.

Marani's second book of the trilogy, *The Last of the Vostyachs*, is again set mainly in Finland, but the protagonist is a Russian survivor of an abruptly abandoned Arctic labour camp. Discovered by a Russian linguist after leaving the labour camp, the survivor is taken to Helsinki, where he becomes entangled with academia and criminalia at Helsinki University. The survivor's ethnicity is found to be that of a long-lost tribe whose language suggests links with Indigenous groups on both sides of the Bering Strait. Following his involvement with two murders, he finds himself the sole remaining member of his tribe, out of reach of the authorities, working as an entertainer aboard an overnight ferry service on the Baltic Sea between Helsinki and Stockholm.

The Interpreter is the third book of Marani's trilogy, anchored in the profession of simultaneous translation for participants in international meetings like the United Nations and European Commission conferences. The hero, slyly bearing the name Felix Bellamy, is a model bureaucrat who finds himself in charge of the professional translators, one of whom begins to develop unusual phonation attacks of glossolalia, or speaking in tongues. The translator is eventually fired and vanishes, but then Bellamy himself begins to experience the same problem. He loses his job and his wife, seeks psychiatric help in a German clinic offering "linguistic training" to re-channel his seizure-like episodes of unwilling glossolalia, but ultimately leaves this bizarre therapeutic environment to search for the missing translator, tracking him around Eastern Europe between the Black and the Baltic Seas. Having many adventures, some criminal, Bellamy finally achieves satisfaction by finding his quarry and the solution to his problem.

The trilogy is a masterful construction of fictional linguistics, and Marani, writing in his own first language of Italian, has received many prizes for his work, most of which has been deftly translated into English by Judith Landry. — *Sept 2020*

137 Europanto and Wordplay

While working as a translator for the Council of the European Union, Diego Marani invented Europanto, a mock international auxiliary language. Strictly for fun, and not a serious language like Esperanto, it was well described by a blurb by Ben Macintyre in the *Times*: "The linguistic recipe used by Diego Marani is broadly the following: take a firm grounding in English and French, toss in chunks of German, Spanish, and Italian; garnish with a dash of Flemish and Euroslang; pour the contents into a language liquidiser and serve when thoroughly pureed."

A book of short stories in Europanto, *Las Adventures des Inspector Cabillot*, like Marani's other novels, has been published by Dedalus. The book, while intelligible, requires at least a fleeting knowledge of modern European languages, as is seen in this description on the back cover, written in Europanto: "Bandidos, villainos, migrantes clandestinas, mafiosos, on your guardia! Voilà arrivante Inspector Cabillot, der beste polizero des Europeane Polizei! Seine intelligente wit shal dismasque alles feine plots, seine legendary genius shal prosecute toi sonder pity zum teine ultime endeavour!"

Marani has also written a number of articles published in Europanto in different European journals, but always in a spirit of amusement and playing with words, not to be taken too seriously.

"Diego Marini habe gewritten manige articulos in Europanto in multiple Europeane journalos, tambien eine videoclip, canzones und some theatre pieces. Diego Marani esse toch best renamed por seine Italianse novellas und collabore in Italianse lingua mit some culturale Italianse journalos." — *Sept 2020*

138 Fausto Squattrinato and C.D. Rose

Squattrinato is an Italian word meaning "poor, down-and-out, penniless." It is also the surname of the character Fausto Squattrinato in two books by English writer C.D. Rose. *The Biographical Dictionary of Literary Failure* (2014) is a mock-literary compendium of authors whose writings failed to achieve acclaim for one reason or another, and *Who's Who When Everyone Is Someone Else* (2017) is a fictional account of a man engaged in a quest for a forgotten author in an unnamed Central European city. C.D. Rose is "delicious," conjuring up images like a mental taste sensation, commanding a licking of the literary chops with the glee of discovery and recognition of a kindred spirit.

The Biographical Dictionary consists of the alphabetized names of fifty-two authors with short accounts of their literary failures, from the unfortunate Casimir Adamowitz-Kostrowicki, whose unpublished masterpiece was consumed by flames ignited by a loyal friend who had promised to destroy it if the author was lost in the Great War (Adamowitz-Kosrowicki returned an invalid, but before contacting his friend was trampled by a horse spooked by fireworks), to the final account of the enigmatic Sara Zeelen-Levallois, "whose works exist purely in the domain of hearsay and rumour . . . showing us . . . words will change nothing. Write how we may, the arrogant and corrupt will still run the world, people will starve needlessly, your lover will still leave you." Rose concludes by reminding us that memorials do nothing for the deceased, but by remembering them we give their words life. This may be true for all authors, both imaginary, as in this book, and real.

Squattrinato appears twice in *The Biographical Dictionary*, once when he claims to have met J.D. "Jack" Ffrench "brokering deals between the New York and Sicilian mafias, but his evidence is always unreliable." The second reference is in the account of the masterpiece of Jürgen Kittler, a manifesto of literary activism: "The Italian poet and performance artist Fausto Squattrinato claimed to have taken part in the kidnapping of Aldo Moro in 1978, but he is a known liar."

In *Who's Who*, Squattrinato appears unexpectedly when the protagonist is searching for a bookshop and Fausto insinuates himself into the quest, even though he "claims to be a performance artist, and that his entire life is his performance. He is an inveterate liar, has no known source of income, and a disturbing habit of appearing when least wanted." Our seeker admits to having first met Squattrinato two decades earlier when living in Naples, and since then he "has continued to crop up with annoying frequency. . . . 'Like old times, this, isn't it?' he grinned back at me, as we were walking and drinking in search of the bookstore, and he wasn't wrong, but they were times best left behind."

The multiple appearances of this bizarre character in Rose's writings suggest Squattrinato is more than merely a comic persona in the mind of the author. It is likely that we, his readers, may also all have some Fausto Squattrinati among the unshared memories of our youth, and prefer to keep them out of sight if we can. But then, I'm a retired shrink and tend to be suspicious of these things . . . — *June 2020*

139 The Cynic's Dictionary

Rummaging through books left by an old friend after his passing, I discovered a small item he obviously had treasured called *The Cynic's Dictionary*. We had shared a similar sense of dark humour over the years in both British Columbia and Yukon, where he worked as a journalist and I as a psychiatrist.

According to the flyleaf, the author of *The Cynic's Dictionary*, Paul "Rick" Bayan (born January 27, 1950), has "held a number of typical jobs for a liberal arts graduate, including assistant editor of *Rubber Age* and managing editor of *Container News.* At Time-Life Books he was assigned to write about plumbing fixtures." More seriously, Bayan is a US author, webmaster and advertising copywriter, also known for his advertising thesaurus *Words That Sell* and his darkly humorous online essays.

Bayan modelled his book on *The Devil's Dictionary* (1911), a satirical glossary written by American Civil War soldier, wit, and writer Ambrose Bierce (1842–c. 1914), which consisted of common words followed by their humorous and satirical definitions. Taking his cue from the more outlandish definitions offered by Samuel Johnson in his 1755 *Dictionary*, Bierce playfully made up his own clever definitions of common words and phrases. In turn, Bierce's *The Devil's Dictionary* became the inspiration for Bayan's opus at the end of the century.

Bayan's collection appeals to modern curmudgeons, who mock the self-important and the purveyors of political correctness. Written in the last decade of the twentieth century, some of its entries now seem dated, though most still retain the tang of a good lampooning directed at attitudes, occupations, behaviours or sacrosanct opinions.

Among his over 900 words are:

denial – How an optimist keeps from becoming a pessimist.
loitering – The crime of doing nothing in particular, particularly in public.
urinal – The one place where all men are peers.
exorcism – Expulsion of the vile demons that hold us in thrall, generally accomplished through medieval rituals and, on rare occasions, psychoanalysis.

I treasure this little book, along with a few others of its ilk, which I regularly rotate through a shelf in the smallest room in my flat, facing the throne, where a few minutes of perusal (longer if constipated) usually fosters a cheerful attitude towards the vicissitudes of life, accompanied by a sense of well-being commensurate with a good dump. — *May 2018*

140 The Portable Curmudgeon

This is the title of a little 1987 compendium by the American writer and editor Jon Winokur. It seems to have been a popular tome when it first appeared thirty-one years ago, for he has penned another four books about curmudgeons since then. A curmudgeon is traditionally known as a churlish, irascible fellow, a cantankerous old codger, though perhaps a not entirely unlikable grouch. Winokur defends curmudgeonry in his introduction: "They have the temerity to comment on the human condition without apology. They not only refuse to applaud mediocrity; they howl it down with morose glee."

Most curmudgeons are older males, suggesting that as language and usage continued to evolve around them, their own speech remained characteristic of their earlier years. Older women no doubt have similar feelings, but many are less assertive and unwilling to express them openly, except to intimate friends and family. I suspect Jan Morris (now in her nineties), though, would be a good example of a curmudgeoness, as was my wife was in her late seventies. There is no fixed lower age limit to merit the title, but it is uncommon in the young. Many teenagers may display typical attitudes of the old grouch, but are usually forgiven, and their negativity is considered to be only a phase of maturing and the need to assert independence.

Winokur's little book is essentially a collection of quotes that typify the temperament of mocking irony characteristic of curmudgeonly comments, and a list of "world class curmudgeons." Being an American writer, Winokur chooses candidates who are primarily, but not exclusively, American. Englishmen G.K. Chesterton, George Bernard Shaw and Quentin Crisp are there, along with continental writers like Voltaire, Nietzsche and August Strindberg. He missed one of my English favourites, though: Lord Chesterfield, who asserted, "Sex: the pleasure is momentary, the position ridiculous, and the expense damnable!"

Top honours in curmudgeonliness are awarded to American writer H.L. Mencken, whose uninhibited and opinionated writings of the 1930s now seem not only a merited assessment of his own times but prophetic of our own: "There's no underestimating the intelligence of the American public." Or "The only way to success in American public life lies in flattering and kowtowing to the mob." One could go on quoting other curmudgeons, but *The Portable Curmudgeon* is like a box of chocolates, not to be gobbled up in one sitting, but savoured intermittently when one needs something relaxing to read, again as when seated in the smallest room in the house.

I have generally regarded myself as a curmudgeon in a psychological sense, though not in behaviour. While mostly reserved in offering opinions to others, I do have a small pin on a jacket stating, *Grumpy Old Fart.* (I don't remember if I once bought it or if it was given to me by an admirer.) But I do not think I am churlish or irascible in demeanour, though there is one situation when I could be accused of acting curmudgeonly: when vexed by misplaced apostrophes, I might ungraciously comment.

Once, when I was walking with an educated and proper Swiss lady in the outskirts of Zurich, we suddenly came upon an English graffitto, presumably scrawled by some disaffected youth: *Fuck the teacher's!* Outraged by the misplaced apostrophe, she hotly demanded, "Fuck the teacher's *what?*" Feeling vindicated, I thought, "Great minds think alike." —*June 2018*

141 Eunoia

Eunoia is the shortest word in English that contains all five vowels, and it literally means "beautiful thinking." It is also the title of the award-winning 2001 book by Canadian experimental poet Christian Bök. Each of the five chapters (designated "A," "E," "I," "O" and "U") is univocalic, composed of meaningful English text constructed entirely from words employing a single vowel.

Examples of sentences from each chapter are:

Chapter A: Awkward grammar appalls a craftsman.

Chapter E: Enfettered, these sentences repress free speech.

Chapter I: Sighing, I sit, scribbling in ink this pidgin script.

Chapter O: Loops on bold fonts now form lots of words for books.

Chapter U: Duluth dump trucks lurch, pull U-turns.

Eunoia was written over a period of seven years and contains additional restraints beyond the use of a single vowel: all chapters must refer in some way to writing, and each chapter must contain a meal, an erotic episode, visions of a bucolic setting and a maritime journey. Internal rhyming is promoted, no less than 98 percent of available words are employed, repetition of words is minimized, and the letter *y* is excluded. The result is a veritable tour de force, a masterpiece of linguistic ingenuity crafted by a wizard of words.

A twenty-page addendum to *Eunoia* is titled "Oiseau," the French word for "bird" and the shortest word in French to contain all the vowels. As a bonus, it proffers further wordplay, including a presentation of every word in English containing only consonants (though perhaps fudged somewhat by including *y*). "Oiseau" shyly presents an anagrammatic text based on the word *vowels*, which is followed by an exuberant homophonic translation of the poem "Voyelle," by the French poet Arthur Rimbaud.

Bök also honours the French novelist Georges Perec, noted for his constrained writing, with a poem titled "W," which echoes Perec's semi-autobiographical book of the same title. Bök was no doubt inspired by Perec's work, which includes a 300-page novel, *La disparition* (1969), which is a lipogram written without ever using the letter *e*. Berec's novella *Les revenentes* (1972) is a complementary univocalic piece in which the letter *e* is the only vowel used. In closing, the "Oiseau" addendum of *Eunoia* presents a section called "Emended Excess," dedicated to Perec, an evocation of the celebrated French logophile that utilizes univocalic *e* words not employed in the Chapter E retelling of the *Iliad*.

And then there's the Czech language, allowing one to exclaim a sentence *lacking* vowels, like "Strc prst skrz krk!" (Thrust finger through neck!), presumably seldom used outside of the anatomy dissection labs at Czech medical schools. —*June 2018*

142 Narrative Constraint

Oulipo was a twentieth-century group of mostly francophone writers who sought to use restricted or constrained writing techniques to create works similar to those described in the previous essay. Similarly to constrained writing, one can also restrict or constrain a narrative, creating a meaningful story from any three given words. A game once played with my three young daughters was devised as a bedtime story: each would suggest an object from which a tale was then constructed, somehow connecting all three in a meaningful narrative.

When describing this scheme to my grandson Hugh over tea one day, I invited him to make a list using this technique, and he wrote *forceps*, *a tricycle* and *a waxing moon*. A waxing moon suggests a gradual increase of light, perhaps a metaphor for the dawning awareness of something previously hidden. A forceps is a handheld, hinged tool used for grasping and holding objects, often referring to a now seldom-used gynecological instrument employed to assist the birth of a child. And a tricycle is a three-wheeled conveyance, usually pedalled by children but sometimes powered by a motorcycle engine, used for personal transportation.

Once I had deconstructed meanings and associations of the three given objects, it became easier to employ them together in a meaningful way, even in one hermeneutic sentence: "From a purely scriptural point of view, unlike the clumsy tricycle of the Holy Trinity, the single forceps of Judaic or Islamic monotheism, like a waxing moon, increasingly illuminates the concept of a single divinity, still mystical, but less impenetrable than the Christian scriptures."

Contrived, I admit, but there's nothing like recreational linguistics to provide one with mental distraction in times of imprisonment, or perhaps of pandemically provoked self-isolation . . . — *Apr 2020*

143 Gallows Humour

So It Goes is the name of a blog by Londoner John Fleming, a writer and historian of comedy who has an encyclopedic knowledge of comedy and comedians active over the past half century. His writing, a rich and humane feast of laughter, compassion and tragedy, was brought to my attention by my eldest daughter, Anna, who performed in British comedy clubs in the 1970s and personally knew many of the artists whose vicissitudes and escapades are exposed with relish by Fleming.

"John's UK Coronavirus Diary – No 1 – Panic buying, leeches and facemasks" refers to behaviours that may be described as gallows humour, which occurs during periods of acute stress. The title of his site is derived from the novel *Slaughterhouse-Five*, by Kurt Vonnegut, containing periodic comments by a fictional survivor of the 1945 bombing raid of the German city of Dresden, which reduced the city to ruins and killed 25,000 people, mostly civilians.

Laughter in the face of adversity is a reactive phenomenon, suggesting defiance, confrontation, and strength of character when confronting certain mortality with humour, like the *New Yorker* cartoon of a bound prisoner before a firing squad being offered a last cigarette by an officer and replying, "No thanks, I'm trying to quit."

This stiff-upper-lip attitude of "keep calm and carry on" has been celebrated in tales dating from the London Blitz in the early years of the Second World War, when the Luftwaffe bombed the city, causing death and destruction among the residents. But the British were not the only ones to suffer so, and the Dresdeners were the victims of payback when the Allies wreaked vengeance on the powerless German civilians once they had air supremacy in the conflict. And then there were Hiroshima and Nagasaki later that year.

Vonnegut immortalized the Dresden raid in his book, and the wry comment "so it goes" is now an apt title for a collection of gallows humour in the face of the global crisis — doubtless there will be more examples of this as the pandemic persists, and they should be welcomed as manifestations of human resilience in the face of adversity.

An example from March 29, 2020, from John Fleming: "Last night, I saw what may have been one of the last comedy shows in London — performed flawlessly by the staggeringly multi-talented Dragos Mostenescu. I would not normally quote from shows directly, but he started with "I used to cover the sound of my farts by coughing, but now I am covering the sound of my coughs with farts." — *Mar 2020*

144 The Colourful Five Percent

The Colourful Five Percent is the name of three oversized softbound volumes by Yukon artist and writer Jim Robb, described as "a unique guide to the Yukon's greatest treasure: her colourful characters and exceptionally fine people, read in all the better cabins in the Yukon." Robb came to the Yukon in 1955 from Montreal at the age of twenty-two, more or less on a whim, "to take a look around." He did summer seasonal work for a few years and enjoyed his knack for painting in the winter, finding his inspiration in late 1957 when he saw "Wigwam Harry" dancing beside the jukebox at the Grill Cafe. He produced a larger-than-life-sized painting, which was proudly hung in a local inn. "I already had the skills of the art, but never really got involved until I saw the Yukon had so many colourful characters."

He picked his subjects by their distinct eccentric photogenic qualities, accomplishments, attitudes and personalities. "Anything that set them apart from the crowd." Yukon writer John Firth described Robb's style as "exaggerated truth — leaning chimneys took on a real tilt and rust became rustier." *The Colourful Five Percent* contains collections of miscellaneous anecdotes and images that together form a picture of those he calls "five percenters," individuals constituting a unique group of men and women who choose to live in the subarctic north of Canada.

The original first edition was published in 1984 and subsequently reprinted ("by popular demand") in 1992. Stories of Wigwam Harry,

Mah Bing and the Hollywood Cafe, Buzz Saw Jimmy and others are told through pictures and sketches. There are stories of Jack London's cabin and of prospector Skookum Jim and his house. Initially sold for $12.95, it can be ordered today, if you want, from Amazon for $119.00. The second edition was released in 1985 and included features on hunting guide Johnnie Johns, Cowboy Larry Smith, the ballad of the famous Sour Toe Cocktail, Skagway's Soapy Smith, and journalist Edith Josie from the village of Old Crow in the far North, celebrated for her column "Here Are the News" in the *Whitehorse Star* newspaper. Many more sketches, cartoons, and photographs enliven this edition.

The third and most recent edition dates to 1998 and continues the style of the first two in an expanded format of sixty-four pages, with new accounts of cold weather stories, business ventures, dance hall girls like Klondike Kate and Diamond Tooth Lil, and some modern characters like Silver Fox (John Howard) and his cross-Canada motorcycle trip, Jaime Smith, the Yukon's only psychiatrist, and the local "reincarnation" of the eccentric entertainer Tagish Elvis. Many photographs and drawings of both pioneers and long-term residents enhance a collection of snapshots, all deemed worthy of belonging to the colourful five percent.

Robb's sketches of Yukon cabins and their residents appear on blankets, coffee mugs and T-shirts, along with framed prints to adorn the walls of your cabin or bear cave. My favourite print is on the wall of my study as I write these lines. It is of the interior of a cabin somewhere in the Yukon, with a table bearing a hoard of gold nuggets overflowing onto a miner's skeleton lying on the floor, with the caption "Got 'er made at last!"

In my sketch on page 38 of the third edition appears the following anecdote about Yukon and psychiatry:

> Although the only psychiatrist in the Yukon, thanks to the internet, there is no more professional isolation; over a thousand psychiatrists worldwide are in contact to share clinical problems and advice every day.
>
> One colleague from New York City wrote me in the late twentieth century, "I've been wondering why you are there — are you being punished for something?
> He probably thought this was a place of exile, like Siberia under the tsars, or Stalin.
>
> I replied, "No, I just have the extraordinary good fortune to be able to live and work in the most wonderful corner of the best country in the world. I note you are in Manhattan.

Are YOU being punished for something?"

He wrote back, "I am Jewish and am married to a Jewish woman. I'm *always* being punished for something . . ."

— *May 2018*

145 Dreamers

We are all dreamers, according to the celebrated Viennese interpreter, who proclaimed dreams to be the "royal road to the unconscious." Some people deny dreaming or, more likely, claim to never recall any dream content, though dreaming is felt to be universal among humans.

A literary acquaintance recently said that he had awakened "in the middle of a dream," and went on to describe the images of bizarre scenery in the nocturnally experienced trip along his personal royal road.

We think of dreams as analogous to cinema or a staged performance of a play, but they are not. One can walk into a theatre before the beginning, in the middle, or after the conclusion of a show, but dreams have no fixed point of departure or final resolution. I wonder about the claim of awakening "in the middle" of a dream — how would one know that? When one awakens from a dream and recalls some of the dream content, must it not *always* be in the middle?

Neurologist Oliver Sacks, in one of his essays, wrote about the physiological activity in the brain associated with dreaming. Researchers in sleep laboratories have identified discrete stages of sleep associated with dreaming, characterized by rapid eye movement. And there is a vast literature about the subject, scientific and literary — sometimes both, as with Sacks.

Enjoyable dreams may lead to regret upon awakening, with the desire of resuming the narrative, as though it were a video presentation that had been interrupted at an inopportune moment. Unpleasant or fearful dreams, however, may yield to relief upon one's awakening and return to perception of the ordinary reality of life, but that depends on the quality of the life one returns to.

Author Vladimir Nabokov investigated "precognitive dreaming" from a literary viewpoint, with inconclusive results, as described in his preserved records. Not surprising, given our unidirectional experience of the dimension of time. But this one-dimensionality can be challenged in fiction, if not in reality, as did blind Jorge Luis Borges, whose labyrinthine prose invites us to transcend the immediacy of the world we perceive when awake.

In my own experiences of dreaming, a common thread seems to have been finding myself in an unfamiliar environment with a task to be accomplished, like locating some particular shop in a town, or a room in some building, often chasing a clue pointing towards a resolution of the quest, but never finding it.

No need to psychoanalyze that one; it's simply the story of my life in a nutshell. — *Aug 2020*

POSTSCRIPT

Die Weltanschauung

It has long been wondered whether the universe has a purpose. Various religious and metaphysical theories have been postulated: Gods, Life-Forces, *Weltgeister*, etc. I rather think that it would be nobler for mankind if the universe had no preconceived plan. Because then, we ourselves might endow it with a purpose. For what is man but a very small and yet complex chunk of the universe come alive and come conscious? For thousands of years, men have set themselves apart from and in opposition to the universe. It simply never occurred to us that we *are* the universe, and what goals we set for ourselves we set for it also.

Consciousness has come in in the middle of the celestial cinema and has just begun to understand the plot. We of this age are living at the very birth of reason, and it is a most critical period indeed. We cannot permit our animal natures to expose the infant, as is indeed possible in this period of internecine war.

Our relations with our fellow men are thus of the greatest importance. Although on the time-scale of the universe a backslide of a thousand or even of a million years might not be important, human beings cannot cope with such time-spans.

Human history, being rational, is cumulative, unlike that of lower species. Great values, scientific, ethical and esthetic, may be irrevocably lost if a reversion to pre-rationality should occur. It is an obligation of every rational creature to have a political and social awareness, and to attempt to preserve from destruction what has already been accomplished.

Above all, let us not become blinded in our specialized ways to universal concepts of truths and of values. Nor must a universal consciousness destroy our immediate experience as human beings. To paraphrase Shaw, we must beware of the pursuit of abstraction; it leads to an indiscriminate contempt for the concrete.

> You know why I struck people funny? I think it was because of the division of labour. Specialization was leaving the likes of me behind. I didn't know spot-welding, I didn't know traffic management, I couldn't remove an appendix, or anything like that. . . . In the world of today your individual man has to be willing to illustrate a more and more narrow and restricted point of existence. And I am not a specialist.
>
> — Saul Bellow (*The Adventures of Augie March*, 1953)

> Barbarism is being lop-sided. Christianity made us barbarians of the soul and now science is making us barbarians of the intellect.
>
> — Aldous Huxley (*Point Counter Point,* 1928)

> A man should be able to play the flute — but not too well.
>
> — Aristotle (*Politics*)

Thus I conclude. This being an overture of sorts, I have performed only a few themes, rondo-fashion, and have not developed them as fully as possible. The development will occur in the opera to come, though it will take many years and will include God knows how many acts. New themes will be found, and old ones will be discarded, but the central idea of the liberal man must remain, for it shall be the presupposed harmony of all my philosophic music. — *May 1954*

Acknowledgements

Because of my advanced age, most of those who I should thank are older and already gone: University of Minnesota political studies professor Mulford Sibley, philosopher Herbert Feigl and humanist Ralph Ross; University of British Columbia psychiatrists Ferdo Knobloch and Hamish Nichol; and American astronomers Willem Luyten and Ira Epstein.

A few younger remain to whom I express my gratitude. For conversations: Peggy Day, Joel Christy, and Hugh Mackie; and for prodding me to assemble my scattered writings into an actual book: Peter Constance, Lorraine Graves, and Ken Quong, along with Al and Richard Mackie.

The finished product was only made possible by Jessica Kaplan, whose substantive editing in organizing and welding together a disparate collection of essays has led to a hopefully coherent account of a Weltanschauung that began in 1954. I am also indebted to designer Jamie Fischer and publisher Jo Blackmore of Granville Island Publishing.

And as always, to Annie, Kjerstin and Emilie, who somehow over the years have tolerated their father's individuality.

Index

A Aarssen, Lonnie, "Dealing with the Absurdity of Human Existence in the Face of Converging Catastrophes," 182–183
Abel, grandson, 51
abortion, 206–207
abseiling, 20–21
abstraction, 144–145
Academia Argüello, 19, 21, 22, 23
Aconcagua, 17
Adamowitz-Kostrowicki, Casimir, 248–249
Adams, Michael, *From Elvish to Klingon: Exploring Invented Languages,* 96–97
aesthetics, 145–146
African American Vernacular English, 94
afterlife, 192
aging, 72, 155–158
AIDS
  clinical care team, 45, 47
  epidemic, 42
  international conferences, 46–50
  patients, 43, 44, 48, 170
  treatment of, 171
Alaska State Ferries, 59
alcohol dependence, 6, 109
Alta Gracia, 14, 16, 17
American Academy of Psychoanalysis (AAP), 162
American Association of Physicians for Human Rights, 44
American Psychiatric Association (APA), 40, 56, 62
American Psychoanalytic Association (APA), 162
anacyclosis, 217–218
anatomy, human, 149–150
Ancient and Mystical Order Rosae Crucis (AMORC). *See* Rosicrucians
ancient world, 195–196
animal behaviour, 135
Anna, daughter, 18, 59
annotation of books, 106
anti-Semitism, 203–204
Appleton, Wisconsin, 5
Apuleius, 119, 198, 200
Araucanian language, 125, 237
Archilochus, 3, 118
Arctic region, Canada, 52
Argenta, Quaker community, 30
Argentina, 56
  conflict in, 222–223
  departure from, 23–24
  revolution in, 15
  travel to, 12–14, 49, 56
  travels in, 124–125
Argüello, move to, 19
Aristarchus of Samos
army conscription, 11, 28
astrology, 162–163
astronomy, 8–9, 162–163
astrophysics, 162–163
Ateneum Museum, 114
atheism, 194–196
Atkins, Peter, *On Being: The Gauguin Questions,* 191–192
atomic theory, 136–137
  See also physics
Auden, W.H., 245
Australia, 45
awareness-raising, 158

B Bach, Johann Sebastian, 240, 241
Barabtarlo, Gennady, 165
Bariloche, 20, 21, 22
Baron, Dennis, *What's Your Pronoun? Beyond He and She,* 91–92
Bartsch, Arthur, 30
Bayan, Paul, *The Cynic's Dictionary,* 249–250
BC Ferries, 59
BC Police Academy, 42
BC Rail, 40
Bear Cave, 74
bedtime stories, 109–110
Beethoven, Ludwig van, 235, 237, 238, 240–241
believing, 82, 187, 192, 194–196, 204
Bell, Julia, 213–214
Bennett, Alan, 94
Benson, Marjorie, 9, 11, 26
Berg, Alban, 238
Bergson, Henri, 142
Berlin, Isaiah, "The Hedgehog and the Fox," 3–4, 118
Bible, the, 227
bibliographies, 98–99
bibliophiles, 102–103, 105–106
Bierce, Ambrose, *The Devil's Dictionary,* 250
big bang, 138, 140
bilingualism, 86–87
biographies, 120–121
biology, 33
biophilia, 172
biophysics, 140–141
bipolar disorder, 52
birth, 228
Bodleian Library, Oxford University, 99–100
Boesky, Ivan, 210–211
Bök, Christian, *Eunoia,* 252–253
Bolshevism, 216
books
  as advice, 130
books (*continued*)
  bibliophiles, 102–103, 105–106
  boring, 244–245
  children's, 174–175
  as companions, 189
  giving as gifts, 130–131
  history of, 98–99
  influential, 190–191
  in libraries, 99–101
  lists of, 101
  reference, 236–238
  See also novels
Borges, Jorge Luis, 102, 103, 258
  "Tlön, Uqbar, Orbis, Tertius," 119
Bosque Alegre
  observatory, 14-18, 21
  estancia (ranch), 15, 18, 19
Brahms, Johannes, 236
British Columbia, 28
  See also individual place names
Britten, Benjamin, 238
Bruckner, Anton, 17, 26, 32, 89, 147, 205, 236, 241
Bruckner Society, 26
Buenos Aires, 15, 18, 103
Buñuel, Luis, *The Exterminating Angel* (film), 177–178
business schools, 211
Byatt, A.S., 82
Byron, Len, 64, 68, 72

C Camus, Albert, 51
Canada, 27–28
Canadian Bible Society, 34
Canadian Border Services Agency, 50
Canadian Legion (Whitehorse), 54
Canadian Museum of Human Rights, 209–210
cannabis, planting, 32
cannibalism, 178–179
capitalism, 126, 212, 225

career advancement, 45, 62–63
carpe diem, 154–155
Castlegar, 32
Cathleen
asthma attack of, 57
as Condom Granny, 170
death of, 64–65, 67
declining health of, 63–64
documentaries made by, 53, 55, 56, 60, 61
education career, 20, 26, 31, 33, 37
first meeting, 11
marriage to, 16
memoriam, 66–67
support from, 63
cenemic writing systems, 85
chaos, 143
Chekhov, Anton, 51, 109, 116
Chernyshevsky, Nikolai, *What Is to Be Done?*, 221–222
Child, Lee, 110
children, 57
China, 127–128, 169–170, 190–191
chinchon, 15
Christianity, 196, 198, 209, 216, 260
Christie, Michael, *Greenwood,* 175–176
Christy, Joel, 30, 58, 70, 73
chronic obstructive pulmonary disease, 57
Chymical Wedding by Johann Valentin Andreae, 202
citizenship, Argentinian, 22
citizenship, Canadian, 33–34
citizenship, renouncing, 17
Ciudad Juárez, 12, 13
civilization, 173
classical mechanics, 137
classical music, interest in
in childhood, 7–8, 238
concerts, 47, 48
and friendships, 16–17
Iannucci on, 234–235
classical music (*continued*)
music critics, 235–237
string quartets, 26, 31
clinical clerkship, 38
Cock-Starkey, Claire, 99–100
Cocteau, Jean, 245
Codex Seraphinianus, 97–98
colonizing space, 180
comedy, 254–255
communism, 126
competition, 216–217, 226–227
computer science, 122
concepts, 81
concreteness, 144–145
conferences
international, 48, 49–50, 51, 60, 165
on neuropsychiatry of HIV, 171
Confucius, 190–191
Conrad, Joseph, 15, 219–220
consciousness, 139, 163
conspiracies, in literature, 119–120
Constance, Peter, 60
Conversation, The, 225–226
cooperatives, 215
Copernicus, Nicolaus, 149–150
Córdoba, Argentina, 11, 14–17, 19, 21, 23, 49
coronavirus, 107
See also Covid-19
correctness, 90–91
cosmology, 150–151
courses, graduate, 26–27
courses, medical school, 35–36, 37
courses, undergraduate, 9, 10, 17
Covid-19, 226, 254–255
crime novels, 111–112
See also novels
cults, 197–199
Curie, Marie, 147–148
curmudgeons, 251–252
curses, 226–227

D Davies, Paul, *The Demon in the Machine,* 139, 144
Dawson City Nuggets (team), 55–56
Day, Peggy, 69
Day House, 40
death, 193–194, 195–196
decay, 157
de Falla, Manuel, 14
Dekkers, Midas, *The Way of All Flesh: A Celebration of Decay,* 156–158
Desert Island books, 101
despair, 227
de Unamuno, Miguel, 22, 125
Dexter, Walter, 31
Diagnostic and Statistical Manual of Mental Disorders, The (*DSM*), 43, 143, 166, 167
Dickens, Charles, 107–108
dictionaries, 236–238, 249–250
Dirac, Paul, 145–146
discrimination, age, 156
dissertation work, 27
divorce, of parents, 6
DNA, 139
Dobzhansky, Theodosius, 182
Donizetti, Gaetano, 240
dorm room, makeshift, 10–11
Dorren, Gaston, *Babel,* 95
Dostoevsky, Fyodor, 194
    The Brothers Karamazov, 114–115
doubt, 187
Douglas College, 50, 66
Drake, David, 72
dreams, 165–166, 257–258
Dryden, John, 246
dystopian novels, 175–177, 209

E early childhood education, 31, 33, 37, 50, 66
earworms, 238–239
Eco, Umberto, 204
    Foucault's Pendulum, 119
economics, 212–213
Economist magazine, 212–213
Efird, James M., 206
ego-dystonic homosexuality, 40, 43
élan vital, 142
Eliot, George, 8
Eliot, T.S., 245
El Tronador, 21
emigration, 11
Emilie, daughter, 23, 57, 74
emoji, 93
end-of-the-road syndrome, 53
England, Jeremy, *Every Life on Fire: How Thermodynamics Explains Origins of Living Things,* 140, 141
English language, 90–91, 95
Enlightenment, 160–161
entropy, 138, 139
environmental degradation, 171–174, 178
environmentalism, 172
envy, 77
Epicurus, 195–196
Epstein, Ira, 18–19, 42–43
Erasmus, 245
Erlösung dem Erlöser, 243
escape from self, 182
Esperanto, 96–97
Espinoza, Señor, 29
Espoo, 114
Esquimalt Recreation Centre, 72
Eunoia, 252–253
Europanto, 247–248
evangelism, 168
Evans, Vyvyan, *The Emoji Code,* 93
exceptionalism, American, 218–219
exercise routines, 59, 61, 65, 68, 72
exiles, 12, 28, 115–116
existence, question of, 193–194
expertise, 188–189

extension of self, 182
extinction, 171–175, 180–181

F faith, in science, 192
Falkland Islands, 222–223
Falstaff, Sir John, 33
families, combined, 26
family day care movement, 66
Farell, Joseph, 204–205
Farmelo, Graham, *The Universe Speaks in Numbers: How Modern Math Reveals Nature's Deepest Secrets,* 145–146
fascism, 218
Feigl, Herbert, 26, 146–147
Fermi, Enrico, 150–151
Fermi paradox, 150–151
Ferryriders, 59–60, 62, 63, 65
Finland, 5, 46, 69, 70–71, 111, 112–114
Finnish crime novels, 111–112
Finnish language, 64, 65, 85, 86, 113, 246
Fiona, granddaughter, 53
Firth, John, 255
Fleming, John, 254
food, Argentine, 23
forensic services, 55
forests, death of, 175–176
Freemasons, 201–202
French language, 91
Freud, Sigmund, 47, 161–162
friends, 189–190
Führer der freien Welt (leader of the free world), 212–213, 218–219
full moons, 163–164
future, visions of, 178, 179–180, 181

G Gallen-Kallela, Akseli, 114
gardening, 55, 59
Gauguin questions, 191–192
Gay and Lesbian Caucus, 40
gay liberation movement, 38
gay men, medical care for, 38
gay, 94
German language, 85
Gesamtkunstwerk, 241
Gibbs, Nicholas, 97
global warming, 179–180, 181, 206, 213
gluttony, 76
Goethe, *Faust,* 188–189
governments, 217–218, 221–222
graduation, high school, 8
graduation, undergraduate, 11
grammar, 85–86, 91–92
grandchildren, 57, 61, 67
Gray, John, 194–195
Greece, ancient, 195–196, 197–198
greed, 77, 210–212
Green, Leon, 25
Green, Marjorie, 25, 26
Greene, Graham, 89
Greene, Robert Lane, *Talk on the Wild Side,* 90
Guardian Weekly, 219, 225
Guevara, Ernesto "Che," 14, 125–126
gun control, 224

H Hamid, Mohsin, "Impure Thoughts," 207–208
Hanslick, Eduard, 236
Haparanda, 46
Harrington, Brooke, *Capital Without Borders,* 214
Hauer, Bradley, 97
Hawkes, David, *A Little Primer of Tu Fu,* 88–89
Hawking, Stephen, *Brief Answers to the Big Questions,* 179–180
Haydn, Franz Jospeh, 240
Hayes, Bill, 121–122
health, 57, 61, 72, 158–159

heliocentrism, 149
hell, 204–206
Helsinki opera house, 69
Helsinki Pride Parade, 70–71
Heppner, Ben, 239
Here Are the News (documentary), 56
hermits, 189–190
Herod the Great, 223–224
Herotodus, 32
Herr, Joelle, 108
Hilkka, Finnish tutor, 69
HIV
  in China, 169
  deaths of friends from, 47
  dementia, 46
  emergence of, 38, 42
  neuropsychiatry of, 46, 48–51, 62, 171
  patients, 45–46, 49
  psychiatry treatment for, 170
hockey, 55–56
Homo cognoscens, 82, 135–136
Homo credens, 82, 187
Homo ludens, 82, 233–234
homophobia, 47, 50–51, 168
Homo scribens, 82, 85
homosexuality
  Alan Turing, 122–123, 162
  of author, 37–38
  in China, 169–170
  classifications of, 166–167
  ego-dystonic, 40
  in Finland, 69
  Frederick William Rolfe, 123–124
  global comparisons of, 167–168
  health clinics, 170
  internalized homophobia and, 47
  Oliver Sacks, 121–122
  presentations on, 43
  rejecting as a mental disorder, 56, 62
hope, 155, 227–228
hora inglés, 152
housing, duplex, 26
Hsing-chen, 120
Hugh, grandson, 60, 75, 143
Hugh-Jones, Stephen, 86
Huizinga, Johan, 233
humanism, 191–192, 194–195
humanities, 81
human rights, 208–210
humour, gallows, 254–255
Hunt, Elle, 130
hydrogen, 147–148

I Iannucci, Armando Giovanni, *Hear Me Out,* 234–235
Ibsen, Henrik, 37
identity expression through books, 102–103
ideologies, 216
Illich, Ivan, 159
impurity, 207–208
Index Librorum Prohibitorum, 99
industrialization, 171–172
internalized homophobia, 47
International Classification of Diseases (ICD), 166, 167
International Neuroscience of HIV conference, 51
  See also conferences, international
internet, 161
Irene, mother, 5–6, 7, 10
irrationality, 160–161
Ixion motorcycle club UK, 70

J Jacob, H., *A Planned Auxiliary Language,* 96
Japanese language, 93
Jasanoff, Maya, *The Dawn Watch: Joseph Conrad in a Global World,* 219–220
Jersey (Island of), 213–214
Jewish peoples, 203–204
John, Elton, 235

Johnson, Alex, 101
Josie, Edith, 55, 56, 57, 61
journalism, 225–226

K *Kalevala* (Finnish poetry), 113–114
Kellogg, Dr J.H., 37
kindness, 129
kings, 217
Kingsnorth, Paul, *Confessions of a Recovering Environmentalist,* 171–174
Kinsey Report, 37–38
Kivi, Aleksis, 113
    Seven Brothers, 112
Kjerstin, daughter, 18, 61–62, 70, 71
Klondyke Medical Clinic, 53, 55, 59, 61, 62
Knights of Templar, 200–201
Kokanee String Quartet, 31, 32
Kondrak, Greg, 97
Kootenay Lake, 36
Kootenay River valley, 32
Krasinski, Josef, 19, 21
Krehbiel, H.E., 236
Kullervo's Curse, 114
Kundry, 243

L Lake Nahuel Huapi, 20, 22, 125
Lamar, Kendrick, 236
Lanchester, John, *The Wall,* 176–177
languages
    comparing, 95, 103–104
    constructed, 96–97
    dictionaries for, 236
    evolving use of, 94
    learning, 85
    See also individual languages
Lanín Volcano, 21
Lapland, 69
Lasswell, H.D., 99
lateness, 152–153
Law Library, 100
learning, 82
lexicography, 236–238
LGBTQ movement, 92
libraries, 100, 102, 103, 131
life, mystery of, 138–141
Linden Manor, 73
Lindren, Minna, *Death in Sunset Grove,* 111
linguistics, 96–97, 246–248
literature reviews, 107
Little Sister's (bookshop), 50–51, 99
lockdown, 107
    See also Covid-19
logical empiricism, 146
London Review of Books, 105
Lönnrot, Elias, 113–114
loss, 228–229
LSD, 32
lucid melancholy, 182–183
lunacy, 163–164
lust, 76
Luyten, Professor, 9, 11, 22
Lyall, Archibald Laurence, *Guide to the Languages of Europe,* 103–104
lycanthropy, 164

M Mack, Katie, *The End of Everything (Astrophysically Speaking),* 140
MacLeish, David, 14–15, 18
Madame Blavatsky, 203
Magee, Bryan, *Ultimate Questions,* 193–194
Mahler, Gustav, 90, 234, 241
Mallon, Mick, 75
Mandarin Chinese language, 71, 72, 85, 86, 87–89, 94
Manguel, Alberto, 102–103
    Fabulous Monsters, 120
    Packing My Library: An Elegy and Ten Digressions, 102
Mann, Thomas, *Doctor Faustus,* 240
Mao's Little Red Book: A Global History, 127
Mao Zedong, *Little Red Book,* 127–128
Marani, Diego, 246–248

Marani, Diego (*continued*)
New Finnish Grammar, 246
The Interpreter, 247
The Last of the Vostyachs, 247
marriage, 16, 64–65, 66
Martel, Frederic, *Global Gay,* 167–168
Marx, Karl, 216–217
Masonic lodges, 201
mathematics, 26, 145–146
MCAT, 34
McGonagall, William, 246
McLeod, Alistair, 54
McLuhan, Marshall, 99
meaning, 191–192, 195
medical care for gay men, 38
medicalization, 158–159
medical school, 35–41, 73
Medical Undergraduate Society, 37
medicine, 34, 158–159
memoirs, 128–129
memories of Argentina, 23–24
Mencken, H.L., 245, 251
Mental Health Centre, Whitehorse, 51
mental illness, 163–164
metaphysics, 239–241
Mexico City, 40
microbiology, 170
Mikusinski, Jan, 26
military order, 17
mind–body problem, 139, 163
Minneapolis, 7
Minnesota, 7, 25, 66
miscellany, 99–101
Monarchist League of Canada, 61–62
monsters, 120
Montaigne, 86–87
morality, 196, 207–208, 218
Morris, Jan, *In My Mind's Eye,* 129–130
Morrison, Blake, *And When Did You Last See Your Father?,* 128
Moscow, 48–49
Moss, Sterling, 15
Mostenescu, Dragos, 255
mother, Irene, 5–6, 7, 10
motorcycles, 18–19, 32, 42, 56–57, 75, 125–126
mountaineering, 19–20, 21
Mt. López, 20–21
Mullaney, Thomas S., *The Chinese Typewriter: A History,* 85
murder stories, 109
Murrin, Alan, 75
music
abstract concrete dichotomies, 144–145
critics, 235–237
dictionaries, 237–238
earworms, 238–239
feelings evoked by, 234–235
metaphysics of, 240–241
pop, 238, 239
taste in, 236–237
See also classical music, interest in
MUSings Quarterly, 37, 38
Mussorgsky, Modest, 241

N Nabokov, Vladimir, 165, 257
Nahuel Huapi National Park, 20
name change, 22, 29
narrative constraint, 253–254
national identity, 25
National Library of Argentina, 102
National Observatory of Argentina, 11, 164
Nazis, 117, 229
negativity, 251–252
Nelson, British Columbia, 29–30, 36, 37
neoliberalism, 212
neonaticide, 206–207
neuropsychiatry of HIV, 46, 48–51, 62, 171
Newbery, Diego, 125
Pampa Grass, 22, 124–125
Newbery, George, 124–125

Newbery, Mrs., 22
news stories, bias in, 225–226
New York Review of Books, 105
Nibelungenlied, 241–242
Nissinen, Martti, 69, 70, 71
nosology, 166–167
Notre Dame University of Nelson (NDU), 29–30, 31–32
novels, 111–112, 175–176, 199, 201–202, 209, 246–247
Nuremberg trials, 229

O observation, 135–136
occultism, 203–204
O'Hagan, Andrew, 152
old age, 155–156, 157–158
Old Crow, Yukon, 55
Olsen, Loren, 71
O'Mahony, Seamus, *Can Medicine Be Cured?,* 158–159
operas, 51, 60, 69, 70, 71, 114, 242
oppression, 209–210
order, 143–144
ordering, 81–82, 143–144
Order of the Knights of Templar, 200–201
Osmothèque, 100
Oulipo, 253
ownership, 215, 217
Ozymandias, 49

P Paca, 20
pampas, 18, 20
Parker, Steve, 164
Parsifal, 19, 241, 243–244
Parsons, Nicholas T., 245
Patagonia, 49, 125
patient referrals, 57, 61, 63
patriotism, 25, 220–221
Payne-Gaposchkin, Cecilia, 147–148
Paz, Octavio, 88
Pender Island Health Centre, 61
people-watching, 190
Perec, Georges, 253
pets, 17, 53, 54, 55, 58, 61, 129
Pfeiffer, Professor, 9
philosophy, 117, 118, 188–189, 193–196, 210–212
photography, 14
physics, 136–137, 145–146
    See also thermodynamics, second law
piano, 7
pictographs, 93
Pigmalion Bookstore, 15, 96, 103–104
plane crash survivors, 178–179
playing, 82, 233–234
pleremic writing systems, 85, 93, 97, 237
poetastery, 245–246
poetry, 87–89, 90, 245–246
poetry, epic, 113–114, 241–242
political power, 217–218
political science, 217–218
political views, development of, 9
politics, 221–222
Polybius, 217–218
polytheism, 195–196
portmanteau words, 94
Poulenc, Francis, 241
pregnancy and parenthood, 17–18
presentations, 49, 51, 63, 171
presocratic philosophers, 136–137
Pride (gay), 69, 70–71, 77
Prime Timers, 64, 65, 68, 70, 71
pronouns, 91–92
property as theft, 215
Protagoras, *On the Gods,* 196
Protocols of the Elders of Zion, 203–204
Proudhon, Pierre-Joseph, *What Is Property?,* 215
pseudoscience, 159–160, 162–163
psychiatry
    beginning practice in, 40

psychiatry (*continued*)
  choice to study, 38
  clinical work of, 39–40
  compared to psychology, 163
  courses in, 36
  private practice in, 41, 43, 44, 59, 60
  retirement from, 62
  sexual orientation and, 166–167
  work in Yukon, 52–57
psychoanalysis, 161–162
  in Russia, 48
psychology, 163
public health, 36
Puccini, Giacomo, 241
pulmonary disease, 57
punctuality, 152–153
purity, 207–208
purpose, 188–189

Q Quaker community, 30
quantum mechanics, 136–137, 138
quasars, 27
Quesnel, 40–41, 45, 51
Quong, Ken, 71

R racism, 207
radioactivity, 147–148
Ravel, Maurice, 240
Raven, James, *What Is the History of the Book?,* 98, 99
reading, 6–7, 105–106, 109
reason, rejection of, 160–161
reference books, 103
regret, 153–154
Rein, Heinz, *Berlin Finale,* 117
religion, 192, 204–206
religious background of childhood, 6
religious belief, 195–196
renewable energy, 172
reporting job, 15
reproduction, 139
retirement, 62, 156
retirement routines, 68, 73, 75
revolutions, 15, 126, 221–222
Rio Negro, 20
Robb, Jim, *The Colourful Five Percent,* 255–257
Rodgers, Ann, 68, 70, 73
Rolfe, Frederick William, 123–124
  Hadrian VII, 124
Rose, C.D., 248–249
Rosicrucians, 202–203
Rosling, Hans, *Factfulness,* 225
Rovelli, Carlo, *The Order of Time,* 151
Russell, Anna, 233, 242
Russia, 48–49
Russian Émigré Short Stories from Bunin to Yanovsky, 116
Russian literature, 114–115, 116–117

S Sacks, Oliver, 121–122, 257
Sand, George, *La Comtesse de Rudolstadt,* 199
Sandburg, Carl, *The People Yes,* 215
Sarmiento, Domingo Faustino, 34
Scandinavia trip, 46
Schleyer, Johann Martin, 96
Schrödinger, Erwin, 137, 139
  What Is Life?, 138
Schumann, Robert, 240
science, 135–136, 188, 191–192
Seattle Psychoanalytic Society, 42
seclusion, 189–190
Second World War, 7, 117, 122
self-criticism, 76–77
Selkirk College, 32
Serafini, Luigi, 97
Sersic, José Luis, 18
Service, Robert (poet), 55
sexually transmitted infections, 38, 170
  See also HIV
sexual orientations, 166–167
  See also homosexuality

Sibelius, Jean, 113, 114
Siberia, 49
Sidney, Vancouver Island, 58, 65
Simenon, Georges, *Police Judiciare,* 109
Simon Fraser University, 40
sin, 205–206, 207
Sipilä, Jarkko,
Seinää Vasten (Against the Wall), 111
Katumurha (Street Murder), 71
slavery, 208–209
sleep disorders, 165
Slezkine, Yuri, *The House of Government,* 216
Slonimsky, Nicolas, *The Lexicon of Musical Invective: Critical Assaults on Composers Since Beethoven's Time,* 235–236
sloth, 76
Smith, Adam, 211
Smith, Alfred, 6, 7, 9
Smith, Alfred, Sr., 7, 9
Smith, Justin E.H., *Irrationality,* 160–161
social collapse, 179
socialism, 198–199, 215
social life, 8, 9–10, 54, 55, 64, 68
societies, secret, 200–203
Solven, Fred, 53
souls, 206–207
Spain, 177–178
Spanish language, 11, 15, 85, 87
speed-reading, 106
Spitzer, Robert, 43
Spotswood, Ken, 51, 73
Squattrinato, Fausto, 248–249
Srinivasan, Amia, 91–92
stardust, 192
statelessness, 17
states, evolution of, 217–218
stellar motions, 26
Steward Observatory, 11
Stoicism, 197
St. Paul's Hospital, 38, 40, 42–62
Strauss, Richard, 236, 238
Stravinsky, Igor, *Rite of Spring,* 236
stress, work, 47
string quartets, 26
suicide, 122
Sweden, 46
Symons, A.J.A., *The Quest for Corvo,* 123–124

T Tang dynasty, 72, 87–90
Tavris, Carol, 155–156
tax, withholding income, 27
tax havens, 213–214
Tchaikovsky, Pyotr Ilyich, 236
teaching career, 19, 28, 29–32
telepsychiatry, 59–60
telescopes, 14
textspeak, 93
theatre productions, 33, 37
theft, 215
thermodynamics, second law, 138, 139, 151, 157, 163, 181, 192
Third Reich, 5, 17
Thucydides, *History of the Peloponnesian War,* 195–196
time, 151–152, 153–154
Times Literary Supplement (TLS), 104–105, 107, 109, 118, 155, 204, 213–214
Tolonen, Anna, 5
Tolonen, Charles, 5, 46
Tolstoy, Leo, 48
tóngzhì, 94, 169–170
Tornio, 46
Toronto, Ontario, 40, 56
translation work, 71, 87, 88–89
Trump, Donald, 212–213
truth, 225–226
Tu Fu, 88–89
Tuleja, Thaddeus F., *The Catalogue of Lost Books,* 244

Turing, Alan, 122–123
Turing Award, 123

U UBC Department of Psychiatry, 45
UFOs, 150–151
uncivilization, 173–174
Unitarian Society, 7–8, 10
United Kingdom, 213–214
United Press news agency, 15, 103
United States, 17
United States Information Service, 17
universe, 188–189, 192
University of Arizona, 11
University of British Columbia, 34
University of Córdoba, 17
University of Minnesota, 8, 23, 25, 66
Uruguay, 15, 16, 22
Ustinov, Peter, *We Were Only Human,* 229
utopian movements, 202–203

V Vancouver, 37, 44, 45, 51
Vancouver Canucks (team), 47
Vancouver General Hospital, 39, 44, 163
Verdi, Giuseppe, 238, 241
Vesalius, Andreas, 149–150
Victoria, BC, 57, 68, 75
Vienna Circle of Logical Empiricism, 146–147
Vietnam War, 27, 28
viola, 8, 11
violence, 109–110, 223–224
viral pathogenesis, 141–143
vitalism, 141–143
Volapük, 96
Voluntary Human Extinction Movement, 181
volunteering, 54–55
von Eschenbach, Wolfram, *Parzival,* 201
Vonnegut, Kurt, 254
Voynich manuscript, 97–98

W Wagner, Richard, 236
    Der Ring des Nibelungen, 241
    Parsifal, 19, 241, 243
    Tristan und Isolde, 235
Wahl, Jan, *Pleasant Fieldmouse,* 174–175
Walhalla, 242
Wang, Jack, 70–75
Wang Wei, 87–88
Warren, James, *Facing Death: Epicurus and His Critics,* 195–196
Watson, Burton, 88
Waugh, Evelyn, "The Man Who Liked Dickens," 107–108
wealth management, 213–214
Weinberger, Eliot, *Nineteen Ways of Looking at Wang Wei,* 87–88
Weltanschauung, 27, 81, 259–260
Weltschmerz, 182
werewolves, 164
Whitehorse, Yukon Territory, 50, 51, 53
Whitehorse Star (newspaper), 56
Whitman, Walt, 245
Whitmarsh, Tim, *Battling the Gods: Atheism in the Ancient World,* 195
Wikström, Emil, 114
Wilcox, Ella Wheeler, 246
Winokur, Jon, *The Portable Curmudgeon,* 251–252
Wittgenstein, Ludwig, *Tractatus Logio-Philosophicus,* 90, 146
woke, 94
World Congress of Psychiatry, 43
wrath, 76
writing
    about reading, 104–105
    essays, 74, 82
    narrative constraint, 253–254

X Xinhua (news agency), 224

Y *Yersinia pestis,* 141

Yle Klassinen (Finnish radio), 64
young men, 223–224
Yukon, 50–51, 52–57, 60, 255, 256
Yukon Medical Council, 50

Z Zamenhof, Ludovic Lazarus, 96–97
Zeelen-Levallois, Sara, 249
Zemlinsky, Alexander, 104
Zheng, Tiantian, *Tongzhi Living: Men Attracted to Men in Postsocialist China,* 169–170
Ziolkowski, Theodore, *The Lure of the Arcane,* 119, 197–199, 200, 201, 203–204
Zurich, Switzerland, 43